INFAMOUS
SCANDALS

INFAMOUS SCANDALS

by
ANNE WILLIAMS
and
VIVIAN HEAD

Futura

A *Futura* Book

First published by Futura in 2008

Copyright © Omnipress 2008

ISBN: 978-0-70880-492-6

Produced by Omnipress, Eastbourne

Printed in Great Britain

Futura
An imprint of
Little, Brown Book Group
Brettenham House
Lancaster Place
London WC2E 7EN

Photo credits: Getty Images

CONTENTS

PART THREE: RADIO/TV PERSONALITIES

PART FOUR: POLITICIANS

PART FIVE: RELIGIOUS SCANDALS

PART SIX: JUDGES AND TEACHERS

PART SEVEN: GOVERNMENT SCANDAL

PART EIGHT: ARISTOCRATIC SCANDALS

PART NINE: SPORTS PERSONALITIES

INTRODUCTION

For the majority of people a minor indiscretion would go unnoticed, but just imagine what the repercussions would be like if you were a major public figure. Over the years pop stars, sportsmen, celebrities, politicians, members of the clergy and members of the royal family have made the headlines by being involved in a wide variety of scandals and controversial issues.

A scandal, put simply, is an incident that becomes widely publicized because it involves allegations of a wrongdoing, a disgrace or something which causes moral outrage. Of course the country in which the incident occurs can have strong implications as to the seriousness of the said moral outrage. A prime example is when a scandal broke after Richard Gere planted a seemingly innocuous kiss on the cheek of Bollywood actress Shilpa Shetty. The couple were appearing together at an AIDS awareness event in India, when Gere embraced Shetty, bent her back in a sort of exaggerated dance and then kissed her on

the cheek. Had this happened in Europe, no one would have turned a hair, but because they were in India's, and the country's Hindu nationalists believed that the act went far beyond anything that is acceptable to their beliefs, it was blown out of all proportion.

Of course a scandal is not always based on fact. Sometimes it is the product of a false allegation which becomes grossly exaggerated. Very often the attempt to cover up the said scandal creates an even greater scandal, when the cover-up fails to do its job and makes the situation even worse.

Years ago a scandal would probably have meant the end of a very prosperous career, but in the 21st century it appears it is easier to ride the storm, but of course this is by no means always the case. A prime example was the scandal surrounding TV presenter and comedian Michael Barrymore, whose madcap personality made him one of the most popular entertainers on British television. However, when a friend was found dead floating in Barrymore's swimming pool after a party in March 2001, it not only tarnished the presenter's reputation, it also ruined his career.

One of the most famous scandals in the 20th century was that of actor Roscoe 'Fatty' Arbuckle, who was accused of rape and murder in 1921. Although he was

apparently innocent of the charges, the scandal still managed to break him. Arbuckle was banned from making films and, although the ban was lifted the same year, his career had already been destroyed.

Sports personalities, who are always in the lime-light, only need to stray slightly from the straight and narrow and the media jump on it. For example, in 1994 Argentina's footballing hero, Diego Maradona, scored a magnificent goal in the World Cup final in the United States against Greece. However, the thrill of the goal was soon quashed when Maradona was sent home after testing positive for the stimulant ephedrene. Although he claimed it must have been in his sports drink, he was not allowed to play any further matches and his team was knocked out of the competition.

Another footballer, Stan Collymore, still bears the scars of an endless string of scandals. In 2004 he once again became the subject of ridicule when he was stopped by undercover reporters for 'dogging' – cruising for anonymous sex – stupidly using a car that bore his own personalized number plates!

The royal family are not immune from scandal – in fact far from it – and if we look back in the annals of time we will see plenty of evidence of 'naughty' behaviour. When kings and queens, princes and princesses play around, everyone wants to know

about it and whispers of their indiscretions reverberate around the world. In 1891 the Duke of Clarence, who was son of the future Edward VII, offered two prostitutes money if they would return two letters he had written to them. Details of this indiscretion did not come to light until the year 2002, when the incriminating letters were auctioned for the sum of £8,220.

In October 2007 two men were charged with attempted blackmail when they demanded £50,000 from an unnamed member of the royal family in exchange for an explicit 'sex tape'.

However, probably the most intriguing scandal to come out about the royal family is that surrounding the marriage of Prince Charles and Lady Diana. When Andrew Morton released his book *Her True Story*, the spell surrounding the fairytale marriage was broken. In the book Morton quotes Diana as saying, 'My wedding day, I think that was the worst day of my life' and she frequently refers to the Prince's 'other woman'. The 'woman' of course was Camilla Parker-Bowles, who has since become the Prince's consort. The scandal surrounding the death of Princess Diana in a high-speed car crash in August 1997 in Paris is still ongoing and various theories continue to emerge regarding the cause of the accident.

Politicians have seen their fair share of scandals

whether they have been involved in illegal, corrupt or unethical practices, or once again the subject of an immoral sexual practice as in the case of John Profumo. At the height of the cold war in the early part of the 1960s, Profumo allegedly had a sordid affair which involved a showgirl named Christine Keeler and a Soviet naval attache.

In September 2006 a respected congressman from Florida – Mark Foley – rocked the Capitol when he resigned over allegations that he sent sexually explicit emails to underage boys working as congressional pages. Further repercussions echoed around Congress when it was believed that several of his fellow House leaders had been aware of his indiscretions for quite some time.

A major political sex scandal broke in 1998 when US president Bill Clinton was accused of having an extramarital affair with a 22-year-old White House intern called Monica Lewinsky. The story made headlines for several days despite denials by Clinton, but the White House were not happy and demanded some answers.

Religious leaders should set a shining example for society on moral issues, or so one would think. However, for decades the sexual misbehaviour of Catholic priests has been shrouded in secrecy.

Jimmy Swaggart, one of the United States' leading

television evangelists was forced to resign from his ministry after it was revealed that he had been consorting with a prostitute. In a tearful confession in front of a large congregation he said 'I have sinned against you and I beg your forgiveness'. Ironically, his confession was all the more scandalous because he had already openly criticized a rival TV evangelist Rev Jim Bakker for committing adultery!

If these snippets have whetted your appetite, then you will enjoy reading about these and many more scandals in greater detail. Of course no one is perfect, but whatever your views about the people concerned it is hard to feel sorry for them when they know the world is watching. We are a sensation-hungry population who revel in the endless supply of headlines that appear in the daily tabloids. After all, scandals sell newspapers, keep journalists and lawyers employed and give us all something to talk about when we get into the office. Access to the internet spreads the gossip faster and further afield, leaving those people at the centre of the scandal to try and pick up the remnants of their shattered reputations.

PART ONE

FILM
STARS

OLIVE THOMAS

If Olive Thomas had a motto, it would certainly have been 'live fast, die young'. As a small town girl from humble stock with beauty and ambition in abundance, it seems that this is exactly what she set out to do. Olive's short life began in ordinaryville USA and ended far too early (just like another notorious beauty and drama queen from across The Pond) after a night of abandon at the Paris Ritz.

Oliva R. Duffy was born into an Irish immigrant family on 20 October 1894 in Charleroi, Pennsylvania. Her father died when she was very young, and she was forced to leave school early in order to help support her mother and two brothers.

At 16 years old, Olive was married to another small-town kid, Bernard Krugh Thomas. The marriage was not destined to last and within two years Olive, who was now working as a store clerk at Kaughman's department store in Pittsburgh, began divorce proceedings. The promise of juicy opportunities in the Big Apple beckoned to the young divorcee. Olive went to stay with a relative in the city where she quickly found employment at a Harlem department store. By this time Olive must have realised that she held at least *some* appeal for the opposite sex, because when she came across a newspaper contest to find New York's most beautiful girl, she entered and won. The accolade saw her modelling for commercial artists such as Howard Christy and Harrison Fisher and she eventually graced the cover of the *Saturday Evening Post*. Olive Thomas had arrived!

The *Ziegfeld Follies* of Broadway were inspired by the Parisian *Follies Bergeres*. They were a series of elaborate vaudeville variety shows conceived and put together by show-biz guru Florenz Ziegfeld at the suggestion of his then wife, the entertainer Anna Held. The show's producers were theatrical legends Klaw and Erlanger. The *Ziegfeld Follies* were most famous for their beautiful and glamorous chorus girls. In 1915, at the recommendation of Harrison Fisher, Olive was invited to join the Ziegfeld girls as part of the line-up. Thomas went on to claim that she'd actually approached Florenz and brazenly asked him for a job, but this version of events was never corroborated. It has also been alleged that Ziegfeld and Thomas were lovers, again there is little evidence to support this theory.

In addition to her role as a Ziegfeld girl, Thomas also performed a much cheekier act afterhours on the roof garden of the New Amsterdam Theatre. The show was called the *Midnight Frolic*, and it did pretty much as its name suggests. The girls had to perform in skimpy costumes, sometimes wearing nothing but colourful balloons which the male patrons took delight in bursting with the lit ends of their cigars. The show was mainly geared towards rich and famous male patrons who had plenty of money to bestow on pretty, nubile young creatures such as Olive. She welcomed the attention.

Before very long Thomas attracted a throng of male admirers from within the New York in-crowd associated with *Vogue* magazine mogul Conde-Naste. They showered her with expensive gifts, one German ambassador apparently bought her a string of pearls worth $10,000. In 1920, she posed nude for the Peruvian artist Alberto Vargas, who painted a titillating portrait of her as a wanton.

Having conquered New York city, Olive negotiated a contract with the International Film Company in Hollywood as the leading lady opposite Harry Fox, the founding father of the foxtrot. She went on to make over 20 Hollywood movies, the first being *A Girl Like That*, which she made straight after her secret wedding to Jack Pickford.

OLIVE AND JACK

Jack Pickford was a Canadian born American actor, and son of the famous Pickford acting dynasty. When Olive and Jack met, Olive was 22 years old and Jack was only 20. There was an instant chemistry between them, and they were married in secret in 1916. Olive later claimed that the reason for their secrecy lay in the fact that she didn't want to trade on the family name – preferring to make it on her own. A highly moral standpoint from a young woman who had for years traded purely on her youth and the sheer beauty of her body!

The famous Pickford family did not approve of the match to begin with, believing that Jack was too young for marriage. They also felt that Olive, whose background was in 'musical comedy' (a euphemistic phrase for burlesque theatre) came from an alien world. In fact this could not have been further from the truth. Both families came from very ordinary, working-class stock. Olive and Jack had both experienced abandonment and poverty as children and both had discovered theatre as a way to escape this life – so in many ways the couple had plenty in common. The Pickfords though, did not want to be reminded of their humble roots – and disliked Olive's coarse and brassy manner.

In Mary Pickford's autobiography *Sunshine and Shadows*, she describes their relationship thus:

The girl had the loveliest violet-blue eyes I had ever seen. They were fringed with long, dark lashes that seemed darker because of the delicate translucent pallor of her skin. I could understand why Florenz Ziegfeld never forgave Jack for taking her away from the Follies. She and Jack were madly in love with one another, but I always thought of them as a couple of children playing together'

(MARY PICKFORD, 1955)

The main reason why the Pickford's did not like Olive, was down to her role in the *Midnight Frolics*. Despite the fact that Olive had graduated from Broadway and was now playing similar roles to her sisters-in-law, they regarded her as little more than a courtesan and not a respectable girl with whom their brother should settle down. Olive was renowned not only for her sexual appeal but also for her potty-mouth. Her language was apparently awful, but she never intended to offend. Jack and Olive didn't seem to care what anyone else thought. They were too besotted with one another.

Olive later commented that 'Jack was a beautiful dancer, he danced his way into my heart. We knew each other for eight months before our marriage and most of that time we gave to dancing. We got along so well on the dance floor that we just naturally decided that we would be able to get along together for the rest of our lives.'

Meanwhile, her Hollywood studio had reinvented Olive as a simple, virginal Irish girl who was devoted to her pet dog and her brothers. This version of Olive may have been closer to the 'real her' for all we know, but it was certainly a different person from the erotically charged sex goddess that Vargas had painted.

America became wrapped up in World War I, and Jack faced a dilemma: join the US military or be draughted into the Canadian army. He opted for the US Navy, and spent the majority of his time in the forces finding young Hollywood hopefuls who would sleep with his Naval superiors in order to keep him out of the firing line. The authorities eventually found about about this little arrangement and Jack was given a dishonourable discharge. The Pickford sisters, ever concerned about the family's reputation, later used their money and influence to have the word 'dishonourable' removed.

While Jack was busy dodging the front-line, Olive drank champagne cocktails and attended celebrity parties in chauffeur driven cars. She had become one of the Hollywood elite. These days we tend to take it for granted that young, beautiful and talented starlets will inevitably brush up against a darker side of

Hollywood – a world where class A drugs and alcohol rule the show. Hardly a day passes when the tabloids are not filled with such goings-on. It may give the likes of Winehouse, Hilton and Spears some comfort to know that things were just the same for Olive Thomas, but ultimately Olive's tale is a cautionary one because it was here, at the height of her fame, that tragedy was waiting in the wings.

OLIVE AND JACK: THE END GAME

In 1920 Jack and Olive decided to take a second honeymoon in Europe, and the couple sailed from New York for Paris on 12 August 1920. The lustre of married life had all but worn off. Jack's philandering and Olive's partying caused enormous arguments, the pair were a volatile combination – one minute they were at each other's throats, the next lavishing apologies, kisses and gifts upon one another. The holiday was aimed at saving their rapidly failing marriage. Jack and Olive checked into the Paris Ritz upon their arrival in the city. On the evening of Saturday, 9 September, Jack and his wife went out on the town – not arriving back at their hotel room until 3 a.m. A couple of hours later, Jack called reception to say that his wife had mistakenly taken an overdose of medicine and required the services of a doctor. A doctor arrived 10 minutes later to find Olive writhing in agony. She had taken a huge dose of mercury bichloride – a medicine prescribed to Jack as treatment for syphillis. There was little he could do to save the young actress.

Mercury bichloride, if taken in large doses, is incredibly corrosive. It basically burns the body from the inside out. Olive died from acute nephritic inflammation as a result of internal corrosion. She suffered in agony for four long days and nights before finally succumbing to death.

Jack's official story behind Olive's accident went something like this: The couple turned out the lights and went to bed, but Olive was unable to sleep. She reached out to grab her bottle of sleeping pills and mistakenly took hold of the mercury bichloride. She gulped-down a number of pills before realising the dreadful mistake she had made. Olive staggered to the ensuite bathroom whereby she exclaimed 'Oh my God!' waking Jack, who came running to her aid, catching her in his arms as she collapsed. It was then that Jack contacted the hotel reception and asked for help. His version of events runs something like a scene from a tacky melodrama of the era, and although the inquest concluded a verdict of accidental death, the papers were rife with alternative theories.

One rumour claimed that Olive had committed

suicide when she discovered that Jack had infected her with syphillis. But if that was the case, why on earth would she choose such a painful way to die? Another rumour stated that Olive was a heroin addict and alcoholic who was so intoxicated that she had no idea what she was doing. The most sinister theories placed the blame squarely with Jack – claiming that he murdered her either for her money or because he discovered that she had been unfaithful.

Olive's body was returned to New York, where she was put to rest at the St Thomas Episcopal Church on 5th Avenue. Over 4,000 people attended the memorial service – it was the first show-biz funeral of its kind. Jack's sisters once again stepped in to help get his life back on track – he continued acting and went on to marry two more Zeigfeld girls, Marylin Miller from 1922-1927 and Mary Mulhern from 1930-1932. He eventually died in 1933, according to his niece Gwen Pickford from 'too many of the right things: women, drink and riotous living' but the reality of his death was not nearly so glamorous. Ultimately he died of syphillis – a virulent and disfiguring venereal disease.

Olive Thomas was the prototype wayward starlet, her sensational but tragically short life went some way towards paving the way for Marilyn Monroe, Anna Nicole Smith *et al*, but today her films have been mostly lost or forgotten, and Olive Thomas is remembered for one thing and one thing only, as the sex siren behind Hollywood's very first major scandal.

JEAN HARLOW

Young, gifted and ravishing, Jean Harlow seemed to have everything – striking platinum blonde hair, a curvaceous figure, natural sensuality and a sharp sense of humour. With all these weapons in her arsenal it is difficult to understand how her short life became so mired in controversy and tragedy.

'BABY' JEAN

Jean Harlow was born Harlean Harlow Carpenter on 3 March 1911, to Jean Poe and Mont Clair Carpenter from Kansas, Missouri. Harlean's mother Jean came from wealthy stock. She was the daughter of successful real-estate broker, Skip Harlow and his wife Ella. Skip and Ella had arranged their daughter's marriage to Mont Clair, and Jean never forgave them for it. She was a dominant, charismatic and free-spirited woman who longed for independence. Consequently she was very unhappy in her marriage to Mont Clair, a suburban dentist with working class roots, so convinced was she that she deserved better.

This depression meant that Jean focused all her attention on the couple's only child, Harlean. Mother and daughter became inseparable. Jean was a controlling and over-protective mother who encouraged her daughter to depend on her for absolutely everything. The entire family referred to pampered Harlean only as 'Baby', and Jean wanted to keep it that way, hence Harlean was five years old when she eventually discovered that her real name was actually Harlean and not in fact 'Baby'.

A BROKEN HOME

When Harlean began attending school, Jean Snr grew ever more frustrated with married life, divorcing Mont Clair in 1922, when Harlean was just ten years old. As a consequence of the separation Mother Jean was granted sole custody of her daughter. Harlean struggled to keep in contact with her father throughout the remaining years of her life.

Jean Snr harboured ambitions to become an actress, and moved herself and Harlean to Hollywood in order to pursue her dream. However, jobs were not forthcoming and so dwindling finances meant they were forced to return to Kansas city after just two years. Jean Snr gave up on the idea of having her own acting career and focused instead on attracting a wealthy husband. Her acting ambitions shifted to that of her daughter. It was largely thanks to the efforts of manager 'Mama Jean', that Harlean would go on to achieve everything her mother had ever wanted for herself and more.

CHILD-BRIDE

At the age of 16, Harlean ran away from home to marry the wealthy 23-year-old Charles McGrew. 'Mama Jean' was now happily remarried to shyster Marino Bello and so the young newlyweds moved from the family's home in Chicago to Berverly Hills. Harlean's true aspiration in life was simply to be a devoted wife and mother. She was never particularly interested in making movies, but at the suggestion of Jean she began to pursue jobs as a film extra. Harlean's obvious sex-appeal made her perfect for Hollywood, and her acting career slowly began to take off. Her marriage, however, was less successful. Harlean's career put pressure on the couple's relationship and before long she had filed for divorce. Little did Harlean know her big break was just around the corner.

DISCOVERED

The story of Harlean's discovery (and her subsequent reinvention as the sex goddess: Jean Harlow) reads like a Hollywood fairy tale, the like of which most struggling young actresses can only dream of. She was spotted by actor, James Hall who was filming Howard Hughes World War I aviation epic *Hells Angels*. The movie mogul was in the process remaking the originally silent *Hells Angels* as a talkie, but the lead actress Greta Nissen, had a thick Norse accent that simply would not work on screen, and so he was on the look out for a replacement. Baby Harlean fitted the bill. A few big movies and a publicity tour later, Jean Harlow's star was firmly on the ascendant and thanks to her new boyfriend, Metro-Goldwyn-Mayer (MGM) big-wig Paul Bern, MGM were looking to buy her contract from Howard Hughes. On 3 March 1932, Jean's 21st birthday, she received news from Bern that MGM had indeed purchased her contract from Hughes for a fee of $30,000 (an exorbitant amount of money at the time). Jean's career was about to go truly stella.

MGM: THE BEHEMOTH

In order to understand the events leading up to the

scandal that followed, it is first important to examine the role of the studio system in Hollywood during the 1930s. A major economic depression had taken its toll on Hollywood, just as it had the rest of America. MGM was the only studio that continued to go from strength to strength despite widespread financial hardship. This was down to the consistently high-quality of their pictures and a number of clever decisions by the studio's board of directors. MGM was therefore the most powerful film studio in America (and therefore the world), and in order to maintain their position they were forced to rule all aspects of the company with an iron fist. They controlled the lives of their actors and actresses, especially the stars such as Greta Garbo, who were their bread and butter. Jean Harlow was already used to being under the thumb, strictly controlled as she had been by her mother for so many years. MGM to her was just like another larger, richer parent figure – constantly pulling-strings and manipulating people and events around her in order to achieve their own objectives.

DOOMED SECOND MARRIAGE

Harlow married Paul Bern at the house of her mother, 'Mama Jean' Harlow, on 2 July 1932. It was an unlikely match to say the very least. Paul Bern had been heralded as a genius by his contemporaries in the industry. He was also known as Hollywood's father confessor, because he was so caring and sensitive that people often went to him with their problems. For all this Bern was also 22 years older than Jean, small and insignificant in stature and physically fairly unattractive. Standing next to his sex-bomb wife they must have looked like the original odd-couple. Despite the apparent mismatch, Harlow seemed radiantly happy in the weeks following the wedding, and all seemed to be going swimmingly. Bern had bought the couple a luxurious house in Beverly Hills surrounded by five acres of ground which was to be the family home. Unfortunately Harlow disliked the house for some reason and wanted to sell it. The couple began arguing about this, and soon the tide changed. Bern began to look haggard and withdrawn, and Jean began spending more and more time at the home of her mother.

BANG BANG: MY BABY SHOT ME DOWN

Jean was at her mother's on 5 September 1932, when the couple's butler found Paul Bern lying face-down on the floor of his wife's all-white bedroom. He was completely naked and drenched in her perfume. A .38 caliber revolver lay at his side. His brains had been blown out. For reasons known only to him, the butler called not the police nor an ambulance, but the studio's security chief. Within minutes he and two top MGM bosses, Louis B Mayer and Irving Thalberg were on their way to the Bern residence. The police were still not called. Mayer arrived at the house first, followed closely by Thalberg and the security chief WP 'Whitey' Hendry. They did not call the authorities until two hours later. What exactly happened during those lost minutes has never been revealed, but many believe that these men manipulated the evidence to suggest Bern had committed suicide. A supposed suicide note was found near the body. It read:

> *Dearest Dear,*
> *Unfortunately this is the only way to make good the frightful wrong I have done you and wipe out my abject humiliation.*
> *I love you*
> *Paul*
> *You realise that last night was only a comedy.*

This was taken by many as evidence to support the rumour that Bern suffered from a physical disability (such as chronic impotence) that made it impossible for him to have intercourse with his bombshell wife.

A condition such as this could certainly have given rise to feelings of abject humiliation – and explain the last line of the note, but was this the case? Upon his autopsy Bern's personal physician supported the claim, stating that Bern suffered from a condition that would have rendered a healthy marital life impossible. However, the couple's gardener later said that he did not believe the note was in his employer's handwriting, and this view was supported by expert handwriting analysts. Perhaps Mayer, Thalberg and Hendry faked the suicide note in order to shift suspicion onto the dead man himself and away from Harlow? They certainly had the abilities, the opportunity and the motive. Jean could not afford to get caught up with a murder enquiry, and her sex-bomb image would falter if it transpired that another lover had committed the murder, as it would imply to her audience that Jean Harlow could not keep a husband satisfied.

CURIOUSER AND CURIOUSER

If things were not mysterious enough already, it soon transpired that Bern had for years kept a common law wife called Dorothy Millette. Dorothy, a struggling actress, had lived with Paul in New York and Toronto for a number of years and she often referred to herself as 'Mrs Paul Bern'. Unfortunately, she began to suffer from severe mental illness and Paul was forced to have her institutionalised. He continued to provide generously for Dorothy's care, but the romance was apparently over when he relocated to Los Angeles. The day after Bern's death, Millette checked out of her room at the Plaza Hotel in San Franscisco and boarded a Sacramento River steamer called the *Delta King*. When the ship docked in Sacramento, Dorothy was no longer on board, but her coat and shoes were found on deck. Dorothy's body was discovered by fishermen a few days later. It seemed that she had jumped overboard.

RUMOURS

Today rumours continue to rage regarding Paul Bern's mysterious death. Some believe that Jean Harlow discovered the truth about Dorothy and furiously murdered her husband; others think that Dorothy Millette became dangerously unhinged and dealt the fatal blow herself. Winifred Charmichael, the Bern's cook was reported as saying that the household staff encountered a strange woman on the night of the murder. She heard an unfamiliar woman's voice in the house and later found a woman's wet swimsuit, as well as two used wine glasses out by the side of the pool. Did Dorothy swing-by for a visit on the day of her expartner's death? Had this clandestine relationship ever actually ended? Was the Harlow-Bern marriage a sham from the beginning? All these questions remain unanswered. One thing is for sure though MGM had the power to manipulate the lives of the A-list's elite, even to criminal ends.

AN UNHAPPY ENDING

Jean Harlow's career did not suffer dreadfully in the days and months following the scandal, but her health certainly did. According to reports Jean attempted suicide shortly after her husband's death, but although she survived, she did not do so for long. At the tender age of 26, whilst filming *Saratoga* with Clarke Gable, Jean began to suffer from kidney problems caused by a childhood bout of scarlet fever. She postponed seeing her doctor because she was busy filming, but by the time her symptoms became serious it was too late. She died of cerebral edema and uremic poisoning caused by a build up of waste products in the blood. Some claimed that her mother, a christian scientist, had kept her from seeing a doctor because of her religious beliefs but this was untrue. It was Jean's other parental influence – her studio who, through the pressures of filming, inadvertently caused her tragic death.

INGRID BERGMAN

Ingrid Bergman will forever be remembered for her role as Ilsa Lund in the unforgettable classic *Casablanca*. In the movie, Ilsa is caught between two men: her war-hero husband, and the nightclub owner and notorious ladies-man Rick Blaine (played by Humphrey Bogart). In her professional life the role of star-crossed-lover Ilsa earned Ingrid extremely high acclaim. However, in her personal life, Ingrid's extramarital transgressions with playboy director Roberto Rosselini cost her nearly everything.

A LONELY CHILDHOOD

Ingrid Bergman was born in Stockholm on 29 August 1915. Her mother, Friedal Adler Bergman – a German native, died when Ingrid was only three years old. Her father, Justus Bergman, owned a photography shop and got his daughter interested in the arts at an early age. He delighted in taking photos and making home movies featuring Ingrid, but unfortunately he died when she was just 12 years old, and Ingrid was passed from pillar-to-post until an elderly uncle and his family took her in.

Ingrid had been introduced to celluloid as a youngster, and clearly felt at home in front of the lens, so when she was 16 years old she began appearing in films as an extra. After graduation she attended the Royal Dramatic Theatre School in Stockholm, during which time she made her professional stage debut.

In 1936, Bergman made the film that would change her life forever. *Intermezzo* was written and directed by Gustav Molander, the man who had given Ingrid her big break in the Swedish film industry. The movie follows the story of a famous violinist who has an affair with his daughter's piano teacher, played by Bergman. Even at this early point in her film career Ingrid was already playing 'the other woman' to great effect. The role brought her to the attention of Hollywood producer David O. Selznick, who bought the rights to remake *Intermezzo*, and cast Bergman as his female lead. Selznick offered Bergman a seven year film contract, and she was soon making the transition from Stockholm starlet to fully-fledged Hollywood star.

ST INGRID THE INPENETRABLE

American audiences soon fell hook, line and sinker for Bergman's angelic beauty, flawless skin, icy demeanour and quintessential good-girl image. The all-powerful Hollywood studios suggested that she change her name to a more American-sounding alternative, have her teeth capped and her eyebrows plucked, but Ingrid point-blank refused to sell-out in this manner. She had worked hard to make a name for herself as an actress in Europe, and her lonely childhood had made her both single-minded and stubborn. It turned out to be a shrewd move on her part. Her natural and unfussy look set her apart from other actresses of the era, most of whom wore heavy make-up. However, it did mean that Selznick tended to cast her in wholesome, virtuous roles and this stereo-typing made the scandal that followed even more difficult for the public to digest.

CASABLANCA

By the time Bergman was offered her most famous role, in *Casablanca*, she had become a dedicated wife and mother. Ingrid married the dentist and neuro-surgeon Peter Lindstrom on 10 July 1937, and the couple had a young daughter Freidal Pia Lindstrom.

Ingrid and Peter met in Sweden when she was just 18 years old and he accompanied her to the United States to pursue a career in Hollywood. Peter found work lecturing on medicine at the University of Pittsburgh and eventually moved to San Francisco, where he became one of America's leading brain surgeons.

BAD BOY ROBERTO

The bubble burst when Ingrid met and fell deeply in love with the director Roberto Rosselini. Rosselini was a reckless Italian playboy with a chequered past. In 1931, he met and pursued an affair with the comedienne Assia Norris. Assia refused to have sex with him before they were married, and so Roberto arranged an elaborate church wedding with all the trimmings, an archbishop, priest and gala celebration. A few years later their marriage was failing and Assia asked her husband for a divorce, only to discover that the entire wedding was actually a staged fake!

When Roberto Rosselini met Ingrid Bergman he was married and already known to be keeping several mistresses, including the actress Anna Magnani. In spite of his terrible reputation, or perhaps because of it (not many women can honestly resist a bad boy!) Bergman was unable to control her feelings for the Italian stallion Roberto.

The two met in Paris while the actress was making the Alfred Hitchcock film, *Under Capricorn* in England. She was accompanied by her husband Peter, who was acting as her manager, but despite this it was love at first sight. She expressed great interest in appearing in Rosselini's next feature. Rosselini later went to visit Ingrid and her husband in the United States, even staying with the couple at their family home. Ingrid later wrote to her husband from Italy, where she and Roberto were filming *Stromboli*, their first feature film together, explaining that:

> *. . . you saw in Hollywood how my enthusiasm for Roberto grew and grew, and you know how much alike we are, with the same desire for the same kind of work and the same understanding of life.*

On 7 February 1950, whilst still married to Peter Lindstrom, Ingrid gave birth to Roberto's son, Robertino Rosselini.

FROM SAINT TO WHORE
AND BACK AGAIN

Today it is difficult to understand the strength of America's reaction to the birth of this illegitimate child, but in 1950 it caused an almighty scandal. Her

American fans, who had been so utterly besotted with her as the virtuous and saintly ice-queen, simply could not accept the disappointment they felt and adulation soon turned to anger. She was preached against from pulpits, cinemas were picketed for showing her films and news of the scandal even reached the floor of the US senate. The Democrat senator for Colorado, Edwin C. Johnson famously denounced her as 'a horrible example of womanhood and a powerful influence for evil'. There was then a floor vote, which saw Bergman made a *persona non grata* in the eyes of the American government and she was effectively expelled from the USA. Ingrid was forced to leave her home, her husband and her daughter in order to seek exile with Rosselini in Italy. One cannot help but wonder if Roberto even got a diplomatic slap on the wrist for his own part in the brouhaha!

While Ingrid was in Italy, American anger continued unabated. As a result her films were widely boycotted in the USA. Ingrid though, ever the single-minded, stubborn and independent woman, evidently forgave herself. She was later quoted as saying 'I have no regrets. I would not have lived my life the way I did if I was going to worry about what people were going to say.'

MARILYN MONROE

Marilyn Monroe is one of the iconic film stars of the 20th century, a Hollywood star whose life was full of sex, lies and scandal. For many years she was considered the most beautiful woman in America, her blonde hair, red lips and curvaceous figure representing the 1950s ideal of womanhood. However, despite her huge success as a movie star, and the fact that she was seen as one of the most desirable women of the age, her life was full of sadness, and throughout her career she suffered a series of mental breakdowns. Her eventual suicide may have simply been the inevitable outcome of this mental instability, but many believed that there was more to the story. There were rumours that she was sexually involved with the president of the USA, John F. Kennedy, or possibly the president's brother, Robert Kennedy, and that she was murdered in an effort to try to hush up the enormous scandal that would have ensued if the affair had become known to the public. However, these were never investigated, so today her death remains something of a mystery.

FOSTER HOMES

Norma Jeane Mortenson was born on 1 June 1 1926, in the charity ward of Los Angeles County Hospital. Right from the start her prospects did not look good. Her mother, Gladys Pearl Monroe, had married twice, divorcing her second husband, Martin Edward Mortenson, a man from a Norwegian background, after only six months. Mortenson played no role in baby Norma Jeane's life, and it was thought by some – including Marilyn herself when she was older – that her real father was in fact one Charles Stanley Gifford, a man that her mother had met while working at RKO pictures as a film cutter.

After the departure of Mortenson, Gladys could not care for her child, so the girl was sent to live with foster parents, where she remained until the age of seven. After that, she went to live with her mother, but it was then that Gladys suffered a serious mental breakdown and was sent to a mental hospital. Norma Jeane moved in with a family friend, Grace McKee, but this did not last and soon she was shuttling between foster homes, since no one wanted to take care of her.

Finally, McKee managed to persuade a young man, James Dougherty, to marry the teenager so that she would at least have a home. The couple moved in to his parents' home, and Norma Jeane began employment spraying aeroplanes in a factory, where she was discovered by a photographer who arranged for her to be signed up by a modelling agency.

MOVIE CAREER

After screen testing for Twentieth Century Fox, Norma Jeane landed a contract and began to make movies under the name of Marilyn Monroe. Little by little, she began to build her movie career, and by the early 1950s had begun to make a considerable name for herself. At this point, some nude photographs of her were picked up and published in *Playboy*. She had posed for these when she was poor and unknown. To the studio's horror, she faced down the scandal by admitting that it was her in the pictures – even joking that all she had had on during the photo shoot was 'the radio'. It was this honesty and lack of hypocrisy that earned her many admirers, and she went on to become the major sex siren of her day, with a ready wit that recalled Mae West. (For example, when asked what she wore in bed, she wittily replied, 'Chanel Number 5'.) She also went on to make some of the classic films of all time, such as *Gentlemen Prefer Blondes, The Seven Year Itch* and *Some Like it Hot.* Yet despite the fact that she had a cracking sense of humour and had proved herself to be a talented actress and comedienne, the film studios she worked for preferred to present her as a 'dumb blonde'.

By the early 1960s, Monroe's erratic behaviour on set – turning up late and failing to learn her lines – was beginning to put studios off hiring her. Eventually, she was dropped by all the major studios and from then on, often expressed her bitterness about the way she had been treated in Hollywood. However, despite the fact that the studios no longer wanted to employ her, she still had many opportunities and admirers in the business, so it came as a shock – both to the industry and to the public – when on 5 August 1962, she was found dead in her home.

PUBLIC SCANDALS

Many speculated on the reasons behind her apparent suicide. Monroe's personal relationships had been very unstable throughout her career, and there had been constant rumours and scandals about her love life. She had divorced her first husband soon after her film career took off and in 1954 married baseball player Joe DiMaggio. However, he became jealous of her and was particularly angry when the crowd yelled their approval as her skirt blew up in *The Seven Year Itch*. They openly fought in public and later Monroe was seen to have bruises on her arms. Less than a year into the marriage the couple split, Monroe filing for divorce on grounds of mental cruelty.

Monroe's second marriage was to the popular American playwright Arthur Miller. The intellectual Miller could not have been a more different man from DiMaggio and the couple at first seemed happy, until Monroe suffered two miscarriages. This was enough to tip her into mental illness once more, and before long this marriage was over, too. Added to this her movie career was now failing. Monroe went to live alone in Brentwood, Los Angeles, where she descended deeper into depression, until on 5 August 1962 she was found dead from an overdose of sleeping pills.

SUSPICIOUS CIRCUMSTANCES

Given her history of mental illness and that of her mother, as well as other members of her family, most people believed that she had committed suicide. After all, she had made numerous suicide attempts over the years, and for many years her behaviour had been extremely erratic. The coroner recorded the case as 'probable suicide' and she was buried at the Westwood Village Memorial Park Cemetery in Los Angeles. However, rumours soon began to circulate that the death was not a suicide and that she had possibly been murdered. There were anomalies in the coroner's report and some aspects of the scene of the crime did not make sense. For example, there was no glass of water near where Monroe's body was found, so how could she have downed an overdose of sleeping tablets? Also, in death, her body looked as though it had been positioned in a certain way; it was not like the usual posture of suicide victims.

Then there were the circumstances surrounding the case. It gradually came out that on the last evening of her life, Monroe had made a number of phone calls, including one to the actor Peter Lawford, who was a close friend of the Kennedys. It was also rumoured that Robert Kennedy, brother of President John Kennedy, had been seen driving away from the house that night. This caused speculation that Monroe might have been having an affair with the president.

A HUGE SCANDAL

The theory was that the president had been worried about Monroe's threats to go public over the affair, and might have had her killed to save a huge scandal, and the end of his political career. Thus – so the theory went – he asked his brother Robert to perform the murder. Additionally, there was speculation that Robert Kennedy, too, might have been having an affair with Monroe. There was also a theory that Monroe was killed by a hitman employed by mafia man Sam Giancana, and that JFK had ordered the killing, or that Giancana himself had been having an affair with Monroe. However, it was not clear, if this was the case, what his motive would have been.

Whatever the truth of the matter, no hard evidence was uncovered that would back up any of these theories. Since that time, there have been many books published on the matter, the most persuasive of which have suggested that Monroe killed herself by accident. It seems that Monroe may have asked her housekeeper to give her an enema containing her medicines, which would explain the lack of a glass of water by the bedside. That would mean that instead of trying to kill herself, she muddled up her tablets, causing the overdose. It is possible that Monroe might have been having an affair with the president, and that knowing this link, whoever found her might have panicked, moving the body around at the scene of the death and delaying calling an ambulance.

The current line of thinking is that, instead of being a murder, Monroe's death was more of a scandal, involving sex, drugs and people in high places. Perhaps the reason that not more was made of it at the time was that, at the heart of the scandal, was a very sad story, about a woman who, despite her success and fame had suffered great unhappiness throughout her life. She was undoubtedly a woman who was held up as an icon of feminine sexuality, but whose talent was never recognised, or so she felt. She was a woman who was adored as a movie star by millions, but who did not feel loved by those closest to her. For, from the outset of her career, Monroe's story was one of sex, lies and scandals; but at the end, at the heart of it, a tale of tragedy.

FATTY ARBUCKLE

One of the most famous Hollywood scandals of all time was that of Roscoe 'Fatty' Arbuckle, a successful Hollywood comedian during the era of silent films. The scandal began when, after a night of carousing with friends at his hotel, a woman at the party died of a ruptured bladder. Arbuckle was accused of raping her so roughly that he caused this injury, though later it transpired that the woman had become ill for other reasons, including imbibing too much alcohol. Whatever the truth of the matter, the scandal ruined the actor's career – tragically, as it turned out – because in the end he was acquitted of the crime. Yet even though Arbuckle received a formal apology for his treatment from the court, his career never recovered and his films were banned. Because of his public disgrace, Arbuckle took to the bottle until, eventually, his reputation was restored and he began to make films again. However, his joy at resuming his acting career was short-lived; the night after being signed up by Warner Brothers to make a feature film, Arbuckle died of a heart attack.

MILLION DOLLAR MAN

Roscoe Conkling Arbuckle was born on 24 March 1887 to Mollie and William Goodrich Arbuckle. As a young man he worked in vaudeville, learning from comedians such as Leon Errol. In July 1909 he broke into films, signing to the Selig Polyscope Company. Four years later he was signed to Universal and made his name as a character in one of the *Keystone Kops* silent films.

During this time he married and appeared with his wife Minta Durfee in many comedies of the period. One of the gags he introduced in his films was that of the 'pie in the face', a piece of slapstick that subsequently became a favourite with audiences, and which has become a staple of knockabout comedy to this day.

Arbuckle also introduced one of the great comic actors of the 20th century to the screen, Buster Keaton, by giving him a role in his 1917 film, *The Butcher Boy*. The pair became firm friends, and Keaton continued to remain loyal to Arbuckle throughout the scandal that followed. Keaton described him as one of the 'kindest souls' he had ever known and declared that he was incapable of committing the cruel act that he was accused of.

Arbuckle's career was by now in full flight and when he moved on to making feature-length movies, leaving the short films to Keaton, he became one of Hollywood's biggest stars. He signed to Paramount for the sum of one million dollars a year, a fee unheard of for those days. He began a hectic schedule of film-making, working on three feature films at the same time. On 3 September he decided to take a short holiday with two friends, Fred Fischbach and Lowell Sherman, both of whom were film directors. The three friends drove to San Fransisco and booked in at the St Francis Hotel. There they threw a party in their suite, inviting several women along, one of whom was an aspiring actress, Virginia Rappe.

ACCIDENTAL DEATH OR RAPE?

Much drinking and merriment ensued and everyone was having fun until Rappe became ill and a doctor had to be called. As Rappe had obviously been drinking, the doctor put her symptoms down to over-indulgence in alcohol. However, he was mistaken; three days later Rappe died, and the cause was found to be peritonitis, which had been caused by a rupture to her bladder.

When Rappe died, her friend Maude Delmont, who had accompanied her to the party, accused Arbuckle of having raped her, causing her death by his rough handling of her. Arbuckle at first responded to the charge dismissively, because he thought he had nothing to worry about, knowing he was innocent of the charge. What he did not realise was that Delmont was out to get money from his attorneys, trying to blackmail them into buying her silence. By the time Arbuckle found out what was going on, the story had become front-page news, and the damage to his career was already done.

Tragically for Arbuckle, it was not long before the story ran out of control and within days, charges were brought against him. When the case came to trial, it became one of the leading newspaper stories of the day. Unfortunately, the timing of the trial also coincided with a major moral panic about the entertainment industry, particularly the behaviour of Hollywood stars. Stories against Arbuckle appeared in all the newspapers owned by William Randolph Hearst, making him out to be guilty as charged. In addition, the Hollywood studios sided against him, eager to ingratiate themselves to the moralists and wanting to distance themselves from the scandal. They also forced actor friends of Arbuckle's, who would have been sympathetic witnesses, to maintain their silence, threatening them that they would lose their jobs if they spoke up in favour of him.

FILM BANNED

To make matters worse, around this time there were several other Hollywood-related scandals that hit the headlines: that of Wallace Reid, an actor and director who overdosed on drugs; Olive Thomas, the wife of a matinee idol, Jack Pickford, who had died from mistakenly drinking his medicine; and William Taylor, a director whose murder cast suspicion on two Hollywood actresses, Mary Miles Minter and Mabel Normand. Coincidentally, Normand had co-starred with Arbuckle in several of his films.

Because of all this, the authorities decided to censor the film industry, believing that the films being made, and the licentious behaviour of the Hollywood stars, were corrupting the nation's morals. As a result, the Hays Code, which ruled on what could legally be shown on screen – in terms of sex, violence and any kind of behaviour considered 'immoral'. This, of course, severely limited the films' subject matter and a series of worthy and very unpopular movies ensued as directors racked their brains as to how to circumvent the rules and yet still make dramatic, action-packed pictures. In the meantime, all of

Arbuckle's movies were banned by the censors, which was another huge blow to his career.

THE FINAL TRAGEDY

The result of the first two trials in the Arbuckle case resulted in a hung jury. At the third trial the jury finally acquitted Arbuckle and issued him with a written apology for the loss to his reputation – by now Arbuckle was unable to find work as an actor and was shunned by all the Hollywood studios. But it was too late; Arbuckle's morale had collapsed under the strain of the scandal and his life was in ruins. He divorced his first wife and married again, to Doris Deane, but after failing to find any work, became an alcoholic. His new wife soon divorced him, unable to cope with his erratic behaviour.

But although Arbuckle's star had fallen, his career was not over yet. Little by little, with the help of his old friend Buster Keaton, he began to find work in the movie industry once more, this time as a writer and director rather than an actor. He used the name William Goodrich (his father's name) as a pseudonym. Things began to look up: he cut down on his drinking and married again, eventually starting to make short films under his own name once more. On 28 June 1933, having completed two short films,

Warner Brothers signed him up to make a feature film. At this point, it seemed that, finally, the terrible scandal that had brought him down was behind him, and that he could now resume his glittering Hollywood career. He is said to have exclaimed, on signing the contract 'This is the best day of my life'.

Sadly, this happiness was not to last. That night Arbuckle suffered a massive heart attack and died. He was aged only 46. Undoubtedly, the fact that he was overweight had contributed to his health problems; but it also seemed likely that the strain of the scandal had taken its toll in the long run.

After his death, many critics cited his influence on comedy, but few prints of his films remained and today there are few examples of his work that still survive. Indeed, for many, the name of Roscoe 'Fatty' Arbuckle name lives on solely as a reminder of the damage that an unfair scandal can inflict on an individual. It wrecked his career, his relationships, his health and his legacy, as well as bringing him to an untimely death.

WOODY ALLEN

Woody Allen was one of the best-loved comedians and directors in Hollywood until a scandal erupted in his personal life that shocked not only the United States but the rest of the world. He began a relationship with his partner Mia Farrow's adopted daughter, Soon-Yi Previn. At the time, Allen was 57 and Soon-Yi was 22. Although Soon-Yi had never been formally adopted by Allen, and he therefore was not technically her stepfather, for many years he had been the partner of her adoptive mother and had obviously taken a parental role, watching the child grow up. Thus, although in purely legal terms Allen had done nothing wrong, the relationship between him and Soon-Yi was viewed by most onlookers as inappropriate, to say the least.

Had the matter stopped there, however, the scandal might have been forgotten; as it was, the situation took a turn for the worse when, during the ensuing custody battle, Farrow accused Allen of sexually abusing the daughter they had adopted together, Dylan (now known as Malone). The charges were later dropped, but the damage had been done, and Allen's reputation never entirely recovered from the scandal.

GIFT FOR COMEDY

Allen was born Allen Stewart Konigsberg to Martin and Nettea Konigsberg in New York City on 1 December 1935. His family were Jewish German immigrants, and Yiddish, as well as German, was spoken at home. In later years this Jewish background proved a constant source of inspiration and comedy for Allen. His parents were hard-working immigrants from the Lower East Side and when they married they moved to Flatbush, Brooklyn, where Allen and his sister Letty were raised.

Allen began his education at Hebrew school, then went to public school and high school, before attending New York University and City College of New York. However, he never took his university education very seriously, and before long was asked to leave both establishments, due to the fact that he hardly ever turned up to lectures or did any work. This was because, since the age of 16, he had been busy honing his career as a comedian.

From an early age, Allen had showed a strong gift for comedy. He wrote jokes for an agent, who sold them to newspaper columnists, and by the age of 16 he was writing for comedians such as Sid Caesar. Three years later, he was writing for TV comedy shows such as *The Ed Sullivan Show* and making a lot of money. In the early 1960s, Allen started a career as a stand-up comedian, making a joke out of his nervousness and playing up his image as a neurotic New York Jewish intellectual.

From there, he moved on to writing plays and screenplays, directing movies and, by the late 1960s, he was making his own films. He became one of the most creative film makers in Hollywood, writing, directing and starring in his own pictures, which ranged from offbeat comedies such as *Bananas, Sleeper* and *Love and Death*, to romantic comedies like *Annie Hall*, to serious dramas such as *Interiors*. On the way, he often broke new ground: *Annie Hall*, which also starred Diane Keaton, marked a new era for romantic comedy; *Manhattan*, made in black and white, was a touching tribute to the city he never left; and *Hannah and Her Sisters*, a romantic comedy with tragic undertones, won three Academy Awards. His output was extraordinary and besides these successes, there were numerous movies that failed at the box office but drew praise from the critics.

However, from the year 2000 onwards, most critics agreed that his movies were not up to his previous standards, until in 2005 he made *Match Point*, starring Scarlett Johansson, which was a box office success and won him another Academy Award. Despite his importance as a film maker, Allen chose never to attend the Academy awards ceremonies in person to collect his accolade.

LEADING LADIES

Throughout his career, Allen had a history of having relationships with his leading ladies, which began after he divorced his first wife, Harlene Rosen. The couple, aged 19 and 16, found they did not have much in common and spent many hours in bitter dispute. Harlene finally lost patience with her husband when he poked fun at her in public after she had been sexually assaulted by a stranger outside their apartment. She sued him for divorce, and after the split, Allen went on to marry actress Louise Lasser. He and Lasser co-starred in a movie called *Take the Money and Run*, but they divorced just three years later, although Lasser continued to star in his movies. His next leading lady was Diane Keaton, whom he cast in his Broadway show, *Play it Again, Sam*, and true to form, the couple became romantically involved. However, this time Allen did not marry his leading lady, although he always referred to her as 'the love of his life'. In 1977, the movie *Annie Hall*, which told of their romance, became a huge hit. Not long afterwards, he and Keaton split up but, like Lasser, she continued to star in his movies.

His next leading lady was Mia Farrow, who starred in many of the movies he made during the 1980s and early 1990s. When he met her, Farrow had six children, three biological children from her previous marriage with composer Andre Previn, and three children she had adopted with Previn, including a young girl called Soon-Yi. Soon-Yi had been found on the streets of Korea and was taken to an orphanage. It was here that she was introduced to her adoptive parents, Farrow and Previn, and taken to the United States.

NUDE PHOTOS

Allen and Farrow never set up home together, but they had a long, close relationship lasting over a decade. During this time, they had a son, whom they named Satchel but who later changed his name to Ronan. They also adopted another son and daughter, although Allen did not formally adopt Farrow's other children. This unconventional domestic arrangement continued until Farrow discovered some nude photographs that Allen had taken of her daughter Soon-Yi. Outraged, she sued Allen for divorce, and a huge scandal broke when the media and the public learned what was going on.

When the couple split, Allen openly continued his relationship with Soon-Yi, despite the many negative comments from the press. Farrow, who was reported to be devastated by the situation, sued Allen for custody of their children and in the process accused Allen of molesting their adopted daughter Dylan (later known as Eliza and then Malone) when she was only seven years old. The charges were later dropped, but the scandal had shocked the world. In the end the judge awarded Farrow custody of the children, and commented that Allen's relationship with Soon-Yi was 'inappropriate'. Allen and Soon-Yi went on to marry in 1997 and later adopted two daughters themselves, whom they named Bechet and Manzie after two of Allen's favourite jazz musicians.

ROCK HUDSON

Rock Hudson was one of the iconic Hollywood stars, a man who, with his good looks and well-built physique, epitomized red-blooded American masculinity during the 1950s and 1960s. Consequently, it was a tremendous shock to the nation when he became one of the first celebrities to die from AIDS, and his life as a homosexual was revealed. For some, it was as though the American Dream itself had died, and the reality of the modern world, with all its complexities and confusions, had taken its place.

HANDSOME NEW STAR

Leroy Harold Scherer Jr was born in Winnetka, Illinois. His father Roy was a car mechanic and his mother Katherine a telephone operator. During the Depression era of the 1930s, his father left home, never to return, and Katherine and her children were left to fend for themselves. When his mother remarried, Leroy took his new stepfather's name and adapted well to school life, graduating from high school and going on to join the navy in World War II. During his time in the war, Leroy worked as an aircraft mechanic, and also served in the Philippines. On his return Leroy decided to pursue a career as an actor, but failed to get into drama school and started to earn a living by truck driving. However, in 1948 his luck changed when he met a talent scout, Henry Willson, who was impressed by his good looks and found him work in the movies. Willson also made up a new, suitably masculine, name for his rising star: Rock, taken from the Rock of Gibraltar, and Hudson, taken from the Hudson River.

Hudson's first screen role was in a film called *Fighter Squadron*, made in 1948. Legend has it that Hudson had so much trouble remembering his one line in the film that it took 38 takes to get it right. But despite this unpromising start, Hudson went on to get more roles in films, primarily because he was an extremely handsome man. Many of his roles were physically demanding ones and he had to take lessons in riding, fencing and dancing. Then, in 1954 his break came in a film called *Magnificent Obsession*, playing a rogue who repented the error of his ways. The film showed that as well as being a matinee idol, Hudson could also act, and he went on become one of Hollywood's most popular stars, working with Elizabeth Taylor, James Dean and many other Hollywood greats.

LIVING A LIE

Unlike other Hollywood stars of the 1950s, Hudson's popularity continued well into the 1960s, and he extended his repertoire with a series of romantic comedies in which he played light-hearted roles with Doris Day as his leading lady. However, by the 1970s his star was beginning to fall, and although he toured the country in the musical *Camelot* and made several TV movies and series, by the end of the decade he was no longer the major movie star that he had once been. This led to a downward spiral of heavy drinking and smoking, until in 1981 he was forced to have heart surgery. In the following years, his health continued to deteriorate and by the time he took a role in the TV drama *Dynasty* in 1984, it was clear that he was seriously ill.

Throughout his career, Hudson had been living a lie. He was a homosexual, yet he was seen as a pin-up idol that women swooned over. Because of his status as a matinee idol, he felt, for obvious reasons, that he could not let his true sexuality be known. In the 1950s homosexuality was taboo in most social circles and it would undoubtedly have harmed his career if his sexual orientation had been revealed.

GAYS IN HOLLYWOOD

In 1955 Hudson married his agent's secretary, a woman named Phyllis Gates, in an effort to persuade his public, and perhaps himself, that he was heterosexual. The real reason for the marriage, which only lasted three years, is still a matter of speculation. In Gates's autobiography she claimed that she and Hudson fell in love and lived together before they married. However, after she died in 2006, some suggested that Gates was a lesbian, and that the pair had made a pact between them. It is thought that as a ploy to restore his reputation, Gates would become his wife, but then they would divorce, and in return, she would receive large sums of money from him for the rest of her life. And indeed, when this happened, her alimony amounted to over $200 a week for a decade. Today, the truth about the marriage remains unknown.

In later biographies of Hudson, there were claims that he had gay relationships with some of the most famous stars in Hollywood, including Marlon Brando and Burt Lancaster. There were other relationships with men such as the novelist Armistead Maupin and the publicist Tom Clark. Later, his co-star and friend Doris Day said she knew nothing of these liaisons, and that as far as she was concerned, her friend Rock Hudson was not gay, nor had she ever had cause to doubt his heterosexuality.

STRUCK DOWN BY AIDS

Whatever the truth of the matter, on 5 June 1984 Hudson was diagnosed with HIV, but chose to keep it a secret. Later, when he became visibly ill, his staff told reporters that he was suffering from liver cancer. That same year, he made an appearance on a TV show called *Doris Day's Best Friends* and the public were shocked by just how sick he was. He could hardly speak and he had become quite emaciated. Such was the public concern that on 25 July 1985, he finally issued a statement to the press saying that he was suffering from AIDS. Even then, he did not refer to his homosexuality, saying that it might be the case that he had contracted the disease during his heart bypass operation in the early 1980s.

Hudson became progressively weaker, until in October of that year, he died at his home in Beverly Hills, aged 59. He was one of the first, and most visible, gay men to die of AIDS and it came as a great shock to the public that this iconic symbol of

American manhood should die in so tragic a fashion. After his death, another scandal broke when his former partner Marc Christian sued Hudson's estate, saying that Hudson had continued to have sex with him after he knew he was HIV positive, thus jeopardising his health. This, however, was later disputed.

Today, Rock Hudson is remembered with a star on the Hollywood Walk of Fame. As one of the most handsome Hollywood stars of his day, he tragically became one of the first famous victim of AIDS; but today, it is his youth, health, fitness and vitality that will forever be captured on screen.

MARLON BRANDO

Marlon Brando was one of the most celebrated actors of the 20th century, introducing a new style of acting on to the screen, and becoming an icon to a rising generation. However, despite his massive success and international stardom, his life was a troubled one. Throughout his career he attracted notoriety: for example, in one instance he sent a Native American woman to pick up his Oscar award and deliver a long speech about America's oppression of the Native American tribes; in another, he was accused of making anti-Semitic remarks in an interview. His behaviour was also erratic to the point of showing mental instability, and his ludicrous demands earned him a reputation for being a spoiled, rich film star – both on and off set – and for this he became legendary. However, all this was nothing compared to the final scandal that seemed to break his spirit when in May 1990, his son Christian shot and killed his half-sister Cheyenne's boyfriend. Not long afterwards, to add to the tragedy, Cheyenne, who was suffering from depression, killed herself. At this point, Brando publicly announced in the courtroom that he had failed his children and went on to spend his declining years in semi-retirement, seldom appearing in films and demanding vast sums when he did. In addition, he grew ever more obese, which limited the number of roles he could take on. His behaviour grew increasingly bizarre and scandals continued to surround his personal life, until his death at the age of 80 in 2004, when it was revealed that he had been suffering from a form of dementia exacerbated by other illnesses.

TURBULENT CHILDHOOD

Brando was born on 3 April 1924 in Omaha, Nebraska, the son of Marlon Brando Sr and Dorothy Brando. He had two younger sisters, Jocelyn and Frances. His parents separated when he was a child, only to reconcile once more when he was 13, and together the family moved to an area north-west of Chicago. There was little security for him and his sisters as they were growing up, since their mother was an alcoholic who often spent long periods away from home, causing their parents' relationship to be somewhat turbulent. However, Brando later recalled his mother with affection as a talented and kind person, who supported him and his sisters in their artistic ambitions.

After dropping out of military school, where he had repeatedly got into trouble for disobedience, Brando's father got him a job digging ditches, but, not surprisingly, he soon tired of this occupation and moved to New York, where his sisters had gone to pursue their careers. His sister Jocelyn was training as an actress and introduced him to the theatrical world in the city. He soon impressed those he met with his personal charisma and began to study under Stella Adler. At her school, he learned method acting, which involved the actor submerging him or herself in the part, recreating the conditions under which the character lived, and drawing on parallel emotions in his or her own life.

In his first screen role for the 1950 movie *The Men*, Brando took this method to extremes, spending a month in bed at a hospital for veterans, so as to prepare himself to play the character of an embittered paraplegic. There was no doubt that he was profoundly committed to his craft and, although his way of achieving his ends was often idiosyncratic to the point of bizarre, most people agreed that he got results – although there were critics who felt that his acting was sometimes rather heavy-handed.

SIMMERING SEXUALITY

Brando's first big success in Hollywood was in the film of *A Streetcar Named Desire*, which he had played to great acclaim as a play on Broadway. The intensity and directness of his acting, together with his portrayal of the rough and ready Stanley Kowalski, completely revolutionised the film industry. He went on to make *Viva Zapata!*, *Julius Caesar*, *On the Waterfront* and *Arms and the Man*, and was soon hailed as the greatest actor of his time. When he played a motorcycle rebel in *The Wild One* he also became an icon for a rising generation – rock'n'roll heroes such as Elvis Presley modelled their style on Brando's in the film and, because of him, for the first time the working-class garb of T-shirt, jeans and boots became hip. Brando's simmering sexuality also earned him many female fans and there were tales of afternoon matinees that sold out because so many women with young children went to see the film. Apparently, not only was he a hit with the mothers but he also appealed to the children, who apparently made motorbike noises while running up and down the aisles. Brando also proved to be a great influence on other actors and film directors. For example, Nick Ray's *Rebel without a Cause*, starring James Dean, borrowed a great deal from *The Wild On*. In fact, many felt that Dean himself had copied a lot of Brando's style, although others pointed out that Dean's approach to acting was a lot more mercurial and had a lighter touch.

Despite all the accolades, however, by the end of the 1950s, Brando seemed to be running out of steam as an actor, and although he continued to be a major draw at the box office, the 1960s saw a slow decline in his career. This was partly because he was very difficult to work with and many studios avoided hiring him, but also because he chose to make films that were considered uncommercial, and consistently overspent when he was making a film.

However, in 1972 his career was revived by his unforgettable role as Vito Corleone in Francis Ford Coppola's *The Godfather*, in which he mumbled his way through the part but nevertheless managed to convey a powerful but tormented Mafia head. He followed this up with another extraordinary performance in Bernardo Bertolucci's *Last Tango in Paris*, in which he played another troubled, ageing man who engages in an affair with a much young woman after the death of his wife. Because of the sexual nature of the film, many missed the fact that Brando had given the performance of a lifetime, but even so, he reinvented his career. After *Last Tango*, his reputation was such that he could command enormous fees for cameo performances in films, and reputedly charged a million dollars a week for his appearance in Coppola's *Apocalypse Now*.

SCANDAL STRIKES

Throughout his film career, Brando's personal life had been extremely turbulent. He had many lovers, both men and women, and married several times. It was reputed that he had had sexual relationships with Rock Hudson and other famous Hollywood stars, but all he would say on the matter was that he was not ashamed of his homosexual encounters. Naturally, many women were drawn to Brando, and he developed a particular liking for exotic looking women. His first wife, Anna Kashfi, convinced him that she was Indian, although in fact she came from Wales and was from an Irish Catholic background. Not surprisingly, their relationship did not last long, and he went on to marry again, first to movie actress Movita Castaneda and then to a Tahitian girl many years his junior, Tarita Teriipia.

Brando had many children, including Christian Brando, by his first wife; Miko C. Brando and Rebecca Brando by his second wife; Teihotu Brando and Cheyenne Brando by his third wife. There were also a number of adopted children as well. But, despite the family's enormous wealth, the excesses of Brando's way of life impacted badly on the children, and in 1990 tragedy struck when his eldest son, Christian, shot a man dead at the family's mansion in Beverly Hills.

MURDER AND SUICIDE

The man was Drag Drollet, the Tahitian boyfriend of Brando's daughter Cheyenne. Christian was arrested, brought to trial, and received a sentence of ten years for voluntary manslaughter and using a gun. Brando gave evidence at the trial, and in a rambling speech that showed his mental imbalance, publicly apologised for having let his son down and announced that if he could have changed places with Drollet, he would. However, the parents of Drollet were not impressed, saying that they believed Brando to be 'acting' and accusing the US judicial system of letting Christian off lightly because he was the son of a movie star.

This was only the start of Brando's troubles, however. Tragically, in 1995 his daughter Cheyenne hanged herself. She was only 25 and had been depressed by the death of her lover at the hands of her half-brother. She also had a history of alcoholism, drug abuse and mental illness, like many other members of her family. To make matters worse, Tarita Teriipia, now divorced from Brando, accused her former husband of sexually abusing Cheyenne, which caused further scandal.

In the years that followed, Brando's behaviour began to decline still further, both on and off screen; he became unable or unwilling to remember his lines, and made ever more absurd, childish demands. He became reclusive, overweight and, in his later years, spent much of his time at his Tahitian refuge, or staying with his friend Michael Jackson on his Neverland Ranch. In 2004 he died and it was later revealed that had been suffering from several illnesses, including pulmonary fibrosis, congestive heart failure, diabetes, liver cancer and dementia. His life had been dogged by scandal and his death was a sad one, yet to this day he remains one of the iconic movie stars of the 20th century.

JAMES DEAN

Since his tragic early death in 1955, James Dean has remained the iconic teenager of American cinema. He embodied the image of the angry, angst-ridden young man and the role that he played with such intensity in *Rebel Without a Cause* focussed on many aspects of his real life, such as his conflicts with his father. Dean was, of course, very attractive to women, but what was less well known at the time of his fame was that he was almost certainly bisexual. The moral climate of the time made it very difficult for Dean to be honest about his sexuality; and the problems were compounded by the fact that he also seemed very unsure of his sexual orientation. Thus, throughout his years as a star, studio heads in Hollywood were always worried that a scandal would break, and did their best to keep the homoerotic elements of his movies under strict control.

Since his death, however, a number of biographies about his life have been written by people he came into contact with, and it seems clear that he was to some degree bisexual. Some have alleged that Dean dispensed his sexual favours so as to advance his career and that he was, therefore, only homosexual 'for trade reasons'. Others, including one of his former lovers, have described him as being attracted to both men and women, and as a person who, in many ways, did not fit in with the conventions of the restrictive society he lived in.

SEXUAL FAVOURS

Dean was born on 8 February 1931. His father Winton and mother Mildren lived in Marion, Indiana, before moving to Santa Monica, California. When he was nine years old, his mother died of cancer, which was a major emotional trauma for the young boy. Dean had been very close to his mother and had got on with her a great deal better than he did with his father. In fact, she was later described as being the only person who could understand him, and it seems that throughout his life Dean, in all his adult relationships with women, was constantly trying to reproduce that sense of understanding, but he was never able to succeed.

After his mother's death, young James was sent to live with his aunt Ortense and uncle Marcus, Quakers who lived on a farm in Indiana. During his high school years, he made friends with a Methodist pastor, Dr James DeWeerd, and became very close to him. Academically, Dean did not do particularly well at school, but he did excel at sports. When he finished high school, he moved back to California to live with his father, who by this time had remarried, and began to study law, but then changed course and transferred to drama lessons. This move resulted in tremendous conflict with his father, so much so that the two eventually became estranged.

However, despite the opposition from his father, it soon became clear that Dean had made the right choice. He seemed to have a natural ability for acting and worked hard on the technical aspects of his new career. Before long, he had dropped out of college to work as a professional actor. To begin with he struggled, gaining only small parts on advertisements and had to earn his living by working as a car park attendant at CBS studios. It was during this time that he allegedly began to exchange sexual favours in exchange for work opportunities in Hollywood, and sometimes so as to have a place to sleep at night. Accounts as to what exactly happened vary; some say that Dean used to boast that he had had sex with five of the major (male) Hollywood stars; others that he was working as a street hustler during this poverty-stricken period of his life. Another commentator, Ron Martinetti, describes Dean as having a homosexual relationship with a radio advertising director, Rogers Brackett, whom he had met while working at the car park. It was allegedly Martinetti who was to help Dean break out of the cycle of failure that he was trapped in.

STARDOM BECKONS

Whatever the truth of these stories, one thing was clear, Dean was not making much headway as an actor in Hollywood. The parts he gained in films were very small, and eventually he left California to try his luck in New York. His aim was to forge a career as a stage actor and after auditioning for the prestigious Lee Strasberg Actors Studio, he gained a place to study there. He was ecstatic and wrote letters to his family telling them how proud he was of being accepted at the studio, which had produced such great actors as Marlon Brando.

Dean began to take on TV roles, and then landed a part in Andre Gide's *The Immoralist*. He received rave reviews and it was then that Hollywood started to sit up and take notice. At last Dean was able to return to California, having at last made a success of his career. His first major role there was for director

Elia Kazan, in the film version of John Steinbeck's novel, *East of Eden*. He played the role of Cal Trask, the rebel son of an authoritarian father and a prostitute mother. Drawing on his actor's studio training, Dean put in an extraordinary performance, often bringing in completely unscripted improvisations, such as the pivotal moment when his father rejects a gift of money. Instead of leaving, as the script required, Dean threw his arms round his screen father in a final attempt to gain his affection. Kazan was so impressed by Dean's performance that he kept the sequence in, which gained added impact because of the other actor's look of surprise when Dean departed from the script.

HOMOEROTIC TENSION

Dean's next film, *Rebel Without a Cause*, truly established his iconic status in the history of American cinema. He played opposite Natalie Wood as his leading lady in the film directed by Nicholas Ray. It was a story of a new generation of young men and women bored and frustrated by small-town America, trying to escape from the misery of their family life and engaging in all manner of illegal, dangerous and anti-social activities, from drinking underage, to stealing cars, to knife fighting and drag racing. Dean and Ray clashed in the making of the film as Dean began to take control, directing his own scenes, and becoming intensely involved in portraying the central emotional conflict of his life – his battle with his father. In one scene Dean almost looked as though he was choking the actor playing his father to death. To add to the intensity, the director played on the homoerotic tension between Dean and the actor playing his young sidekick, Sal Mineo, even suggesting at one stage that they kiss, although this was banned by the studio heads.

After the success of *Rebel Without a Cause*, Dean sought to extend his acting career by playing a completely different kind of role, that of a bad-tempered, racist Southerner given to drinking and violence. For this part, Dean dyed his hair grey to look older, and shaved his hairline so that it would look as though he was going bald. He gave another intense performance, though in one scene, his drunken mumbling was so incoherent that it had to be re-recorded later, but he never lived long enough to see the reviews of the film.

HEAD-ON CRASH

On 30 September 1955, Dean set out with his mechanic Rolf Wutherich in his Porsche 550 Spyder to compete in a sports car race at Salinas, California. Now a hugely wealthy Hollywood star, Dean had taken up car racing, although he had been banned from doing so while filming. Having finished his work on *Giant*, an epic film directed by George Stevens covering the life of a Texas cattle rancher and his family, Dean celebrated by driving his car down to the rally, gaining a speeding ticket while doing so. On the way there, a car driven by a 23-year-old university student crossed into his lane on the highway and although Dean tried to take evasive action, it was too late. The two cars crashed head on. An ambulance arrived on the scene and rushed Dean to hospital, but by the time he got there, he was already dead. The student, Donald Turnupseed, escaped with his life and only sustained minor injuries.

After his death, Dean became a legend of American cinema. His status was undoubtedly enhanced by the fact that he had died early, in a manner befitting the careless young daredevil of *Rebel Without a Cause*. Not surprisingly, in the years to come, a lot of biographies were written about him, many of them focussing on his ambivalent sexuality. He became a major gay icon, and his films were constantly reanalysed, particularly the scenes between him and Sal Mineo, in which he shows a touching tenderness and love towards his young admirer.

In 2006 William Bast, who was at one time Dean's college room mate and close friend, finally admitted that he and Dean had had a homosexual relationship in his book *Surviving James Dean*. Bast describes the problems they had in pursuing the relationship in the moralistic culture of 1950s America, and also writes about Dean's relationship with producer Rogers Brackett, who was very important in helping Dean to forge his career in the movie industry. Some commentators, such as journalist Joe Hyams, maintain that Dean only involved himself in homosexual relationships to advance his career, but Bast disputes this, pointing out that in many cases, Dean's homosexual lovers were not able to help him in that way. Others who knew Dean, such as Gavin Lambert, Nicholas Ray and Elia Kazan, have described him as bisexual. Moreover, several women who had affairs with him, such as actress Liz Sheridan, confirm this, and it seems likely that, had Dean lived longer, the scandals about his sexuality would have seriously damaged his career.

HUGH GRANT

Actor Hugh Grant, known for his many film roles as the bumbling, feckless but charming British upper-class twit, became the subject of one of Hollywood's biggest scandals, when in 1995 he was arrested by police on Sunset Strip in Los Angeles. He was in his car with prostitute Divine Brown, who was apparently performing oral sex on him. The officer who arrested him charged him with lewd conduct in a public place and Grant later admitted that he had paid Brown $50 to perform the act. When the story came out, a police mug shot of Grant, looking somewhat dishevelled, appeared in newspapers all over the world, along with one of Ms Brown, who also looked somewhat the worse for wear.

The scandal was such that it looked as though Grant's reputation would be seriously damaged by the incident, especially as his long-time partner Liz Hurley, another Hollywood star, publicly admitted how upset she was by what had happened. However, in the event, the affair did not damage Grant too badly; in fact, some commentators felt it had actually helped his cause. After the event, Grant made no attempt to defend his behaviour, as many Hollywood stars would have done, and wasn't even afraid of being interviewed on the subject. Instead, he 'faced the music', taking the opportunity to apologise gallantly to all concerned, including Hurley. Indeed, he handled the scandal so well that he may, ironically, have increased his popularity among his female fans. Once the sordid details of his amorous tryst had emerged, his image of a flawed but lovable young man getting himself into scrapes – in the tradition of 'boys will be boys' – was not substantially altered. As his grandmother reportedly put it to her friends, explaining his behaviour, 'He had a few drinks and got fresh with the girls'. Sadly, however, his relationship with Hurley did not survive the scandal, and the couple parted, although they later went on to become close friends.

COMIC TALENT

Hugh John Mungo Grant was born in London, the second son of Fynvola MacLean, a teacher, and James Grant, a businessman and aspiring artist. The family had military connections, his grandfather being a member of the Seaforth Highlanders regiment, whose tradition was always to die in combat rather than ever to surrender. As a child, Grant was told the story of how his grandfather broke with the tradition to save hundreds of lives. Many years later, Grant spoke about his wish to make a film about his grandfather, but said this would be impossible as his father regarded all films as a 'vulgarisation of the truth'.

The Grants had no wish for their son to become an actor and were pleased when Hugh gained a place at Oxford University to study English. On completing his degree, however, he failed to do well enough to follow through with a doctorate, and instead began to trade on his good looks and charm. Before long, he had landed a part in a Merchant-Ivory film, *Maurice*, and proved that he wasn't just a pretty face but that he could actually act as well. More choice roles followed, until in 1994 he revealed his talent for comedy in the film that really made his name, *Four Weddings and a Funeral.* By this time he had developed an engaging film persona of an easily embarrassed, disorganised, rather selfish young man who seeks to avoid responsibility and entrapment in a domestic relationship at all costs. The role was undoubtedly based on the famous character of Bertie Wooster created by P. G. Wodehouse, but Grant's genius was to update it for the 1990s, which he did to great comic effect in the film.

ORAL SEX IN A CAR

Four Weddings was a huge success, and became the highest grossing British film ever. After its release, Grant became a major star, not only in Britain but internationally. He was seen as a golden boy and he and his partner, the glamorous Liz Hurley, became one of the most feted couples in Hollywood. However, the good times were about to end.

On 27 June 1995, Grant went for a drive down Sunset Strip, one of the main thoroughfares of Los Angeles. That evening, he was arrested by an officer of the LAPD as a black prostitute, Divine Brown, performed oral sex on him in his car. He was taken to the police station for identification, and when it became clear that he was one of the biggest film stars on the planet, his photograph was released to the newspapers. Grant was fined $1,180 and was put on two years' probation. Later, he explained what had happened. He had given 12 interviews that day for his newly released film, *Nine Months,* and had emerged in a state of confusion. Not surprisingly, few regarded this as a persuasive explanation of his behaviour.

Immediately after the incident, Hurley was reported to be very upset, and asked the media to give her some time to herself. Grant did the opposite, however, appearing on chat shows and giving interviews, in a move that – in retrospect – possibly saved his career. Instead of going into hiding, or blaming his childhood problems, as most Hollywood stars would have done, Grant decided to issue a full apology and to take the blame for his bad behaviour. On one show, *Larry King Live*, he said, 'In the end you have to come clean and say I did something dishonourable, shabby and goatish'. To Jay Leno he remarked, 'I think you know in life what's a good thing to do and what's a bad thing, and I did a bad thing, and . . . there you have it'.

FALL . . . AND RISE

Curiously enough, the film that Grant had just made, *Nine Months*, featured a character, Tom Arnold, who constantly got into trouble with the tabloid press, and Grant remarked that his 'nemesis' helped him through a difficult time. However, although the public forgave him – one woman even turned up to see him with a banner reading 'I would have paid you, Hugh' – Hurley did not, and the relationship came to an end.

Fortunately for Grant, the incident on Sunset Strip did not damage his career and, despite the scandal, the parts continued to come in thick and fast. Another major film triumph was *Notting Hill*, in which he starred with Julia Roberts, a movie that confirmed his increasingly stereotypical image as a British upper-class twit. Other successful romantic comedies followed, such as *Bridget Jones' Diary*, in which he began to emphasise the more selfish aspects of his screen personality, but like so many of Grant's movies, the film continued to rely on portraying stereotypes for its comic effect. In 2002's *About a Boy*, Grant extended his range somewhat by sporting a more modern hairstyle, and playing a disaffected wealthy bachelor who helps a young boy to mature, and in the process, grows up himself.

Today, Hugh Grant is one of Britain's most popular, highly paid actors. He continues to maintain a public image of bewilderment and ambivalence about his success, remarking in one interview that the only film he had starred in that didn't make him cringe was *About a Boy*.

Since his relationship with Hurley, his name has been linked romantically with several other women, including celebrity Jemima Khan, but he currently remains a bachelor. He affects a disdain for the film world and says he is writing a novel in case his acting career falls apart in the near future. However, that seems unlikely to happen: the self-deprecating, charming, yet selfish bachelor is a character that the public love, and that Hugh Grant plays to perfection.

As Julia Roberts once said of him, 'His silliness has grace. He could say, "I have foot fungus" and it would sound charming. It's the accent, the manner, the Oxford education.'

Hugh Grant is one of the few victims of scandal that has emerged unscathed, largely because of the stylish way in which he handled this crisis. Since then he has had to face allegations of attacking members of the paparazzi, but in true Hollywood style Hugh Grant has come out without losing any credibility.

WINONA RYDER

Winona Ryder is an American actress who has achieved notoriety for the portrayal of her roles, receiving a Golden Globe Award, a Screen Actor's Guild Award and two Academy Award nominations in 1993 and 1994. She has her own Star on the Hollywood Walk of Fame and is also known for her high profile romance with actor Johnny Depp in the early 1990s. In 2001, however, Ryder took on her most challenging role as a real-life defendant when she was arrested in Saks Fifth Avenue in Beverly Hills, suspected of taking several thousand dollars' worth of designer merchandise.

CLIMBING THE LADDER OF SUCCESS

Winona Laura Horowitz was born on 29 October 1971, being named after her hometown in Minnesota. When she was seven years old, the family moved to a commune in the town of Elk in northern California, where they lived with several other families. There was no television and Winona became an avid reader, losing herself in the characters from the books. From time to time movies were shown in the main barn on the commune and it was from these that Winona developed a strong desire to act.

Three years later the family were on the move again to Petaluma, just north of San Francisco. These were not happy days for Ryder as she suffered bullying at school, and life didn't improve until her parents gave her permission to enrol at the American Conservatory Theatre. Ryder was serious about carving herself a career in acting and luckily success came quickly. At the young age of 13, she was spotted by a talent scout and given a role in the film *Lucas*, starring alongside Charlie Sheen and Corey Haim. When asked how she would like her name to appear in the credits, she thought for a while and then chose the surname 'Ryder', after Mitch Ryder and the Detroit Wheels, which was one of her father's favourite bands.

Ryder gained real recognition when she was chosen by director Tim Burton to play in his movie *Beetlejuice*. She excelled in the part of Lydia Deitz, who was a gothic bookworm who defied her yuppie parents. The film was a major hit and so was Ryder, putting her firmly on the ladder of success. After

Beetlejuice the offers came in fast and she played a teenage bride in *Great Balls of Fire*, Cher's long-suffering daughter in *Mermaids* and another gothic character in *The Addams Family*.

TROUBLED LOVE LIFE

Ryder first met actor Johnny Depp at the premier of *Great Balls of Fire*. They were immediately attracted to one another and began a love affair which survived three years. Depp was infatuated and even had 'Winona Forever' tattooed on his arm. They appeared together in Tim Burton's next project, *Edward Scissorhands*, which was a huge box office success and once again secured her popularity with her fans.

Due to her tempestuous relationship with Depp, although she put it down to exhaustion and over-work, Ryder missed a big opportunity when she pulled out of role in *Godfather 3*. Ryder took other roles, gradually losing her teenage image, but the pressure slowly started to show. Her relationship with Depp was on the rocks, she was suffering from insomnia, and Ryder decided to check herself into a psychiatric clinic for a short period.

After a few years of sticking to mainly literary works, Ryder got her life back on track and started a new relationship with the singer from the group Soul

Asylum. While working on the set of *Alien: Resurrection*, the fourth in the Alien saga, Ryder struggled with her part and, to add to her troubles, fell and injured her back. She was prescribed painkillers, but little did she realise at the time that these would cause her no end of problems.

BAD TIMES

In 2001 Ryder boosted the ratings of the television show *Friends*, when she was seen kissing Jennifer Aniston in a lesbian embrace. However, the gossip this stirred up in the press was nothing compared to what was happening in her private life. In August that same year, Ryder was forced to go into a clinic suffering from acute stomach pains, forcing her to drop out of her latest movie. The following month she went to visit Dr Jules Lusman, breaking down in his office because she said she was in so much pain. He diagnosed it as a spinal condition that had been caused by the fall during her filming of *Alien*, and recommended that she took an opiate-based painkiller to kill the pain. However, the painkiller itself was known to be highly addictive and, added to this he prescribed her Valium, a fashionable drug among the celebrity set. The doctor had been recommended to her by one of her friends, but little did Ryder realise at the time that the physician was not actually doing her any favours. In fact, Lusman had been under investigation for 'over-prescribing' since 1997, but it was too late for Ryder, who was already on a slippery slope.

In December 2001 Ryder was caught up in a scandal when she was caught shoplifting at Saks Fifth Avenue. Having already paid around $4,000 for purchases, she was found to have a further 20 items on her for which she had no receipts. These items included a Gucci dress, five handbags and four hairpieces, valued at around $5,500. It was alleged that not only had she taken tissue paper with her to wrap the goods up, but that she also carried scissors to cut off the security tags. Worse still, when she was searched, the police found she was in the possession a variety of toxic drugs, and couldn't produce a prescription for one of them.

Ryder tried to explain her actions by saying that she was just acting out a role for a part in Steve Martin's *Shopgirl*. However, but with public opinion high that celebrities could get away with anything, the prosecutors were determined to make an example of her. If found guilty, Ryder could face up to three years in jail.

At the trial, the jury heard a lot of damning evidence and it was said that Ryder had received 37 prescriptions from as many as 20 different doctors between January 1996 and December 1998. Lusman, whose offices had been searched after Ryder's arrest, was himself being charged for over-prescribing, but backed his patient's claim that he had actually prescribed her the Endocet. Lusman had prescribed Endocet to relieve the pain, but not only was it a highly addictive substance, it was although known to have other side effects such as impairing a person's thinking or reactions.

On the same say that Lusman had his licence revoked – 6 December 2002 – Ryder was acquitted of burglary, but was found guilty of vandalism and grand theft. She was sentenced to 480 hours of community service and three years' probation. She was ordered to pay $3,700 in fines and $6,355 in compensation.

For a while Ryder's life was in disarray, with a string of broken relationships and a struggle to give up the drugs prescribed to allegedly help her health. After a series of either collapsed or delayed projects, Ryder eventually returned to successful film roles in 2006. Although seriously rocked by scandal, it would appear that Ryder eventually survived and has continued to be a hit with her fans. Six years after her infamous shoplifting incident, Wynona Ryder graces the cover of *Vogue* magazine and proves what a tough cookie she really is.

RIVER PHOENIX

The tragic death of River Phoenix at the age of only 23 caused a huge scandal in the United States. Firstly, because the young actor had always stressed his healthy lifestyle as a vegan and as a person who stayed away from drugs of any kind. Secondly, because it highlighted how troubled he was, having been a victim of child sexual abuse that he had suffered when he was only four years old. This information did not come to light until shortly before his death. His parents had been part of a cult organisation known as the Children of God, and a scandal had erupted during the 1970s and 1980s when it became known that their leaders advocated sexual contact between adults and children, and even proposed that incest was acceptable. By the 1990s, River Phoenix himself had taken to making angry remarks on the subject of the cult, but it was not until his death that the American press and public realised just how severely disturbed his mental state had become as a result of this, and other pressures.

THE RISE OF A STAR

He was born River Jude Bottom in Metolius, Oregon, on 23 August 1970 to John Lee Bottom and Arlyn Sharon Dunetz. His parents had adopted the name Phoenix and were missionaries of the Children of God and travelled throughout South America, trying to convert people to the cause. River was named after the River of Life in Herman Hesse's novel *Siddhartha*, and his middle name came from the song 'Hey Jude' by the Beatles. He and his siblings, Joaquin, Rain, Summer and Liberty, grew up without the usual trappings of modern life, and the family lived most of their time with very little money. Travelling around the world, the children witnessed scenes that made them grow up very fast. Legend has it that Joaquin, aged four, persuaded his family to stop eating meat after seeing fishermen killing fish on a trawler by banging their heads against the boat. As an adult, River continued to be a vegan, and refused to wear leather, even using a rope instead of a belt to hold up his trousers.

All the siblings pursued careers in the entertainment business: like River, Joaquin, Rain, Summer and Liberty became actors, although Liberty gave up acting while still only a child. This path was encouraged by their parents. While still in his teens,

River had a major role in the movie *Stand By Me*, which brought him public acclaim in 1986. After this success, he went on to garner more important roles and at the age of only 18 was nominated for an Oscar for his role in *Running on Empty* in 1988. River went on to star in films such as *My Own Private Idaho*, *Sneakers*, and *The Thing Called Love*, becoming one of America's most successful young actors, and making friends with such stars as Keanu Reeves. On the set of *The Thing Called Love* he met his girlfriend Samantha Mathis, who was present on the night he died.

AN EMBARRASSED IDOL

As well as his career as a movie star, River also had his own band, Aleka's Attic, and became friends with artists such as Flea of the Red Hot Chili Peppers and Michael Stipe of REM. According to many sources, it was music rather than acting that was his real passion. However, the income he was making from his movie career was helping to keep his family, so he continued to make films. He was not very happy about being presented as a teen idol, and actually found his fame embarrassing. He very seldom smiled in photographs and was reported to be disgusted by representations of himself as a sex symbol.

Unlike many young movie stars on the 1990s,

River Phoenix was extremely critical of the drug culture pervading Hollywood, and he made a point of discussing the virtues of a vegan diet and holistic medicine when he was interviewed. He was also critical of the political and social system of the United States, at a time when radicalism was very unpopular in the country. He made it clear that he considered the prevailing culture to be morally corrupt and had tried to live differently from his peers by refusing to take drugs, eat meat, or medicate himself in the conventional way.

Towards the end of his life, he began to criticise the way he was brought up, alleging that he had lost his virginity when aged only four, and saying that he found the Children of God cult disgusting because 'it ruined people's lives'. He went on to add that, although the sexual abuse happened when he was still under five, after that he had remained celibate until he reached adulthood.

DRUG OVERDOSE

Although he was so successful, River suffered from depression and was also given to compulsive behaviour at times, which included substance abuse. Commentators have suggested that this was due to his childhood trauma of sexual abuse, although the exact details of what happened have never become clear. After the public outcry that met their views, the Children of God changed their argument and began to teach otherwise, but there was always the suspicion that a great deal of harm had been done while they espoused their bizarre beliefs – just at the time, in the 1970s, when River was growing up.

Given his adherence to an ascetic lifestyle, the American public were shocked when news came that River Phoenix had died on 31 October 1993 of a drug overdose. According to those present, he had been partying at the Viper Room, a Hollywood nightclub owned by movie star Johnny Depp. He had been indulging in speedballs, a dangerous mixture of heroin and cocaine, and had also been smoking cannabis. After he died, a coroner's report showed that he also had an unusually large amount of cough syrup in his stomach.

SCANDAL BREAKS

As details of the evening's activities came out, it became clear that Phoenix had engaged on a drug spree that Halloween night. Shortly before one o'clock on the morning of 31 October, River had been in the bathroom of the Viper Room doing drugs with some friends who were known dealers. One of his friends offered him a snort of a high-grade drug called 'Persian Brown', which contained opiates and methamphetamine. The so-called friends told River that it would make him feel on top of the world. However, almost immediately after he had snorted the drug, River started to tremble and shake and vomited violently after screaming at his friends to help him. One of the men splashed his face with cold water and then offered him a Valium to help him calm down, probably not realising that it was the worst thing they could have done. River staggered back into the bar and then over to his sister Rain and his girlfriend Samantha. He started to complain that he couldn't breathe and passed out for a few minutes. When he came round he asked his girlfriend to help him outside to get some fresh air. However, once outside the club River collapsed on the pavement and started to have seizures. A photographer, Ron Davis, aware that something was seriously wrong, went to call 911 at a nearby payphone and River's brother, Joaquin, also called for help. Because River was thrashing around so violently, Rain threw herself on top of his body to try and control the seizure, but it was all in vain because by this time River had stopped breathing. By the time the paramedics arrived at 1.14 a.m. he was in cardiac arrest, his skin had turned blue and all efforts of revival failed.

When the news of his death broke, it was all the more shocking because Phoenix had portrayed such a clean image, and seemed, more than most young Hollywood actors, to have his life under control. His friends and family did not, on the whole, speak to the press about the matter and have continued to maintain a dignified silence about it ever since.

Critics, however, have discussed it a great deal and have been struck by the uncanny similarities between the stories told in many of his movies and his own life – in particular, the way he died so suddenly, and tragically, at such a young age. River Phoenix, who had everything to live for, tragically died at a time when he had fame, money, friends and at 23, supposedly plenty of time to enjoy it. Instead, his untimely death was surrounded by scandal, which his family have worked their hardest to survive.

ROBERT BLAKE

'This really was a story out of a bad novel,' CNN legal analyst Jeffrey Toobin commented when details of the scandal surrounding actor Robert Blake began to emerge. Blake had been arrested for the murder of his wife Bonnie Lee Bakley, but just how contorted their relationship had been was not generally known until news of the incident reached the media. And, indeed, once the story was out, it really did seem extraordinary that such a tale of deception, stupidity and callous behaviour between two people could ever have taken place.

A RISING CHILD STAR

Robert Blake, most famous for his role in the US television series *Baretta*, was born Michael Gubitosi on 19 September 1933 in Nutley, New Jersey. He was one of three children, with a brother James and a sister Giovanna. His father Giacomo, an Italian immigrant, who worked as a die setter in a can factory. His mother, Elizabeth, performed with her son James as a song and dance act. Later, coached by their mother while still very young, the three children began performing together as a group called *The Three Little Hillbillies*. In 1938, the family moved to California, where Elizabeth began to find work for the children as movie extras.

When he was only six, Michael began to act in MGM movies, appearing regularly in shorts such as *Our Gang*. Eventually, he became the lead character in the series, and by the time he was ten, he was a seasoned actor. He found a new stage name, Bobby Blake, and started to work in westerns and comedies, appearing with Humphrey Bogart in *The Treasure of the Sierra Madre*.

A TROUBLED CHILDHOOD

His career flourished, but he later claimed that his childhood had been miserable due to the fact that his father was an alcoholic and was often violent towards him. He got into trouble at school for fighting and was expelled, after which he ran away from home, eventually joining the army.

After his spell in the army, Blake returned to California with the intention of becoming a serious actor. As Robert Blake, his career in TV and movies was extremely successful, and he made a name for himself playing tough, violent characters whose lives were in emotional turmoil. During the 1970s, he became a household name as Tony Baretta, the undercover detective in the TV series *Baretta*, whose motto was 'don't do the crime if you can't do the time' – a phrase that was, ironically, to become apt to his personal life in later years.

LONELY HEARTS SWINDLE

In 1962 Blake married actress Sondra Kerr and the couple had two children. However, during the 1980s the couple divorced and Blake's career also began to wane. In 1999, he met Bonnie Lee Bakley. Bakley had an extremely unsavoury past as a con woman. For many years, she made a living running a lonely hearts scheme, sending naked pictures of herself to men and promising to visit them for a fee. She had numerous brushes with the law, and had been under investigation for fraud. In several cases, Bakley swindled men out of their savings and made a good deal of money out of her scam, allowing her to buy land and property. She used some of her ill-gotten gains to fund a career as a Hollywood entertainer, using the stage name Leebonny, however, this was largely unsuccessful.

By all accounts, Bakley was obsessed with celebrity status, and made it her business to date famous men whenever she could. At the time when she met Blake, Bakley was dating Christian Brando, the son of Marlon Brando.

MARRIAGE TRAP

After having only known Blake for a short period of time, she told him she was pregnant, but she couldn't be sure who the father was. When a DNA test determined that Blake was in fact the father, Blake agreed to marry her. The reasons for this remain under dispute, but the outcome was that, after the marriage, Blake set Bakley up in a small guest house next to his home in the San Fernando Valley. Rumours circulated that Blake wanted the child to give to his eldest daughter to raise, which – as it turned out – is exactly what happened in the final outcome.

Bakley's history as a wife and mother left a lot to be desired, to put it mildly. She had been married ten times and Blake was her tenth husband. She had two children by her second husband, Paul Gawron, who was also her cousin. She also had a daughter whose father she claimed was Jerry Lee Lewis, the rock 'n'roll star, even naming the child Jeri Lee Lewis after him. Her fourth child, a girl, was initially named

Christian Shannon Brando, and later renamed Rose Lenore Sophia Blake.

SHOT IN THE HEAD

Not surprisingly, Blake soon fell out with his new wife. It was rumoured that Blake bitterly regretted the marriage, hated Bakley and was desperate to get rid of her. On 4 May 2004, he took her out to dinner at Vitello's Restaurant on Tujunga Boulevard in Studio City. After the meal, Bakley was found sitting in a car parked round the corner from the restaurant – she had been shot in the head. When questioned, Blake's excuse was hardly reassuring; he said that he had not been present when Bakley was killed because he had gone back to the restaurant to fetch a gun that he had left lying on the table there.

On the face of it, there seemed to be a clear motive as to why Blake should want to murder Bakley. He had a history of violence and Bakley had tricked him into marriage through her pregnancy, or so he claimed. However, despite the circumstantial evidence against him, the situation was not, in fact, as clear cut as it appeared. First of all, it was difficult to find hard evidence that Blake had actually shot his wife as there were no witnesses to the actual murder. In addition, her past history as a con woman meant that there were a lot of men who might want to kill her – men that she had lied to, swindled money out of and become sexually involved with. Many claimed that Bakley had had a voracious, some would say perverted, sexual appetite and it was argued that this might have laid her open to violence by numerous ex-lovers. Not only this, but according to the defence lawyers in the case, Bakley was a drug addict who had in the past used her older daughter as a prostitute to earn money to fuel her addiction. This meant that there were many people who had, allegedly, been victims of Bakley's selfish behaviour in her desperate desire for drugs, money, sex and celebrity status.

EX-LOVER'S PRISON RECORD

There was one past lover who looked, like Blake, as though he could have had something to do with the murder. Christian Brando, whom Bakley was dating when she met Blake, was noted for his out-of-control behaviour. In fact, he had served eight years in prison for the manslaughter of his half-sister's lover. The Christian Brando case was well known and had shocked America, because his father was one of the country's most famous actors, Marlon Brando. When details of the incident came out, they revealed just how far the Hollywood star's family life had descended into chaos. Like Blake, Christian Brando was part of a Hollywood B list of celebrities renowned for their wild behaviour, and the stories that surrounded his life involved the usual litany of dysfunctional families, drugs, drink, sexual abuse and violence. So it was not unreasonable to suspect that Christian Brando, whom Bakley claimed had fathered her baby, might have been incensed by her behaviour and taken revenge.

'A MISERABLE HUMAN BEING'

Despite the uncertainties and lack of evidence, Blake was charged with the murder of his wife Bonny Lee Bakley. However, when the case came to trial, largely because of the complications mentioned above, the prosecution was unsuccessful. On 16 March 2005, Blake was found not guilty. Blake had also been charged on two counts of hiring a former stuntman to murder her. He was cleared on one of these charges, and the other was dropped after the deadlocked jury finally came to a decision and acquitted him.

After the trial, many commentators felt that the decision had been unfair. Los Angeles District Attorney Steve Cooley went so far as to call the jury 'incredibly stupid' and gave his opinion that Blake was a 'miserable human being'. However, none of this altered the fact that Blake was allowed to go free. On 18 November 2005, Bakley's children sued Robert Blake in a civil trial, claiming that he was responsible for their mother's death. This time, the charge stuck, and Blake was found liable for her wrongful death. He was ordered to pay a fine of 30 million dollars. Since then, Robert Blake has filed for bankruptcy, but Bakley's children believe that this is just a ploy to evade payment of the fine, and that he is hiding his money. To date the conflict continues, as Blake seeks a retrial of the case and continues to claim that he is penniless.

ROB LOWE

The American actor Robert Lowe is perhaps best known today for his role as Sam Seaborn in the popular TV series *West Wing*. During the 1980s, as one of the so-called 'Brat Pack' of good-looking young actors, he made a series of movies that increased his already high profile. However, in 1988 his career hit a low patch when it was revealed that a videotape was circulating which showed him having sex with two young women. It later transpired that one of the young women was underage, and even though he argued that he did not realise this at the time, he was shunned by powerful elements in the film world for a considerable period after the scandal hit the headlines.

THE GOLDEN BOY

Robert Hepler Lowe was born on 17 March 1964 in Charlottesville, Virginia. He was the son of a lawyer,

Charles Lowe and a teacher, Barbara Hepler. While he was growing up, his parents divorced and Lowe and his brother were brought up in the Episcopalian church. His mother moved the children around, first to Dayton, Ohio, and then to Los Angeles, where Lowe attended Santa Monica High School, making friends with a number of other young would-be actors. These included Sean Penn and Robert Downey Jnr, while living next door to them was the Sheen family. Not surprisingly, Robert, who was a good-looking boy, gravitated towards acting as his chosen career.

When he was 19, he was cast in the TV show *Thursday's Child*. His big break came in 1983, in Francis Ford Coppola's *The Outsiders*, which also launched the careers of other big names in the film world, such as Tom Cruise and Patrick Swayze. By his early 20s, Lowe had the kind of life most people can only dream of – he was good-looking, he was rich, he dated women like Princess Stephanie of Monaco and Nastassja Kinski and on top of that he was a film star. But then, he made a big mistake.

A 'LESBIAN CLINCH'

Lowe was involved in politics and he attended the Democratic convention in Atlanta, campaigning on behalf of Michael Dukakis. While he was there, he met two women in a nightclub and took them to his hotel for a sex session. What he did not know, he claims, was that one of the girls was only 16 and had got into the club under false pretences.

At the hotel, he filmed the two women in what the media dubbed a 'lesbian clinch', but what the actor did not foresee was that the women would steal the tape from him. A year later, the mother of the youngest girl found out about the tape and sued him. Since the girl was only 16, she was underage by the law of Georgia, which forbids lesbian sex until the age of 18.

As it turned out, the case did not come to court. Lowe settled out of court with the girl's mother and completed a term of community service as punishment. However, that was not the end of the matter because the tape was later released by pornographer Al Goldstein, which further harmed Lowe's career. The 'Sex Video', as it became known, appeared on Lowe's filmography on the Internet, and was jokingly called the best film he had ever made. For a while, it seemed that the episode had tarnished his film career to such a degree that he was no longer in demand. Offers from the major studios dried up and he was forced to take small parts in television to keep his head above water.

ADDICTIONS TO ALCOHOL AND SEX

Lowe himself saw the episode as a watershed in his personal life. As he tells the story, it was a wake-up call to end a life which had been blighted by an addiction to alcohol, sex and constant partying. It was during this time that he met his future wife, make-up artist Sheryl Berkoff. Initially, she was dating Emilio Estevez, another member of the Brat Pack, who had been a friend of Lowe's at school. She and Lowe had a one-night stand together, but later fell out when Lowe admitted this liaison to Estevez. However, when the scandal of the Atlanta tape hit the headlines, Sheryl befriended Lowe and stuck by him as he became the butt of humour for actors and directors in the film world and the media pundits. At her request, Lowe entered a rehabilitation clinic for alcohol and sex addiction. The couple married in 1991, after he promised her that he would give up the lifestyle that had led to these problems. Today, they have two children, Edward and John.

After the scandal, Lowe slowly began to rebuild his career. As he grew older, he was cast in parts that demanded more from him and he began to relish the fact that he was no longer just playing a handsome hunk. He began to land comedy roles, in films like *Wayne's World* and *Austin Powers*, and also had a spot presenting *Saturday Night Live*, which showed that he had a quick sense of humour.

His most successful part was the character Sam Seaborn in *West Wing*, written by Aaaron Sorkin. He said of the part, 'Sam has been a gift, in that Aaron was smart enough to see that you can be a handsome person as well as a brain. He has never traded on the sexuality of the character. If I had been on *Ally McBeal*, I would have been seen coming out of the shower on the first show'. Like Lowe, Sorkin himself was no stranger to scandal; at various times he had been arrested for being in possession of marijuana, mushrooms and crack cocaine.

The *West Wing* became one of the most popular shows on American television, but disputes arose over the way Sorkin wrote the shows. Lowe felt that his character was being marginalised and eventually left the series. He was quickly followed by Sorkin, and after their departure the show's rating plummeted. Lowe returned for two more episodes and then moved on. He produced and starred in two more drama series, but neither of these managed to engage the public. Later, he returned to working with Sorkin, in a play in London's West End. He also starred in several mini-series.

Today, Lowe sees himself as being very lucky, in that not only was he able to regain his acting career after the scandal, but he also made drastic changes in his personal life that, he says, have brought him great happiness.

When interviewed about his past life, Lowe admitted that he regrets nothing, saying, 'I wouldn't be where I am today without my mistakes. Particularly my mistakes. Exclusively my mistakes.' Rob Lowe seems to have learned how to survive a scandal and the once, so-called 'good time boy' seems to have manage to have fixed himself firmly in the affections of his fans.

LANA TURNER

The sultry film star Lana Turner, whose heyday was in the 1940s and 1950s, had a turbulent love life, both on and off screen. As she once put it succinctly, 'I liked the boys, and the boys liked me'. She had seven husbands and many lovers, and scandal and rumour were very much part of her life. However, there was a scandal that reached epic proportions when she and her 14-year-old daughter, Cheryl, became involved in the murder of her lover Johnny Stompanato, a Los Angeles gangster, with whom she had a characteristically stormy relationship.

FATHER MURDERED FOR MONEY

The story of Lana Turner was a rags-to-riches one which epitomised the excitement of Hollywood in its glory days. She was born Julia Jean Mildred Frances Turner in Wallace, Idaho, on 8 February 1921. Her father, John Virgil Turner, was a miner from

Tennessee, and her mother Mildred Frances Cowan, was a 16-year-old girl from Alabama. Growing up, Lana was known as 'Judy' and her parents struggled to make a living, eventually moving to San Francisco to try and improve their life. Shortly after moving, her father was murdered after winning a small sum of money in a craps game. Apparently, he had stuffed his winnings in his sock and was found dead on a street corner. His murderer was never caught.

Lana and her mother, who was now suffering health problems, moved to Los Angeles. By the age of 16, Lana was attending Hollywood High School, and one day, instead of taking her usual typing class, she decided to go down to the Top Hat Café on Sunset Boulevard for a soda. It turned out to be the best decision she ever made.

'THE SWEATER GIRL'

While she was at the café, she caught the eye of the publisher of the *Hollywood Reporter*, William R. Wilkerson. Wilkerson and his wife were struck by Lana's outstanding beauty and curvaceous figure. They introduced her to talent agent Zeppo Marx, who in turn took her to see film director Mervyn LeRoy. She made her debut appearance in the 1937 film *They Won't Forget*. In this film, she famously wore a very tight sweater and her highly alluring appearance created a sensation. After this, she was known as 'the sweater girl' and became a pin-up. Following this performance with equally glamorous film appearances throughout the 1940s and 1950s. Her most memorable film was the 1946 film noir classic, *The Postman Always Rings Twice*. She continued to make films during the 1950s, but by the end of the decade her popularity was starting to decline, in part due to a huge scandal that had broken out about her private life.

A ROCKY RELATIONSHIP

The scandal involved Turner's relationship with Johnny Stompanato, a man she had met during the spring of 1957 after ending her marriage to Lex Barker. She had divorced Barker because her daughter Cheryl, by a former marriage, claimed that Barker had repeatedly molested and raped her. She now became involved with Stompanato, who was good looking and apparently a great lover. However, after learning of his links with the gangsters of Los Angeles, in particular, Mickey Cohen, Lana decided to break off the relationship. This proved difficult to do: Stompanato did not want her to leave, and the pair continued to fight, sometimes violently, occasionally reconciling their differences.

STABBED TO DEATH

Towards the end of that year, Turner travelled to England to star in a film with Sean Connery. Stompanato was worried that she was amorously involved with Connery and stormed on to the film set waving a gun, intending to put a stop to the imagined liaison. As the story goes, Connery leapt dramatically to Turner's defense and punched Stompanato in the mouth, also managing to take away the gangster's gun. On this occasion, Stompanato was arrested and deported back to the United States.

However, that was not the end of the sordid affair between Stompanato and Turner. On 4 April 1958, the couple started to argue violently in her house on Bedford Drive, Beverly Hills. By this time, Turner's daughter Cheryl was aged 14. Fearing that her mother's life was in danger, Cheryl took a kitchen knife and ran to help her. In the fracas that followed, Stompanato was fatally stabbed.

Not surprisingly, the incident caused a huge furore in the press. Many theories were advanced as to what had happened, but of course no one other than Turner, Cheryl and Stompanato had been present at the time of the killing. Some believed that Turner was in fact guilty and called her testimony in the witness box at the trial 'the performance of her life', and undoubtedly, she brought her dramatic skills into play while giving her evidence. But whatever the truth of the matter, in the end Cheryl was thought to have committed the act, and it was judged to be a justifiable homicide. Neither mother nor daughter were charged with the murder.

MARRIED EIGHT TIMES

In typical style, Turner managed to rebound from this horrifying episode, and went on to rebuild her career, havinge some of her biggest hits shortly afterwards. Indeed, the notoriety she gained from the Stompanato affair seemed to enhance her popularity. In 1959, she starred in *Imitation of Life*, a film directed by Douglas Sirk, which was a remake of Ross Hunter's classic. Turner made a fortune from the film, since she had elected to take a share of the box-office receipts instead of a fee. One of the most dramatic elements of the film was that it dealt with the issue of a single mother and her troubled teenage daughter, which closely resembled Turner's own situation in her private life. This was also the case with another of her films, an adaptation of the novel *Peyton Place*.

Turner was famous for her sexual allure, and was married eight times, remarrying the same man once. This in itself caused constant scandal and rumour about her private life, though not on the scale of the Stompanato murder. Her first husband was bandleader Artie Shaw, whom she eloped with on their first date when she was only 19 years old. The marriage lasted only four months. Like many of her other romantic involvements, her relationship with Shaw was characterised by dramatic arguments and reconciliations.

Next up was actor-restaurateur Josef Crane. This marriage was annulled when it became clear that Turner's previous divorce to Shaw had not come through. The couple separated, during which time Crane attempted suicide. They then remarried as Turner had given birth to their daughter, Cheryl.

DIAMOND RING IN MARTINI

Turner's third husband was millionaire playboy Henry J. Topping, and legend has it that he proposed to her by dropping a huge diamond ring into her martini. However, although both of them were extremely rich, Topping managed to run through their joint income at an alarming rate, making foolish investments and gambling heavily. When the money finally began to run out, Turner divorced her spendthrift husband.

The next three husbands did not last much longer. Actor Lex Barker, whom Turner married in 1953, received his marching orders only four years later, when Turner's daughter Cheryl accused him of molestation and rape. Subsequently, Rancher Fred May found himself out on his ear after only two years of marriage, between 1960 and 1962. The next husband, writer Robert P. Eaton, married Turner in 1965 but by 1969 the relationship was over. Eaton did, however, salvage something out of the marriage; his novel *The Body Brokers*, about the sordid truth behind the Hollywood myth, featured a character called Marla Jordan, who bore more than a passing similarity to his former wife. The final husband was Ronald Peller, also known as Ronald Dante, a nightclub hypnotist whose short period of tenure was between 1969 and 1972.

By the 1970s and 1980s, Turner's years on the silver screen as a sex siren were over, but she continued to act in television. A heavy smoker throughout her life, she died of throat cancer in 1995, at the age of 74. She left some of her estate to her daughter Cheryl and Cheryl's lesbian life partner Joyce LeRoy, whom Turner had accepted as a second daughter. The bulk of it, however, was left to her maid, Carmen Lopez Cruz. Today, Lana Turner is remembered as one of the legendary Hollywood stars, whose turbulent private life provided her adoring public with a never-ending supply of gossip, rumour and scandal.

RUDOLPH VALENTINO

Silent film actor Rudolph Valentino was given the nickname 'The Great Lover' and was a Latin sex symbol and a popular heart throb in the 1920s. Perhaps the label of a great lover was a little hypocritical, as the question of his sexuality reared its ugly head from time to time and many of his relationships ended in misery. Valentino became involved with a scandal that involved people of high society, after which he resorted to changing his name to avoid losing his reputation.

Rudolfo Alfonzo Raffaelo Pierre Filibert Guglielmi de Valentina d'Antonguolla was born on 6 May 1895 in Castellaneta, Italy. His mother, Marie Berthe Gabrielle Barbin was French and his father, Giovanni Antonio Giuseppe Fidele Gugliemi was a veterinary practitioner from Castellaneta. He had three siblings, an older brother, Alberto, an older sister Beatrice who died at in infancy and a younger sister, Maria. Despite being raised in a loving family, Valentino was spoiled and became a troublesome child. From an early age his dream was to leave the restraints of Castellaneta and see the rest of the world. His father died in 1906 and despite being sent to the nearest town, Taranto, to further his education, Valentinto could not settle. He became very disruptive at school, failed to concentrate in his lessons and constantly pleaded with his mother to allow him to leave Italy. By the time Valentino was 18, his mother had had enough and gave him the money his father had put by for his education. The excited young man set sail for the United States with stars in his eyes.

It was 23 December 1913 when Valentino set foot in New York. At first he stayed with some friends of the family and made his living by taking menial jobs. He struggled hard with the language and persevered to try and improve his English. After obtaining a job as a gardener on an estate owned by a millionaire, Valentino started to see how the rich and famous lived and vowed that one day he himself would be among the elite. However, due to his daydreaming and delusions of grandeur, Valentino neglected his duties and was fired.

After being sacked, Valentino was down on his luck for a while taking a stream of low-paid jobs, and with nowhere to live his dreams turned to that of suicide.

However, his luck was about to change after he took a job as a helper in an Italian restaurant. Amid his chores of clearing dirty dishes, setting tables and helping the waiters, Valentino started to learn about the excitting world of cabaret and dance halls. One of the older waiters took the young man under his wing and taught him how to dance. He seemed to have a natural aptitude and was soon employed as a full-time dancer at the restaurant, thrilling the crowds with his spectacular tango.

Desperate to earn more money, Valentino played on his good looks and became a gigolo. He soon learned what pleased women and he became adept at the art of seduction.

INVOLVED IN A SCANDAL

In 1915 Valentino became the main attraction at a high-class dance club in New York called Maxim's. He was a big hit with people of high society and in particular one woman, Blanca de Saulles. Blanca, an heiress from Chile, was already married, albeit unhappily, to a prominent businessman by the name of John de Saulles. Although it is uncertain whether Valentino and Blanca actually had an affair, one thing that was in no doubt was Valentino's feelings towards her. When Blanca told Valentino that she had decided to start divorce proceedings, he said he would be prepared to stand up in court and give evidence about her husband's infidelities. In particular, the affair he was having with Valentino's dancing partner, Joan Sawyer.

John de Saulles was furious when Valentino turned evidence against him and, once the divorce was granted in December 1916, he used his political connections and had Valentino arrested along with a known 'madam' of a brothel, Mrs Thyme, on vice charges. Although the evidence against Valentino was very flimsy, the police demanded a $10,000 bail, which was later lowered to $1,500 when they realised they had too little evidence.

The scandal hit Valentino hard and he felt thoroughly degraded. No one seemed prepared to hire him and most of his old friends simply turned their back on him. Even Blanca showed no gratitude for his testimony and had very little contact.

THE MURDER

After the divorce Blanca and John were given joint custody of their son, but Blanca was refusing to accept the court's decision. On the evening of 3 August 1917, Blanca drove to her ex-husband's house in Roslyn, New York. When she arrived she found him sitting on the porch and a violent argument broke out. Blanca reached into her handbag and took out a gun, which she pointed at John's head, demanding that he immediately handed over their son. When he tried to take the gun from Blanca, she lost her control and shot him five times from close range. John was rushed to the nearest hospital, but they failed to resuscitate him and he died at 10.20 p.m. of his gunshot wounds. Blanca, rather than try and run, had waited at the house for the police to arrive and she was taken into custody having admitted that she had fired the shots. She was charged with first-degree murder and held in Nassau County Jail in New York, to await trial.

The trial turned out to be a sensation and lingered on for months, making headline news despite the fact that war was raging in Europe. Blanca became the darling of the court and portrayed herself as a victim of a very male chauvinist society. Blanca was unanimously acquitted of all charges and was released on 1 December 1917.

RISE TO STARDOM

Despite the fact that Valentino had had nothing to do with Blanca since her divorce, his name got dragged through the courts and once again he became the victim of scandal. To try and free himself of the bad reputation he had received, Valentino changed his name at this stage from Rodolfo Guglielmi to Rudolph Valentino and headed off to Hollywood to see if that would change his luck. His first role was as a dancer in a film called *Alimony,* and once again his agility and natural aptitude for dancing caught the eye of a movie star, Mae Murray. She asked Valentino to play the leading role in her next movie, *The Big Little Person,* which was followed by another leading part in *The Delicious Little Devil.* The union between Valentino and Murray was to be short-lived because Murray's husband became jealous of the steamy love scenes, and so the association came to an end.

Murray had given Valentino the opening he needed and he was approached to lead in two more films, *A Society Sensation* and *All Night,* both of which were box office successes. At last Valentino had achieved his dream – he was rich, famous and always had an attractive woman on his arm.

UNLUCKY IN LOVE

In 1919, following his two successes, Valentino met a woman named Jean Acker. Acker was just a small time actress who got her parts due to her lesbian relationship with the Russian film star, Alla

Nazimova. This was a relationship that Valentino apparently was completely unaware of. The three of them became close friends, but Acker was in a difficult predicament and wasn't sure how to get out of it. She was caught in a love triangle with Nazimova and another lesbian by the name of Grace Darmond, both of whom threatened to destroy Acker's career if she left either of them. Seeing her chance to get out of the situation without damaging her reputation, Acker agreed to marry Valentino.

However, the marriage was a sham and was never consummated. Valentino's new wife locked him out of their hotel suite on their honeymoon night and later fled into the arms of Darmond. Valentino followed her and begged Acker to give him another chance, but she wasn't prepared to listen and he went away with his tail between his legs.

Valentino soon pulled himself together and his star was to rise once again. In 1921 he was cast in the coveted role of Julio in *The Four Men of the Apocalypse*. He capitalised on his good looks and exotic dance moves and wowed the hearts of his audience, earning himself the title as the 'Great Italian Lover'.

By the time Valentino starred in *The Sheik*, also in 1921, Valentino had become the first real Hollywood male sex symbol. With his graceful style and seductive blend of passion, he literally had women fainting in the aisles. To them this handsome young man represented forbidden eroticism fulfilling their dreams of illicit love. Unfortunately, Valentino was not so lucky with love in real life.

Valentino and Acker remained legally married until 1921, when he met a rather domineering woman by the name of Natacha Rambova. She soon took over as Valentino's adviser and in fact manipulated him for the remainder of his life. She demanded to be present on all the film sets and frequently caused disruption with her unreasonable demands. Despite this, Valentino was desperately in love with her and asked her to marry him. The couple were married on 13 May 1922, but Valentino had not waited the allotted time for his divorce to be finalised and was subsequently arrested for bigamy. However, after telling the courts that his first marriage had never even been consummated and that he had been deserted on his wedding night, the charges were dropped and Valentino was free to go.

Determined to make things right with Rambova, the couple remarried the following year and honeymooned in Europe. But the passion was to be short-lived as Rambova stormed out one night after a violent argument and went to live with her mother. Rather than let the failed marriage get him down, Valentino threw himself into his work and got a part in a 1925 film called *The Eagle*, which firmly placed him firmly on top of the Hollywood ladder. *The Eagle* and *The Son of the Sheik*, which followed, were two of Valentino's most critically acclaimed and most successful films. A single man once again, Valentino embarked on a lifestyle of wild parties and womanising, repairing many of the friendships that had been ruined by Rambova.

However, the lifestyle proved to be too much for Valentino and on 14 August 1926, after attending an all-night party, he was found writhing on the floor in excruciating pain. He was rushed to hospital and underwent surgery for acute apendicitis. Valentino never really recovered from the operation and after various complications, the Great Italian Lover died on 23 August 1926, at the young age of 31.

INSECURITIES

There is no question that Valentino's life was clouded by a number of scandals that took their toll and left him full of insecurities about his own identity. His masculinity was frequently slandered by the media, which made him very sensitive about the way other people saw him. Although women adored him and dreamed of having him as their lover, men felt threatened by his sexual allure and would frequently walk out of his films in disgust. His sexuality was frequently the subject of speculation and it has even been suggested that he had several homosexual relationships, but there is no real evidence to prove this point. It is thought that most of the rumours spread because of the company he kept – many of his theatrical friends had quite low morals when it came to their sexual exploits.

In 1926 Valentino was the brunt of another defamation of character when he was dubbed the 'Powder Puff'. This came about because of a vending machine dispensing pink talcuum powder being placed in the washroom of a high-class hotel. The newspapers had a heyday, questioning the masculinity of American men and blaming Valentino and his sheik movies for feminising his gender. Valentino challenged the writer of the article to a duel and then a boxing match, but neither challenge was ever met. The powder puff comment continued to bother Valentino, and it was something he could not get out of his head. It is alleged that even on his death bed he referred to the incident:

'Am I a powder puff now, doctor?' he asked.

'No sir, you've been very brave,' was the doctor's reply.

PART TWO

POP STARS
AND
CELEBRITIES

JERRY LEE LEWIS

Jerry Lee Lewis was one of the great pioneers of rock 'n' roll, and is considered a leading figure in the history of rock. However, his career faltered when, in 1958, it was revealed that his third wife, whom he had recently married, was only 13 years old. What made it even worse was the fact that she was distantly related to him, being his second cousin twice removed. So negative was the publicity surrounding this that the star had to cancel his British tour and returned home in disgrace.

'PLAYING FOR THE DEVIL'

Jerry Lee Lewis was born on 29 September 1935 to a poor Southern family in the town of Ferriday, Louisiana. His parents, Elmo and Mamie Lewis, were both farmers. As a boy Jerry Lee showed a natural flair for music and played piano with his cousins, Mickey Gilley and Jimmy Swaggart. Swaggart later became an evangelical religious leader, whose own sex scandal hit the headlines in later years.

Jerry Lee showed such talent that his parents bought him a piano, apparently mortgaging their farm to do so. As he grew up, he continued to absorb influences from all around him, which came out in his piano playing. He had a cousin, Carl McVoy, who was a talented pianist and he also visited a black juke joint in the neighborhood, Haney's Big House, where he learnt a number of different piano styles. Listening to the radio as well, he began to mix all these sounds together, adapting it to his own style, which encompassed boogie woogie, gospel, country and rhythm and blues.

By the time Jerry Lee reached adulthood, he was playing the piano professionally. His mother, worried about the possible bad influence of the entertainment industry on her son, enrolled him into a religious university in Texas, but at a concert there, he began to play *My God is Real* in a boogie woogie style, resulting in his expulsion. He later said that he always knew he was 'playing for the devil', rather than for God.

Having given up any idea of making religious music, Lewis set out for a life on the road, playing at clubs around the south, and making his first recording in 1954. He then went to Nashville and tried to make an impact on the country music scene, but met with little enthusiasm from producers there. One of them told him he should take up guitar instead of playing piano, whereupon he apparently replied, 'You can take your guitar and ram it up your ass.'

Not surprisingly, his aggressive, erratic behaviour did not make him very popular among the smooth executives of the Nashville music industry, and it was not until Sam Phillips of the legendary Sun label discovered him, that Lewis's career really took off. Legend has it that when Elvis Presley heard him play, he remarked, 'If I could play the piano like that, I'd quit singing'.

THE UNDER-AGE BRIDE

Lewis initially began working for Phillips as a session musician, playing on hits by Carl Perkins and other artists. Then, billed as 'Jerry Lee Lewis and his Pumping Piano', he began to tour the country as an artist in his own right. He soon found an audience for his exciting stage shows, which combined all the Pentecostal fervour of his church upbringing with his commitment to 'playing for the devil'. He soon had a hit record, *Great Balls of Fire*, which became a rock 'n' roll classic. His piano style was imitated by many musicians, and came to be known as 'piano rock'. In live performances, he would often stand up at the piano, and was known for antics such as sitting on the instrument, kicking it and banging it with his foot. In later years, artists such as Billy Joel and Elton John would copy this style, to great effect, and this manic behaviour at the keyboard became one of the staple crowd pleasers of rock shows.

Jerry Lee Lewis's personal life was, throughout his early career, dogged by scandal. He married his second wife before the divorce from his first wife became final, but the scandal that really rocked his career was to do with his third wife, Myra Gale Brown. Brown, a distant relative, was just 13 years old when Jerry Lee married her. This was more or less accepted in America at the time, where very young brides were common enough in the South; but in Britain, where the scandal broke, that was not the case. When it was discovered just how young Lewis's 'child bride' really was, the press were outraged, and Lewis became so unpopular in the media that his British tour was cancelled after just three shows, to the disappointment of many of his fans.

THE SHUNNED MUSICIAN

On his return to the United States, Lewis found himself shunned by people who had previously accepted his marriage, and felt himself to have been betrayed. He was not invited to play on TV music shows, such as the *Dick Clark Show*, the most important teenage pop show on television at the time, and was angered when Sam Phillips of Sun Records released a single, *The Return of Jerry Lee*, poking fun at his troubles. One of his few remaining allies in the music business was Alan Freed, the pioneering rock 'n' roll DJ, but Freed had a scandal of his own looming, and was kicked off the air for allegedly accepting bribes to play records.

During the 1960s, Lewis went back to record for Phillips, and had a hit with a cover of the Ray Charles classic, *What'd I Say*. However, by 1963 his contract with Sun was over, and although he continued to record and tour, especially in Europe, he failed to make a comeback in the United States.

PLAYING WITH GUNS

During the late 1960s and early 1970s, Jerry Lee Lewis reinvented himself as a country singer and had more success, but by now his behaviour was beginning to veer seriously out of control. His wife Myra divorced him in 1970, and from then on his mental and physical health began to deteriorate. His older son was killed in a car accident, and then another son drowned in a swimming pool. He began to drink heavily, so much so that he developed severe stomach ulcers and nearly died from a perforated stomach. He was known to play with guns, and on one occasion, injured his bass player, Butch Owens, while shooting at empty bottles.

Today, in his 70s, Jerry Lee Lewis continues to tour, and by all accounts, his performances have lost little of their passion and intensity over the years. His importance as one of the great exponents of rock 'n' roll has been recognised, and it seems that, for many, this has blotted out the scandal of his marriage to an under-age girl during the 1950s. However, the scandal certainly cast a shadow over Lewis's career for a long time, even though today he has taken his place in the Rock and Roll Hall of Fame alongside great pioneers of rock 'n' roll such as Chuck Berry, Little Richard and Elvis Presley.

CHUCK BERRY

As one of the founding fathers of rock 'n' roll, Chuck Berry is revered by music fans all over the world. There were many scandals surrounding him during his long career, and these are often reported as mischievous pranks, as befits a rock star. However, some of his antics revealed an extremely unpleasant streak in his nature, especially in his sexual relationships with women.

TEENAGE JOY RIDER

Chuck Berry was born to a relatively well-to-do black family. His father worked as a contractor and was deacon of a Baptist church, while his mother was a successful head teacher. The third child in a family of six, he grew up in St Louis, Missouri, in a middle-class area called The Ville. He was a choir boy in the church and a bass singer in his high school glee club. Berry excelled at music as a boy and his music teacher, realising the special talent he had, urged him to take up the guitar. He taught himself how to play and gave his first public performance while he was still in high school. However, even at this early stage in his career, he got into trouble.

In 1944 Berry was arrested for armed robbery, having stolen a car and ridden to Kansas City, Missouri. He was convicted of the crime and sent to a reformatory institution near Jefferson, Missouri, and it was here that he sang with a gospel group. He was released in 1947 on his 21st birthday.

On his release, Berry married Themetta 'Toddy' Suggs and began work in an automobile factory. He also attended night school and learned how to be a hairdresser, playing in local groups in his spare time to supplement his wages. Berry found work in night clubs and having been spotted for his talent was asked to play with a band called the Johnnie Johnson Trio. Although already an experienced blues player, Berry began experimenting with country music, or 'hillbilly' as it was called at the time. He found that black people attending the clubs enjoyed the sounds, which were new to them, and that it also drew a crowd of whites. He became known as the 'black hillbilly' and also began to sing material by a range of black singers, from the smooth sounds of Nat King Cole to the down-home blues of Muddy Waters, mixing up the styles as he went.

UNDER-AGE PROSTITUTION

In 1955 Berry secured a recording contract with Chess Records in Chicago, who were impressed by the unusual style of his songs. That year he recorded an old country and western song, 'Ida Red', retitling it 'Maybelline'. It was a number one hit for him on the black charts and also reached the pop charts. His next hit was 'Roll over Beethoven', after which he began to tour relentlessly, joining white stars such as Buddy Holly and the Everly Brothers, thus breaking down racial barriers in the musical world for the first time. From 1957 to 1959 he wrote many of his major hits, in an extraordinary rush of creativity. These included such classics such as 'Johnny B. Goode' and 'Sweet Little Sixteen'.

However, off stage Berry was running into trouble again. This time, his criminal activity was to do with a young girl he had become involved with, Janice Escalanti. After Berry fired her from her job as a hat check girl in his club, Escalanti went to the police and told them that Berry had met her when she was only 14 years old, during a trip to Juárez, Mexico. She recounted how he had introduced her to a life of prostitution. Berry was accused of transporting her across state lines for the purpose of prostitution, which was a crime under the Mann Act, a federal statute. He was brought to court and convicted of the crime, receiving a prison sentence of three years and a fine of $10,000. Berry did not served the full term of his sentence, and was realeased after less than two years.

CYNICAL MONEY MAKER

After his release in 1963, Berry went back to touring and playing, having written more songs while in jail. These were difficult years for him, since he had quarrelled with his family and alienated many of his former friends. On the other hand, his career was flourishing, and he was making successful chart records again. During this period he had six hit singles in the charts, including, 'You Never Can Tell' and 'Nadine'. In 1972 he had a major hit with the double-entendre song, 'My Ding-A-Ling'. This song reached the number one spot, and from then on Berry became a stalwart of the rock 'n' roll revival circuit.

As many recount, by this time his attitude towards playing rock 'n' roll had become completely cynical, and he concentrated on making as much money as he could, without being very concerned about the quality of his performances. He often hired back-up bands and refused to rehearse with them before the shows, leading to a steep decline in the quality of his performances. This disappointed many of his fans, both young and old. In addition, Berry was known for his bad temper and arrogant behaviour towards other musicians. One of his former backing musicians, Bruce Springsteen, recounts how Berry never gave the band a set list before the show, or thanked them for playing afterwards. Even so, such was Berry's musical reputation that when he appeared at the Rock and Roll Hall of Fame in 1995, Springsteen agreed to back him once again.

TAX EVASION

Although Berry's career as a musical innovator was over by the 1970s, he was still making large amounts of money on the revival circuit. The Internal Revenue Service was convinced that he was evading tax and prosecuted him for the crime. He pleaded guilty to the charge and was convicted. His sentence was four months' imprisonment, and 1000 hours of community service, which in his case consisted of doing benefit concerts. By now he had become one of the 'bad boys' of rock 'n' roll, but in some quarters this only enhanced his reputation.

Much as Berry was disliked by those who came across him in the show-business world, his fans still adored him. However, his reputation took something of a battering when in 1990 he was sued by over 50 women. The women alleged that he had installed a video camera in the ladies' room of his restaurant, *The Southern Air*, so that he could watch them as they used the toilets, believing that they were doing so in private. Berry denied that he had indulged in this distasteful voyeurism, but offered to settle the matter out of court, which is thought to have cost him over a million dollars. In the same year his house was raided and the police found a cache of home-made pornographic videos, including one in which, according to some reports, he was depicted urinating on a young woman in a bathtub.

GUNPOINT HITCHHIKER

In his later years Berry's erratic behaviour became legendary. There was one story circulating that, on one occasion, when his car broke down, he hitchhiked a lift so that he could get home. He persuaded the driver of the car to give him a lift by pointing a gun at him. Berry himself recounted this story in his autobiography, published in 1987. Unusually for a rock star, Berry actually wrote the autobiography himself, instead of employing a ghost writer, and showed some skill as a literary writer.

Despite his many faults as a human being, Berry is

still regarded as a great musician, and today he continues to be admired as a pioneer of rock 'n' roll. Only two years after the restaurant debacle, he performed at President Bill Clinton's inaugural celebration. Along with Jerry Lee Lewis and other stellar performers in the rock world, he has survived many scandals and is set to remain one of the legendary performers of 20th-century popular music.

MICHAEL JACKSON

After years of controversy and speculation about his personal life, Michael Jackson's status as an international pop icon was seriously undermined when, during the 1990s, allegations of child molestation were brought against him. Up until that point, his erratic behaviour, his increasingly strange appearance as the result of cosmetic surgery, and his odd family life had been viewed as the foibles of a superstar; but the claim that he had actually sexually abused children at his home shocked the United States and the rest of the world.

THE JACKSON FAMILY

Jackson was born in Gary, Indiana, and from the age of five sang the lead with his brothers in the family group the Jackson 5, which formed in 1964. In the early years the five brothers – Jackie, Jermaine, Tito, Marlon and Michael – played the local clubs and bars, but as their talent grew so did their venues.

In 1968 the group was granted an audition with Berry Gordy, who was in control of Motown Records. Gordy was so impressed with their music that he signed them up and the Jackson 5 moved to California. Their first four singles were 'I Want You Back', 'ABC', 'The Love You Sav'e and 'I'll Be There', all of which made number one in the United States.

In 1971, Michael Jackson decied to begin a solo career and had several hits before appearing with Diana Ross in the film The Wiz. It was on the set of this film that Jackson met music producer Quincy Jones. Jones proved the ideal producer for Jackson, and their 1979 album Off The Wall yielded many hit singles, such as 'Don't Stop (Till You Get Enough)' and 'Rock With You'. This was followed by the groundbreaking *Thriller* in 1981, six of whose nine tracks were hit singles, including the title track, 'Billie Jean', and 'Beat It'.

Jackson then signed a multi-million dollar advertising deal with Pepsi Cola and went on to make three more successful albums *Bad*, *Dangerous*, and *History*. From 1985, when he co-wrote 'We Are the World' with Lionel Ritchie for the United States for Africa charity, he attempted to introduce serious social and ecological concerns into his music, but from then on, his sincerity was called into question by his increasingly bizarre private life.

ALIEN SUPERHUMAN BEING

Michael Jackson had plenty of reasons to be emotionally disturbed, having never lived a normal family life and not given the opportunity to be a child. From the age of six, as lead singer of the Jackson 5, he had been managed by his tyrannical father, Joe, who was later alleged to have terrorised him and the rest of his children, with beatings and punishments. As a result, Michael, who was highly sensitive and gifted, became very withdrawn, to the point, in later years, of becoming a recluse.

Not only was his personal life highly unusual, but there were concerns about his appearance. Over the years, Jackson's skin colour had changed from brown to white and there were rumours that he was bleaching his skin. Critics claimed that this was setting a bad example to his black fans all over the world and that he was providing a poor role model to many black children and teenagers, to whom he was an idol. Interestingly, Jackson himself seemed to feel he did not belong to any ethnic group, but was in some sense superhuman, writing lyrics that stressed the unimportance of colour. The video of *Thriller* shows Jackson acting the role of a werewolf, presaging his later fascination with adopting fantasy roles.

Jackson's apparent vision of himself as a kind of

alien superhuman being gave rise to a great deal of controversy, especially over his skin lightening treatments, which some critics felt was an attempt to disguise his physical characteristics as an African-American. However, it was also argued that Jackson was attempting to liberate himself, both in his image and his music, from the constraints of race and culture, by presenting himself first and foremost as a human being. To this degree he has been a positive role model for racially mixed and culturally displaced young people in today's world. When questioned about his skin, Jackson denied that he had had any skin lightening treatments, saying that the colour change was due to a skin disease, vitiligo. He also announced that he had hardly had any cosmetic surgery at all, blaming the changes in his facial characteristics on puberty and diet, which seems extremely unlikely.

CHILD MOLESTATION CHARGES

As well as concerns about his appearance, his marriages and children surprised and shocked the public. In 1994, Jackson married Lisa Marie Presley, the daughter of Elvis Presley, but two years later the couple were divorced. Next, in a very unlikely pairing, he married his dermatologist's nurse, Debbie Rowe, with whom he had two children, Michael Jr, and a daughter, Paris. Rumours were rife that Jackson was not the father of the children, and many people surmised that the children were not even conceived naturally. His family life grew increasingly odd until, in November 2002, he responded to members of the press clamouring for a picture outside his hotel window by holding his baby out over the balcony, in what many people regarded as a highly dangerous manner. The fact that he covered his children in face veils to prevent them getting airborne diseases also worried the public.

Jackson's liking for children, and his belief that he himself was still a child, was well known. He liked to host charity events for children, and often invited children to sleep over at his Neverland ranch. But in 1993, a former Beverly Hills dentist, Evan Chandler, accused Jackson of molesting his child Jordan, who had stayed with Jackson at the ranch on several occasions. The case did not come to court, as Jackson settled the matter out of court for a very large sum.

HIGH-PROFILE TRIAL

Many felt, at this stage, that although Jackson's behaviour was odd, he had actually done nothing wrong. Indeed, many criticised the parents of the children who were allowed to sleep over at the ranch, pointing out that that there were those in Hollywood who were opportunistically taking advantage of Jackson's wealth and hospitality.

However, it was in 2003, when journalist Martin Bashir made a documentary about his private life that public anxiety reached a new level. Jackson was shown conducting sleepovers with a number of children, including a cancer victim, Gavin Arvizo, in which he shared the children's bedroom and sometimes even their beds. After the film was broadcasted, Jackson was charged with child molestation on seven counts, and also accused of administering an intoxicating agent to commit the crimes. Naturally enough, he denied the claims, and was supported by his friend, the actress Liz Taylor, who said she had been present at some of the sleepovers.

In 2005 the case came to court and the trial of Michael Jackson began. It became one of the most high-profile cases ever to take place, with thousands of journalists fighting for coverage. As well as members of the press, thousands of Jackson's fans flooded Santa Maria, California, where the trial was held. In the end, the star was acquitted on all counts, and his fans celebrated by cheering as each of the ten not guilty verdicts were read out for all to hear outside the courthouse.

However, despite the fact that he had been acquitted of all the crimes, Jackson's reputation had been tarnished, and in later years it was not helped by the fact that, as well as his usual idiosyncracies, he showed increasing signs of delusions of grandeur, seeing himself as some kind of messiah. In 1996 he performed in London at the Brit Awards, adopting Christ-like poses while surrounded by actors portraying starving children and the like. British pop star Jarvis Cocker was so incensed by the tastelessness of this display that he leapt on stage and pretended to show his bottom to the audience. This in itself angered some viewers, and there were claims that in the fracas that followed, some child actors were injured.

Today, it is certainly true to say that the many scandals surrounding 'Wacko Jacko', as the British newspapers dubbed him, particularly the charges of child molestation, have harmed his career; and sadly, there is no doubt that, as well as being one of pop's greatest ever stars, Michael Jackson is also, in the evident unhappiness of his personal life, one of its greatest casualties. That said, few today can dispute Michael Jackson's extraordinary talent and his pioneering role as one of the giants of 20th century pop music.

GEORGE MICHAEL

Singer George Michael has had more than his fair share of scandal in his life. Yet he has weathered each of the many storms that have come his way with surprising honesty, in most cases admitting candidly to the accusations raised against him. In 1998, after being arrested in a public toilet for 'lewd behaviour' by an undercover policeman, he came out about his homosexuality. Since then, he has remained un-apologetic about the incident, even going so far as to make a video about it. In addition, he has been open about his problems with depression and drug abuse, admitting his weaknesses rather than being ashamed of them. Interestingly, the fact that Michael has been so straightforward about these issues, refusing to lie about them, has meant that the scandals surrounding his behaviour have had little overall effect on his career. He has shown by his example that if the person at the centre of a scandal is honest, much of the shock value of the sordid details are lost. What the tabloids and, increasingly, the quality newspapers seek is to expose the bad behaviour of someone who presents a respectable image to society, and in this way, try to reveal their hypocrisy. However, when the person they are hounding refuses to play this game, and is open about their sexuality and their problems, in many cases the story ceases to be so much of a scandal, and can be tackled in a more serious, thoughtful way that raises issues for everyone about the way we live in modern society.

INTERNATIONAL SUPERSTAR

George Michael was born Georgios Kyriacos Panayiotou in East Finchley, North London. His father was the manager of a Greek Cypriot restaurant, and his mother was a dancer. The family was socially diverse; one of his grandmothers was from a wealthy Jewish family, while one of his grandfathers came from a poor, working-class background. Michael grew up in North London and attended Kingsbury High School, along with his sisters. As a teenager he formed his first band The Executive with his friends Paul and Andrew Ridgeley, David Austin and Andrew Leaver. In 1981 he went on to form a duo with Andrew Ridgeley, and it was then that his group, now named Wham!, hit the charts.

The pair released an album which gave rise to a string of hit singles on the British charts. Their image was one of two best friends, 'young guns' as they called themselves, out on the town looking for love, laughter and a good time. They often used female backing singers and dancers to emphasise their masculinity. The upbeat style of music, their 1980s' fashion sense, their good looks and their energetic dancing made them one of the most popular acts of the day, so much so that their second album became not only a British bestseller, but a worldwide hit.

As well as touring America, Wham! became the first Western pop group to tour China, and Michael went on to become an international superstar. The following year, however, tensions began to develop between Michael and Ridgeley as a result of the attention being lavished on Michael, and Wham! split up. Their farewell show at Wembley Stadium attracted thousands of fans, and it was clear that Michael had a brilliant career still ahead of him.

After the break-up of the group, Michael became a huge solo act, and his debut album Faith charted at number one both in the United States and Britain. Hit single after hit single followed, and many of his songs, such as 'Careless Whisper', became timeless classics. Still at a young age, Michael seemed to have achieved everything that any singer could possibly want.

However, trouble lay ahead as he began to argue with his new record company bosses at Sony, who had taken over CBE, the record label that had pioneered his career up to that point. Michael accused the enormous new corporation of mishandling his career, and indeed many pop acts were critical of the way they were treated as commodities by the new Sony management. In particular, Michael was angry about some homophobic remarks made by one of the executives at the company, which he overheard on the phone one day, in which he was referred to as a 'faggot'.

SCANDAL BREAKS

Everyone who knew George Michael personally realised that he was gay. However, at this stage Michael had still not come out in public about his sexual orientation for fear of harming his career. As far as most members of the public were concerned, he was a poster boy for heterosexuality; girls swooned over him, and he traded on the image of himself as a young man about town who lived for the high life of wine, women and song. To keep this image alive, there were constant rumours in the tabloids about him dating female film stars, dancers and other women in the entertainment world, but his close associates knew that for many years he had been having a stable relationship with a male Brazilian designer, Anselmo Feleppa. Sadly, Feleppa died in 1993 of a brain haemorrhage, prompting a deep emotional crisis for Michael, which was made more severe by the death of his mother from cancer four years later. The death of these two loved ones had a sobering effect on Michael, who later dedicated his album, *Older* to Feleppa. In his music, he acknowledged the changes that the death of his lover and his mother had made in his life, but he continued to keep his private life a secret, away from the prying eyes of his fans.

In reality, however, he was in a state of emotional turmoil, and matters reached a head when on 7 April 1998 he was arrested for masturbating in a public toilet in Beverly Hills, California. The man who arrested him was an undercover policeman, who Michael claimed had encouraged him in the act and had also joined in the sexual behavior. However, the courts did not believe him and Michael was fined and sentenced to community service. Afterwards, he was unrepentant and made angry comments to the press. He felt that he had been conned and accordingly made a video for his next single, 'Outside', in which two men dressed as policemen were seen kissing. After this, the policeman sued Michael for a huge sum of money. The whole affair blew up into a huge scandal, but Michael continued to maintain that he had done nothing wrong, and for the first time openly declared himself to be a homosexual. He began to be seen in public with his partner Kenny Goss, a former coach and sports clothing executive, and spoke openly about their relationship in interviews.

A LIFE IN TURMOIL

From this point, it seemed that Michael might have reached a new period of stability in his life. In 2006, however, scandal broke once again when Michael was arrested for possession of minor drugs. There followed a number of incidents in which Michael was seen driving cars under the influence of drugs or alcohol, and on May 2007 he pleaded guilty to driving while under the influence of drugs. The following month his partner Goss checked into a rehabilitation clinic because of his problems with dependence on prescribed drugs. It became blatantly obvious that Michael's life was still in turmoil, or at least that the pressures of stardom never receded very far away.

However, despite all the bad publicity and inner turmoil, Michael has continued working and today continues to tour the world, reaching an ever-increasing army of fans worldwide. In the new millennium he is still regarded as one of the major stars of popular music, despite the many scandals that have at times threatened to ruin his career. Today, he is widely respected among the gay community and other groups for his courageous, honest stance about his sexuality, and his refusal to be intimidated by the authorities in the case of the incident at the public toilet. As a result, the affair has now largely been forgotten, and he remains one of the best loved acts in the pop world to this day.

GARY GLITTER

One of the biggest scandals to hit the British headlines in recent years was that of international entertainer Gary Glitter. After several run-ins with the law regarding allegations of sex with under-age girls, in 1997 Glitter was convicted of possession of child pornography and served several months in prison for the offence. However far worse was yet to come . . .

ILLEGITIMATE CHILD

Paul Francis Gadd was born on 8 May 1944 in Banbury, Oxfordshire. He was an illegitimate child who never knew his father, and his young mother struggled to raise him, helped by his grandmother. After a difficult early childhood, he was taken into care at the age of ten, along with his brother. However, the experience of being brought up in a home failed to quell his restless spirit, and by 14 he set off to London to see fame and fortune, carving a career for himself as a singer in the city's night clubs.

At 14, Gadd cut a record for Decca, which failed to make the chart, but undeterred, he went on to adopt a number of stage names, calling himself Paul Russell, Paul Raven and even Rubber Bucket, in his attempt to attract attention. However, his career stalled and it was not until he jumped on the bandwagon of glam rock in the early 1970s that he finally became successful.

Gadd chose himself a new name to match the glam era, picking Gary Glitter from a number of options, including Terry Tinsel and Stanley Sparkle. He overhauled his image, wearing ridiculously over-the-top stage clothing, including glitter boots with high heels and an Elvis-style cape. His hair was styled into an enormous quiff, parodying the rock 'n' roll style of the 1950s' singers.

RISE . . . AND FALL

With producer-arranger Mike Leander, Glitter released a record called 'Rock and Roll, Parts One and Two'. The disc was a hit, both in Britain and in the United States. Finally, at the age of 28, Gadd had found success as Gary Glitter and from then on, the hits came thick and fast. In the years that followed, Glitter became one of the top glam rock acts, releasing many more hits such as 'I'm the Leader of the Gang (I Am)', 'I Love You Love Me Love' and' I Didn't Know I Loved You Till I saw You Rock and Roll', and gained a loyal fan base in the process. 'Rock and Roll (Part Two)' became a popular anthem in the world of American sport, with fans shouting out the 'hey' in the chorus (in some parts of America, the song is now known as the 'hey' song.) Glitter was soon able to release serious ballads with far more success than he had in his early career, and these met with chart success, including the ballad 'Remember Me this Way', which reached number three in the hit parade. By 1975, he had sold a total of 18 million records, making Gary Glitter one of Britain's biggest stars.

Sadly, however, Glitter's meteoric rise to fame was swiftly followed by failure. By 1976, with the advent of punk, which replaced glam rock as the music of youth culture, Glitter's records were failing to reach the top ten and he announced his retirement. This was a big mistake – by the end of the decade, his life was in ruins. He began to drink heavily and left his wife and two children. After a sojourn in Australia, he went bankrupt, leaving huge debts, and it was during this period, as he later recounted, that he seriously considered taking his own life.

HIGH CAMP

It was not until the dance music of the 1980s became popular that Glitter was back in the limelight once more, bouncing back with a hit single called 'Dance Me Up'. The success of the record was enough to turn his career around, encouraging him to improve his lifestyle. He not only gave up drinking, he also became a vegetarian and a Buddhist in an effort to keep on the straight and narrow. However, it was not long before his demons came back to haunt him and in 1986 he overdosed accidentally on sleeping pills and was taken to hospital. The same year, he was convicted of drinking and driving for the third time and was banned from driving.

During the 1990s, he became something of a figure of fun and found himself supported by college students, who enjoyed his ironical, high camp pose. He toured university campuses and also appeared in advertisements for British Rail, the joke being that he was pretending to look younger than he was. When the British band Oasis used some lines from one of his songs on their album, he gained sizeable royalties, which he used to buy a yacht. But by the end of the decade, his star had lost its sparkle once again, and he had become unpopular – this time for something much more serious than releasing bad records.

CHILD PORNOGRAPHY

In November 1997 Glitter was arrested for downloading child pornography on his computer. He had taken it in to a Bristol branch of PC World to be repaired and, during the process, the images had been discovered by staff working there. It is not clear whether the discovery was made by accident, or whether members of staff had accessed the contents of the hard drive on purpose, to find out what was on it. Whatever the reason, once the news was out, Glitter's reputation was severely damaged. His status as a lovable entertainer, somewhat akin to the old British stars of pantomime, was completely undermined; instead of being seen as eccentric, his high-camp pose was now seen as creepy and menacing, especially as his music had appealed greatly to children. Glitters bookings declined and soon he was unable to find work. But his troubles were far from over.

Two years later, Glitter was convicted of possessing child pornography and formally classified as a sex offender. He received a prison sentence of four months, of which he served two. A young woman named Alison Brown accused him of having sex with her when she was under-age, and he was charged accordingly. However, the charge was revoked when it was discovered that Brown was being paid large sums of money to tell her story to a tabloid newspaper. It later evolved that the paper had offered her a further sum if Glitter was convicted of the charges that she had made.

CHILD SEXUAL ABUSE

After this debacle, Glitter travelled to Spain, but was hounded by the British press there, so decided to make Cuba his home instead. Not surprisingly, the Cuban government was not keen to have him, so he went to Cambodia instead. When news got out that he was a convicted sex offender, the Cambodian government were forced to expel him. His next port of call was Vietnam, where in 2005 he was arrested and charged with raping of under-age girls, a crime that carried with it the death penalty. He attempted to escape to Thailand but he was arrested at the airport before he was able to board his flight.

When victims of his alleged crimes were called in for questioning, it emerged that six girls and women aged between 11 and 23, had admitted to having sexual relations with Glitter. He was taken into custody and remained there until the end of the investigation on 26 December 2005. Throughout the proceedings, Glitter claimed that he was innocent, and was bitter about what he saw as inhumane treatment at the hands of the authorities.

OBSCENE ACTS

Eventually, the charge of raping under-age girls was dropped, which was just as well for Glitter because if he had been found guilty he would have faced death by firing squad. Instead, he was charged with committing obscene acts against the two young girls, and after a summary trial, was convicted on 3 March 2006. He received a prison sentence of three years, which he continues to serve today.

Glitter has consistently denied any wrongdoing, and has blamed the tabloid press for his downfall, citing them as 'the worst enemy in the world'. In an interview with the BBC, he continued to maintain that he was innocent, blaming the press for the fact that he could not, as he put it, put his life back on track. However, in the interview he failed to address such issues as why he had been in possession of child pornography, or why he had tried to escape from Vietnam if he was innocent.

In June 2006, Glitter appealed against his sentence, but the appeal was rejected. Afterwards, Glitter commented angrily, 'There is no justice here in Vietnam'. The same year, the National Football League asked teams to stop singing the 'hey' song at their matches. It remains to be seen what Glitter will make of his life when he is released in August 2008, as an entertainer whose reputation has been completely ruined by a series of shocking sex scandals over the last decade.

R. KELLY

R. Kelly was one of the United State's most popular black entertainers until 2002, when it was revealed that a videotape of him apparently having sex with a 14-year-old girl was circulating among the public. Not surprisingly, the scandal has seriously damaged his reputation as an entertainer, changing his image from that of oversexed crooner to that of cold, manipulative paedophile. However, he still succeeds in making million-selling records, showing that the damage to his reputation has not seriously dented his income to date.

SEXUAL LYRICS

Robert Sylvester Kelly was born in the south of Chicago on 8 January 1969. From a young age, it was clear that he had great talent as a singer, and at high school, his teacher encouraged him to pursue a career in music. He began by singing in the street and on trains in the city of Chicago, winning over audiences with his beautiful voice. Encouraged by his success in entertaining audiences, he joined a group called Public Announcement, and by the early 1990s he was beginning to make records with them. Their first hit was an album called *Born Into the 90s*, and he followed this up with a solo album, *12 Play*. His songs were light, smooth and full of sexual lyrics, and soon made him one of the most successful artists in rythm & blues.

In 1994, R. Kelly produced the debut album of a 15-year-old singer, Aaliyah. Later, it turned out that Kelly and she had married, after Aaliyah feigned to be 18 years old. Because of the controversy that followed, the wedding was annulled and the pair separated, on non-speaking terms. The incident was to be recalled later, when R. Kelly's dealings with under-age girls once again created a public scandal.

PAEDOPHILE SEX VIDEO

Although this episode provoked a scandal, Kelly continued to be a popular act and also made his name as a producer and songwriter, working with Michael Jackson and other famous artists. He made another album, and wrote a hit song for the Michael Jordan film *Space Jam*, 'I Believe I can Fly', following this up with 'Gotham City' for the 1997 movie *Batman and Robin*. In 1998, his career hit the heights with a new album on which he sang a duet with Celine Dion, and which eschewed the explicitly sexual lyrics of his former records.

In the new millennium Kelly teamed up with Jay-Z and went back to his old style of sexualised lyrics, with great success. However, it was during the advertising campaign for the album *Best of Both Worlds*, featuring Kelly and Jay-Z, that a huge scandal broke. In February 2002, the *Chicago Sun-Times* reported that it had been sent a videotape of R. Kelly having sex with a girl who appeared to be under 16 years of age. In the video Kelly performs various sexual acts, including urinating on the girl. The girl was thought to be the daughter of an associate, and the niece of an artist called Sparkle that Kelly had championed at one time. Both Kelly and the girl – along with her parents – denied that they were the individuals in the video. However, after the Aaliyah episode, few believed Kelly, and he was indicted in Chicago on 21 charges of having sex with a minor.

Viewing of the tape later showed that there was no actual sexual intercourse involved and the charges were reduced to soliciting a minor for child pornography, videotaping the act and producing child pornography.

In 2003 he was charged in Polk County, Florida, on 12 counts of possession of child pornography when it was found that he had a digital camera showing him having sex with an under-age girl. The charges were later dropped. Several more girls and young women sued him for circulating pictures of them having sex with him without their consent, and one woman accused him of having got her pregnant when she was only 16, and then forcing her to have an abortion. He settled most of these cases out of court, claiming that this was to protect his career.

ASSAULT AND FALSE IMPRISONMENT

By 2005, Kelly's reputation had hit rock bottom as his girlfriend Andrea – originally his backup dancer and the mother of his children – sought a restraining order on him, claiming that he had attacked her. However, she later dropped the charges. She went on to marry him, only to sue for divorce shortly afterwards. The following year, his close friend, mentor and former employee, Henry 'Love' Vaughn sued him for assault, false imprisonment and a breach of contract concerning songwriting royalties. According to Vaughn, Kelly had taken him to the basement of his house and had punched him hard in the face and on the body. However, there was some dispute as to what had really happened, as a police investigation did not find any evidence to support Vaughn's claims.

Next, trouble broke out between Kelly and Jay-Z. Kelly behaved erratically during a tour and Jay-Z eventually threw him off the tour. Kelly responded by announcing that a friend of Jay-Z's, Tyran Smith, had attacked him and members of his entourage with mace or pepper spray. The two artists fell out in no uncertain terms, and each of them launched a massive lawsuit against each other, which involved millions of dollars.

After the paedophile scandal, Kelly's career took a nosedive as a result of the negative publicity that followed. Several radio stations refused to play his records, and some record shops even refused to sell them. Sales on his album immediately dropped.

In 2002 he was charged on the counts of child pornography and released on bail to the tune of $750,000. Currently, he is banned from associating with Michael Jackson and has to seek permission from the courts each time he wants to go on tour. However, he has refused to let the scandal over-shadow him, and has continued to release successful albums, despite the public humiliation following the revelations of his sexual proclivities, his manipulative behaviour towards women and his circulation of images of him having sex with under-age girls.

ANNA NICOLE SMITH

Anna Nicole Smith, a *Playboy* model, became famous when she married oil billionare J. Howard Marshall, who was 63 years older than herself. After his death, she fought his son for a share of her deceased husband's estate. She was also the subject of many sex scandals after the birth of her daughter, when several of her former lovers claimed paternity for the child. Other scandals erupted and her various legal battles over money, paternity and custody of her children, as well as her increasingly exhibitionist behaviour in public, ensured that she was constantly featured in the tabloid press throughout her dramatic career as an all-American sex symbol.

BREAST IMPLANTS

Smith was born Vickie Lynn Hogan in Houston, Texas, the only child of Donald and Virgie Hogan. During her childhood, her father left the family home, and Anna Nicole was raised by her mother and aunt. When her mother remarried, Smith ·took her new stepfather's name before adopting her stage name. As a teenager, she went to live with another aunt and dropped out of high school, working in a restaurant instead. There she met her first husband, cook Billy Wayne Smith, and the couple married when she was 17 and he only 16. They had one child, Daniel Wayne Smith, before separating two years later.

As a young mother with a child to support, Vickie found work as a stripper, and also took dance and singing lessons in the hopes of furthering her career in show business. Her break came when she auditioned for *Playboy* magazine and was picked out by Hugh Hefner to work as one of his star models, becoming Playmate of the Year for 1993.

Anna Nicole Smith, as she now became known, attracted attention because of her large breasts, harking back to the glamour of 1950s' sex symbols like Jayne Mansfield. Unlike them, however, her breasts were surgically enhanced by implants, and her popularity set a trend, decried by many, for women to enlarge their breasts in this way. In a series of advertisements for jeans and underwear, Smith played on her 1950s' image, which created a good deal of controversy in the media. This got out of hand when, in 1994 *New York* magazine issued a picture of her wearing Western cowboy clothing, under the headline 'White Trash'. Smith took objection to this and sued the magazine, claiming that they had not told her they were going to use this headline.

GOLD DIGGER?

By now, Smith was a well-known sex symbol and had embarked on a film career, but in 1991 she met an elderly oil billionaire, J. Howard Marshall, at a strip club in Houston, and began a two-year affair with him. During this time, he reportedly wooed her with expensive gifts and then proposed marriage. The wedding took place in 1993, when Smith was 26 years old and Marshall was 89 and in poor health. This union provoked outrage from the media, but in response Smith told the press that she loved her husband and that 'age did not matter to her'.

Just over a year into the marriage, during which time Smith did not live with her husband, Marshall died, leaving an enormous estate behind him, valued at millions. Only a few weeks later, instead of mourning him, Smith and Marshall's son became locked in a battle for the estate, in which Smith claimed half the proceeds. The legal proceedings were extremely long, drawn out and complicated, and to this day the battle continues.

PATERNITY CLAIMS

While the negotiations for the money were continuing, Smith's career began to decline. She began to put on weight and to make an embarrassing display of herself on screen, sometimes shedding her clothes to attract attention and slurring her speech, as though under the influence of drugs. Her reality TV series, *The Anna Nicole Show*, initially attracted good ratings, but critics panned it and eventually it only retained a cult following among college students.

In 2006 Smith announced that she was pregnant, and her attorney Howard K. Stern claimed that he was the child's father. On 2 September 2006 Smith's daughter Dannielynn Hope Marshall Stern was born. There followed a series of counter-claims by Smith's former lovers, including photographer and journalist Larry Birkhead, Zsa Zsa Gabor's husband Frédéric Prinz von Anhalt, former bodyguard Alexander Denk and Hollywood bad boy Mark Hatten, who all claimed paternity.

DRUGS OVERDOSE

Scandals about Smith continued to entertain readers of the tabloid press, although by now her story was becoming a tragic one. On 10 September 2006, while visiting his mother and new baby half-sister in hospital, Smith's son Daniel died suddenly. It was later found that he was suffering from an overdose of various drugs, including methadone. That same month, Smith and Stern threw a party and got married, although no formal marriage certificate was ever registered. Some were shocked at the hastiness of the celebrations, given that Smith's son had only recently died.

After the ceremony, Smith and Stern decided to stay in their holiday home in the Bahamas to avoid Birkhead suing for custody of the child in the United States. Another scandal erupted when, after gaining the right to stay in the country, Smith was photographed lying in bed embracing Immigration Minister Shane Gibson. As a result of the ensuing row, Gibson was forced to resign his position.

DEAD ON ARRIVAL

The final scandal came when Anna Nicole Smith herself was found dead in a hotel room in Florida. A bodyguard found her unconscious and although she was rushed to hospital, she was pronounced dead on arrival on 8 February 2007. After seven weeks of investigation, news came that Smith had died of a combination of prescribed drugs, among them chloral hydrate, a sleeping medicine that Smith consumed in large quantities. She had also taken several kinds of benzodiazepines, including lorezapam and diazepam, as well as injecting vitamins and growth hormone into her buttocks.

After her death her estate was valued at over a million, although some of her property was heavily mortgaged. Today, legal disputes over her claim of Marshall's estate continue, in the name of her daughter, and the paternity status of the child is still being contested. Even her place of burial continues to be a source of conflict among her family and friends. Smith was eventually buried in the Bahamas next to her son Daniel, despite his grandmother's persistent attempts to have them both brought to Texas for burial. Various scandals persist to this day, and look set to continue, even after the death of Anna Nicole herself.

PETE DOHERTY

Pete Doherty is used to living life on the edge – drugs, alcohol, fights, prison and sex with a supermodel – have all been part of his daily routine. And yet, despite all the scandal that has haunted his life, Doherty has still managed to produce some of the most exciting punk-style music to come out of Britain in the past few years. His picture is very rarely out of the tabloids with news both good and bad, but despite the damning reports Doherty still manages to survive, maybe the reason is because he refuses to lie taking the criticism like a man.

Doherty was born on 3 December 1979 in Hexham, Northumberland, the second of three children. His father was a major in the army and a strict disciplinarian and Doherty spent much of his childhood travelling around due to his father's assignments. Doherty did not respond well to the constant moving and at the age of 17 went to live with his grandmother in North London. Settling into a regular routine, Doherty started to excel as a student and achieved top grades – 11 A grades at GSCE level and 4 A grades at A Level, earning himself a place at Oxford University to study English. However, in his first year Doherty dropped out and moved into a London flat with his friend Carl Barat, because he shared his love of music. Together they wrote songs and by 1996 had started to play as an acoustic duo in pubs around London. Other musicians, who were impressed by their talent, joined them and by 2001 the punk band known as the Libertines was formed. Doherty and Barat were joined by a drummer, Gary Powell and a bassist John Hassall.

In 2002 the band were spotted by a talent scout and signed up to the Rough Trade label. Their first single, 'What A Waster', caused quite a stir in the music press and their second single a year later, 'Up The Bracket', received a similarly enthusiastic reception.

However, along with the fame, came the self-destructive lifestyle, embracing the behaviour of one of his heroes, Sid Vicious from the band the Sex Pistols. Doherty's behaviour started to cause problems with the other band members and the situation became volatile. When Doherty failed to turn up for a scheduled European tour, it was the cherry on top of the cake and he was expelled from The Libertines.

With his unquenchable appetite for living in the fast lane, Doherty's problems with drug addiction continued to get worse and his behaviour became more erratic. In 2003, while the rest of the Libertines were on tour, Doherty was arrested for breaking into Barat's flat. During his brief spell in prison, Doherty managed to pull himself together and patched things up witt Barat, and when he was released the Libertines said they were prepared to give him another chance. Not surprisingly, their reunion was short-lived, when Doherty's behaviour threatened the future of the band. Again he was expelled, being told that he needed to do something about his drug addiction before they would be prepared to take him back.

Friends and family pleaded with Doherty to go into rehab, but on two occasions he walked out before completing his treatment. Then his manager, Alan McGee, paid for him to go on a strict rehabilitation programme in a Thai monastery, but again the troubled star fled and drifted with no real purpose to his life.

BABYSHAMBLES

With the Libertines seemingly unaffected by the loss of their front man, Doherty decided to form a new band called Babyshambles, which many believed at the time was due to his need to fund his drug addiction, rather than his obsession with music. However, his new musical career didn't manage to keep him out of trouble and in the summer of 2004 Doherty was arrested again and charged with possessing a flick knife that the police found in his car.

This was followed by several drug and assault charges in 2005 and despite all odds, Doherty and the Babyshambles were signed up by his old record label Rough Trade. Many people said they were even better than the Libertines, but their success constantly teetered between triumph and disaster. Their fans were never certain whether their hero would turn up, and if he did what his behaviour and performance on stage would be like. Several disruptions and even cancellations have only served to reinforce Doherty's reputation for unreliability. Many people have said of Doherty, 'If Pete wasn't a junkie he would be ten times bigger than he is now!'

AN EXPLOSIVE COUPLE

Pete Doherty's name has long been romantically linked with supermodel Kate Moss, who herself has been the subject of constant scandal. Doherty tried to help Moss to launch her music career by teaching her to play guitar and inviting her to sing on Babyshambles' debut album. After a very volatile romance, which was off as much as it was on, Doherty announced in April 2007 that the couple were engaged. The announcement took place during one of Babyshambles' concerts when Moss was appearing on stage with the band, and shortly afterwards the couple were seen house hunting in trendy areas of London. However, by July the romance was in tatters after Doherty was seen leaving a nightclub with another girl on his arm.

Pete Doherty is a vulnerable, yet talented young man, who has been unusually honest about this substance abuse. He continues to be in trouble with the law, even though his friends and family have pleaded with him to try and get on top of his addiction. It appears that everything about his lifestyle is not only self-destructive but bent on destroying people around him as well, and yet for some reason he continues to be more and more successful. Maybe he is just one of the few people who actually survives on the scandal that follows him wherever he goes.

PART THREE

RADIO AND TV PERSONALITIES

ALAN FREED

Alan Freed was a pioneering disc jockey, or DJ, who made his name as one of the seminal figures that introduced the new sound of rock 'n' roll to white teenagers in the 1950s. In fact, he is credited with having introduced the term 'rock 'n' roll' to the mainstream, deriving it from a slang term in rhythm and blues (R & B) meaning to make love. However, early in the following decade, Freed found himself at the centre of a huge scandal about 'payola', or the practise of bribing DJs to play records. Although the practise was widespread in the broadcasting industry at the time, it was Freed who took the rap for it and it destroyed his career.

THE MOONDOG CORONATION BALL

Alan Freed was born Albert James Freed on 15 December 1921. His early years were spent in Johnstown, Pennsylvania, and when he was 12 the family moved to Salem, Ohio. There, he formed a band in high school and called it the Sultans of Swing, a name that Mark Knopfler of Dire Straits later used in the hit song of that name. Freed played trombone in the band.

On leaving school, Freed went to work in the broadcasting industry, beginning by working as a sports commentator. However, he soon gravitated towards music and became known for his exciting selections of new jazz and pop sounds. By 1949 he had made a name for himself as a music DJ and moved to Cleveland, where he began to host an R & B show on air, calling himself 'Moondog' after a way-out experimental street musician in New York. The first Moondog show was broadcast on 11 July 1951 and caused a sensation, so much so that when he decided to host a big show for more than 10,000 fans at the Cleveland Arena, calling it 'The Moondog Coronation Ball', an audience of more than 20,000 fans crashed the gates. The show was cancelled by the authorities, but it was clear that Freed's music was hugely popular, and the episode went down in history as the first genuine 'rock' concert.

INTER-RACIAL ROCK 'N' ROLL

After this Freed moved to New York, where he took

a job at WINS radio, playing what he termed rock 'n' roll, which basically meant R & B for a teenage audience. He put together theatre shows all over the city, featuring black performers – whom he termed rock 'n' roll artists – and almost single-handedly created a new genre in music. Soon, the music papers were advertising rock 'n' roll records and there were several movies featuring the music, in which Freed himself starred. So popular was the new music that in 1957, Freed got his own TV show on ABC, which was broadcast throughout the nation. However, when one of the rock'n'roll's youngest stars, Frankie Lymon, was seen dancing with a white girl, the southern states were infuriated, and ABC chose to cancel the show.

It was clear that all Freed wanted to do was play the music he loved and introduce it to new fans, but the success of the new craze, and its appeal to both black and white audiences, created enormous controversy around the country. The authorities tried to find different means of stopping him in his tracks, cancelling shows and blaming him for any disturbances that occurred at his concerts. In 1958 a fight broke out at a stage show near Boston, and the authorities there accused Freed of inciting audience members to riot. However, the charges were dropped when it became obvious that he had had no intention of causing such violence, but the radio station he worked for, WINS, still decided not to renew his contract. Undaunted, Freed found another job on a New York radio station and hosted a dance show that was televised in the area.

THE 'PAYOLA' SCANDAL BREAKS

However, this period of stability did not last long. Towards the end of the 1950s, a major investigation into the dealings of the recording industry was launched, and Freed's dealings came under scrutiny. It was found that he had received payments from record companies to play certain records. He tried to mount a defence that the payments were for 'consultations', but nobody believed him, and he was fired from both his radio and TV positions as presenter.

It seems likely that Freed did, in fact, accept bribes to play records, since this was common practice throughout the music industry at the time. By focussing on Freed, and using him as a scapegoat, the leaders of the industry were able to show that they were doing something about the illegal financial activities that characterised it. A further benefit, for the authorities at least, was that they got rid of someone who was threatening to break down the barriers of race that had so carefully been erected in American society, over hundreds of years, both in the north and the south, for a new generation of teenagers.

FREED FOUND GUILTY

Freed continued his controversial career in Los Angeles, at the radio station KDAY, which was owned by the same company as WINS. However, he soon fell foul of the powers that be when he tried to promote live shows in the city. The station forbade him to do, so and in response he handed in his resignation. He went back to New York where he presented a live twist show, but when the twist craze died down, he found himself out of a job again. Unable to find work in the city, he moved to Miami and began to drink heavily. Before long he had been fired from his job there as well.

Meanwhile, the payola investigation was grinding on, and in December 1962 he was finally found guilty on two counts of commercial bribery. He received a fine of $300. From then on he was unable to find work at all, and went to live in Palm Springs, California. There, his drinking increased, until he developed cirrhosis of the liver. He died on 20 January 1965, ostensibly of the disease, but his friends attested to the fact that he died a broken man, in a state of deep despair.

Since his death, his impact on contemporary rock music has been reassessed, and he is now recognised as one of the leading figures of rock 'n' roll. In 1986, he was inducted into the Rock and Roll Hall of Fame, and in 1991 he was commemorated with a star on Hollywood's Walk of Fame. Today, numerous music books cite his influence on the development of rock 'n' roll as paramount. Sadly, he was only given credit for launching the new sound after he died; instead, during his life he took the blame for the financial irregularities surrounding the music industry, rather than being celebrated for playing great music to a new generation of fans, and in so doing attempting to foster better relationships between black and white people in America.

MARTHA STEWART

Martha Stewart, a former stockbroker and fashion model, is a wealthy woman who was named America's third most powerful female in 2001 by the *Ladies Home Journal*. She is the author of several books and magazines and has hosted two popular daytime television programmes – the last person you would expect to become involved in a scandal. However, in 2002 Stewart's world started to fall apart when she was accused of insider trading and other felonies.

BRIEF BACKGROUND

Martha Helen Kostyra was born on 3 August 1941 in the industrial city of Jersey in New Jersey, USA. Her mother, Martha, was a schoolteacher and her father, Edward, worked as a pharmaceuticals salesman. Martha proved to be a hardworking student and won herself a partial scholarship to Barnard College in New York. To help try and pay her way through college Martha did a small amount of modelling, which turned into a successful career after her graduation. In her second year at college, Martha married Andrew Stewart, who was studying law. In 1965 Martha had a baby girl and was forced to give up modelling, but always being a career girl at heart she didn't let this hold her back. In 1967 she started a new career as a stockbroker – working for her father-in-law. Her husband formed a publishing house but when Wall Street was hit by the recession in 1973, the Stewarts decided to leave New York and moved to a 17th-century farmhouse in Westport, Connecticut. They undertook the ambition job of restoring the property, which they did to such high standards it still appears in Martha's television programmes.

Martha had another change of career in 1976 and opened a catering business with a friend from her college days. She ran the business from the basement of her home and within a very short time the enterprise was worth over one million dollars. Using the profits from her business, Martha opened a retail store in Wesport and sold speciality foods for entertaining.

A PROLIFIC WRITER

Martha was a prolific writer and several of her articles appeared in the *New York Times*. Her flair for writing was noticed and she became editor and columnist for the *House Beautiful* magazine. This was followed by several books on food for entertaining, weddings, Christmas, gardening and restoring old properties.

Regular appearance on television soon made Martha Stewart a household name in the United States and with her own magazine, *Martha Stewart Living*, it appeared she couldn't put a foot wrong.

THE SCANDAL BREAKS

Needless to say people who are constantly in the limelight have to face unfair criticism and bad press, but in 2002 Martha Stewart was faced with a far greater challenge. The Justice Department and Securities Exchange Department started an investigation into her personal stock trading, which resulted in her being charged with insider trading.

Martha was visibly shaken when charges were brought against her for selling shares in a pharmaceutical company, ImClone, just days before its application for a new drug were turned down. Despite maintaining her innocence, Martha's reputation suffered greatly over the next couple of years and she had to face trial in early 2004.

The indictments against her included: selling some stock because someone told her an insider was selling; lying to investigators; and conspiring with someone else to lie to investigators. Despite the fact the course dismissed the original accusation of insider trading from which the other two charges stemmed, the trial still took place and Martha Stewart was forced to defend herself.

She told the court that she had sold her stock in ImClone because of a previous instruction she had given to her stockbroker to sell stocks if they dropped below $60 dollars. Unfortunately, the jury didn't believe her story. In the end the whole case rested on the testimony of a broker's assistant, Douglas Faneuil, who claimed that he had been told by his boss to contact Mrs Stewart because the head of ImClone was selling his stock and that she should do the same.

The government then decided to charge Faneuil as being a participant in the conspiracy, and hey presto, the broker's assistant changed his story! In theory this made a mock of the entire trial.

Despite all the uncertainties and lies that had obviously been told, the jury still found Martha Stewart guilty of misleading federal investigators and was given a five-month prison sentence, to be followed by a two-year period of supervision.

While waiting for her appeal, Martha served her time in a minimum security prison, Alderson Federal Prison Camp, and was finally released on 4 March

2005. On 6 January 2006 the appeals court turned down her appeal and upheld the jury's verdict.

SURVIVING THE SCANDAL

After being released from prison, Martha was forced to home confinement and was required to wear an electronic ankle bracelet to monitor her at all times. Despite all the scandal, Martha Stewart made an amazing comeback and returned to daytime television without any loss to the viewing figures.

Although her marriage did not survive the scandal, she has gone on to bigger and better things. It has been said many times that not many people could have pulled off such an amazing comeback. Martha Stewart has everything it takes to be successful and a scandal – whatever the scale – will not stop her in her tracks.

MICHAEL BARRYMORE

One of the biggest scandals to hit British show-business in recent times is that of entertainer Michael Barrymore. Barrymore's zany personality and catch-phrase 'all right', pronounced in a strong cockney London accent, made him a favourite as a TV game show presenter, comedian and actor, until a major scandal rocked his career and left him a broken man.

COMING OUT

Barrymore was born Michael Ciaran Parker on 4 May 1952 in Bermondsey, then a working-class area of London. He lived with his parents on the Dickens Estate but his childhood was marred by sadness. Barrymore was only 11 years old when his father packed up and left, which left a big rift in his life. At the age of 15, he left school and took a job as a Butlins

Redcoat, entertaining the public at a local holiday camp. Barrymore showed a natural talent for the work and began to put together an act as a stand-up comic. His skill soon became evident and he was soon appearing on television talent shows. As a result of his successful performances on these shows, he was hired as the warm-up act for television audiences, and by the early 1980s had become a regular face on television comedy shows.

Michael's career really started to take off under the guidenace of his wife and manager, Cheryl, whom he married in 1976. In 1986 Barrymore made a name for himself with his quirky type of humour on the entertainment show, *Strike It Lucky*. Other shows followed, and he was voted the UK's top television star as well as earning enormous sums of money. The crowds loved him, they couldn't get enough of him, but fame was starting to take its toll.

It was during this time that Barrymore started to have problems with an alcohol addiction. According to his account of the period, he wanted to stop drinking, but his wife Cheryl, also his manager, did not feel he had a problem. However, in 1995, after years of rumours, Barrymore announced that he was gay when being interviewed on the radio. Aware that the news was now out, Barrymore went into a gay pub in London's east end and told a surprised crowd of drinkers that he was a homosexual, advising them to start spreading the news. Needless to say it wasn't long before the tabloids got hold of the story, and it was splashed across the front pages of every newspaper.

SEXUAL ABUSE

Barrymore and Cheryl separated shortly after he broke the news of his sexuality. Despite several attempts at reunions, it soon became clear that there was not much hope of sustaining the relationship. After the couple divorced in 1997, Cheryl Barrymore published her autobiography *Catch a Falling Star*, in which she revealed the negative side of Barrymore's personality.

His career took a nosedive when viewing figures started to decline on his television shows. He went on to present two more programmes for London Weekend Television – *My Kind of Music* and *Kids Do the Funniest Things* – and even tried his hand at acting. But gossip and scandal were never far from his door.

In 2000 Barrymore received a police warning when they found some drugs in a hotel room, and in 2001 allegedly he appeared drunk on stage at a fund-raising event for a children's charity. It was evident that Barrymore had long been in a mentally fragile state, and matters came to a head in 2001, when on March

31 a young man named Stuart Lubbock was found dead at Barrymore's home. Witnesses claimed that the man had died in Barrymore's swimming pool; some thought he had been seen floating on the top of the water, while others claimed he had sunk to the bottom. The scandal reached a high point when it was reported that Lubbock had injuries to his anal area, suggesting that he had been the victim of sexual abuse before he died. Witnesses reported that Barrymore had been seen rubbing cocaine on to Lubbock's gums that evening, but there was no evidence that he had been forcing him to take the drug. In the end Barrymore was cautioned for possession of cannabis, but there were no other charges.

The following day, Barrymore voluntarily checked himself into the Marchwood Priory in Southampton where he hoped he could conquer his problems with addiction and depression.

SORDID SCANDAL

On 6 June 2001 drag queen Jonathan Kenney, who was Barrymore's lover, and an unemployed ex-dustman called Justin Merritt were arrested on suspicion of murder. There was an inquest, but an open verdict was reached because of lack of evidence. At this stage, Cheryl Barrymore intervened and claimed that her ex-husband had lied under oath, saying that he had rubbed cocaine onto several friends' gums, and that he could have swum into the pool to save Lubbock. Barrymore's lawyers countered this claim by saying that Lubbock had died accidentally and that he might have been attacked as his body lay in the mortuary, in an instance of necrophilia. The police issued a statement to the effect that this was an absurd suggestion – leaving the case wide open and unsolved.

Relations between Barrymore and his ex-wife had reached an all-time low by this point. Sadly, Cheryl Barrymore was then diagnosed with lung cancer and died at the age of only 55 in April 2005. After her death, Barrymore published his own autobiography, *Awight Now: Setting the Record Straight*, in which he claimed that Cheryl was a controlling person who had suppressed his true personality to the extent that he was forced to take solace in drugs, alcohol and gay sex. Not surprisingly, the sordid scandal surrounding Barrymore's social life ruined his career as a 'family' entertainer, and he was no longer able to function as a TV game show host.

Barrymore moved to New Zealand for a time, with his partner Shaun Davis, in an attempt to escape the press. But his problems were not over – there would be no running away. In January 2006, a lawyer named

Anthony Bennett began a private prosecution of Barrymore, teaming up with Lubbock's father to form The Lubbock Trust. Barrymore and Lubbock's father, Terry, met up in a hotel to discuss the matter, and reportedly Terry was persuaded that Barrymore was not responsible for the death of his son. However, the disputes continued, and eventually it became clear that the Essex Police had bungled the investigation, and that there had been some sort of cover-up.

THE FUTURE

As all this was going on, Barrymore made a high-profile appearance on a reality TV show, *Celebrity Big Brother*, in which it became clear that he was in an extremely highly strung state. There was some controversy surrounding his relationship with another contestant, Jodie Marsh, and he was dubbed 'Bullymore' by her, but he proved popular among the viewers, mainly because he was one of the few people on the show to display any talent as an entertainer.

On 14 June 2007 the police announced that they had arrested Michael Barrymore on suspicion of murder, along with Kenney and Merritt. This was over six years since the death of Stuart Lubbock. However, they were all later released without charges. Since that time, Barrymore has shown signs of wanting to resume his show-business career, although tabloid newspapers continue to report his drink and drug-fuelled antics on the gay scene. Whatever the future holds for the 54-year-old entertainer, it is clear that the scandal surrounding the death of Stuart Lubbock will continue to haunt him until what really happened that fateful night is made clear.

HEIDI FLEISS

Heidi Fleiss became famous in the 1990s as the madame of a high-class brothel in Hollywood, a favourite haunt of many stars and wealthy entrepreneurs from the entertainment world. As the owner of a little black book full of names of the rich and famous, Fleiss was notorious for some years, before being jailed on various charges, including tax evasion. On her release she publicised her plans to run a 'Stud Farm' in the Nevada desert, where it is legal, under certain circumstances, for prostitutes to work in brothels. However, Fleiss' plan was to have a brothel with a difference . . .

BORN ENTREPRENEUR

Heidi Lynn Fleiss was born on 30 December 1965. Her father, Doctor Paul M. Fleiss, was a famous Hollywood paediatrician who made a name for himself by publicly opposing the practise of circumcision on infants and young boys. Her family was wealthy, and she came into contact with many rich, famous people from the world of entertainment.

As a teenager, Fleiss became a babysitter and started a business hiring out herself and her friends to look after children. With her wealthy connections, she found she was earning a good living, so decided to drop out of high school in the tenth grade. At the age of 19, she went to a Beverly Hills party and met Bernie Cornfield, a famous financier. She fell in love with him, and the couple began dating, even though he was 40 years her senior. She later said that she was attracted to his intelligence: 'He was this genius in so many ways . . . he was always trying to make me a better person and make me understand things.' Despite her enthusiasm for her new lover, the affair did not last and she found herself single again.

At the age of 22 Fleiss met another influential figure in her life – Madame Alex – a well-known brothel keeper in Hollywood. She was surprised to find that, far from being elegant and beautiful, Madame Alex was short, bald and not at all glamorous. However, she joined forces with her and was soon running the business for her new employer. Heidi found all sorts of ways to revamp the enterprise; for example, instead of employing the same girls year after, she used new prostitutes, thus making sure that the clientele had a variety of girls at their disposal. She also brought in young women that she had met as part of her social circle, as well as through Bernie Cornfield. Within a matter of months, according to Fleiss, the earnings of the business shot up from around $50,000 a month to $300,000.

TOP CALL-GIRL RING

Despite the obvious success of the business, it was not long before Fleiss and Madame Alex fell out. Fleiss claims that Madame Alex did not pay her fairly, and did not value her managerial acumen highly enough. So, instead, Fleiss moved on to launch her own call-girl ring, with a stable of girls who became the most sought after in Hollywood.

Fleiss took her work seriously and went to great lengths to find out the fantasies of all her clients, and to match them to the right women with the right wardrobe and accessories. She even arranged travel and payment details, as well as booking accommodation. For this, she earned a handsome salary. She went on record for her refusal to accept that her earnings were immoral in any way, saying, 'I think it's unfair men put laws on a woman's body. I think a woman has a right to choose with her own body. I don't think prostitution is a career . . . but maybe it is a little stepping stone.' She added: 'I don't regret what I did at all. It's consensual sex. These are men who are billionaires and these are women in their 20s. They are old enough to make adult decisions, adult choices.'

In Fleiss' eyes she was providing a service and helping her employees to meet the right men, who would possibly advance their careers in the entertainment industry.

PRISON SENTENCE

In 1993 Fleiss was arrested as part of an undercover operation to root out prostitution in Hollywood. Not surprisingly, some individuals on her extensive client list came to light, causing a scandal that rocked Tinseltown. One of the most prominent of her clients was the actor Charlie Sheen. Later, Sheen became known as a 'living legend of sex' after he claimed that he had had sex with five girls at once.

'It was very organised,' he commented. 'Very ordered. All six people in that room came out of it pretty satisfied.' Sheen also claimed to have had sex with a total of 5000 women. Naturally, with such a busy schedule, the services of a well-organised madame such as Heidi Fleiss would have been invaluable to him.

Despite her protestations of innocence, Fleiss was brought to trial on federal charges of conspiracy, tax evasion and money laundering. She was also charged with attempted pandering, a type of pimping. She was convicted of the charges and received a prison sentence of 37 months, although she only served 21. Many commentators were outraged by the severity of her sentence, especially as none of her clients or employees were charged. Her father, Doctor Fleiss, was also convicted of money laundering and sentenced to serve one day in prison, as well as three years of probation and over 600 hours community service.

THE STUD FARM

On her release from prison in 1999, Fleiss made the most of her new-found notoriety, and began a series of commercial enterprises. One of these was a line of clothing called Heidi Wear; another involved selling sex aids. She appeared regularly on television to talk about her experiences, and was interviewed in many leading newspapers and magazines. She then announced her intention to open a stud farm in the Nevada desert, where in some areas brothel keeping is a legal activity, subject to state scrutinisation of the operation. The proposed brothel was due to be located about an hour's drive away from Las Vegas.

Instead of offering the sexual services of women to male clients, the brothel would offer an array of handsome men to provide sex for women.

Fleiss' vision of this pleasure palace was that it would be shaped like a castle, with marble-floored rooms, a spa, a sex-toy shop and secluded bungalows for love play to take place. The men she proposed hiring would be handsome, physically fit with a muscled physique, charming and well-mannered. They would also be issued with generous amounts of Viagra to cope with up to ten female clients a day, some of them not in their first youth or in good shape physically. In return, the women clients would pay a fee of around 250 dollars an hour.

DIRTY LAUNDRY

As Fleiss has admitted, the obstacles to launching the stud farm remain daunting. State laws require all prostitutes to have regular cervical STD tests, which obviously in the case of the stud farm would not apply. The statutes will need to be reworded to cover Fleiss' stud farm operation. In addition, Fleiss faces considerable opposition from other brothel keepers in the area, who are worried that adverse publicity will ruin their business. Already her business partner, a successful Nevada brothel owner, has backed out of the project. Funding for the palace of sin, which will require around $1.5 million, is also lacking at present. However, Fleiss remains optimistic. She claims to have received over 1,000 applications from men who wish to work at the farm, including former soap opera stars and Hollywood actors. She also says that a number of wealthy, beautiful women have contacted her to arrange appointments. Fleiss maintains that her idea is 'perfect for bachelorette parties or for women wanting uncomplicated, STD-free hook-ups'.

At present, the stud farm is set only to cater for women, not for men. Interestingly, some gay men have asked for a legal opinion as to whether the brothel would be violating discrimination laws by letting only women use the stud farm's services. In response, Fleiss has suggested the opening of a separate gay brothel.

Despite these grand ideas, to date, plans for the stud farm have foundered. Instead, Fleiss has opened a laundromat named 'Dirty Laundry', a far more modest enterprise than her fantasy of a luxury bordello in the desert. She also sells sex aids in her 'Little Shop of Sex' in Los Angeles, and over the Internet. However, Fleiss continues to insist that one day the stud farm will be a reality, and the media continues to watch her activities and listen to her opinions with interest.

THÉRÈSE HUMBERT

The life of the French woman, Thérèse Humbert, was one of fantasy and pure illusion. A peasant girl from the Languedoc region of France, she dreamed of a life of wealth and luxury and to fulfil this dream she pretended to be the heir of an imaginary millionaire. The scandal that was exposed in 1902 nearly destroyed the French Third Republic, and ruined the lives of thousands of creditors.

Thérèse Daurignac was born in 1856 and her delusions of grandeur began at a very young age. She convinced her friends to pool all their jewellery so that she could fool people into believing she was rich. Her main stepping stone to success, however, was when she married her first cousin Frédéric Humbert, who was the son of the French politician Gustave Humbert. Although under normal circumstances her cousin would probably not have paid any attention to the poor peasant girl, Thérèse started to woo Frédéric with her fantastic story.

DEADLY DECEPTION

Thérèse told Frédéric that she had received a large inheritance under rather unusual circumstances. She claimed that she was on a train in 1879, when she heard someone groaning in the next carriage. Thérèse said she was able to gain access into the carriage by climbing along the outside of the train and crawling in through the window. Inside the compartment she found a man laying on the floor writhing in agony. She claimed to have aided the man by giving him some of her smelling salts, for which he said he was eternally grateful. The man told Thérèse that he was a wealthy American millionaire and that his name was Robert Henry Crawford.

Thérèse went on to tell Frédéric that she thought that was the end of the matter and gave it no further thought. However, to her surprise, two years later she received a letter from a solicitor saying that Crawford had died and had made Thérèse a beneficiary of his will. To get round the fact that Thérèse was not actually in possession of any money, she said that the money had been put in trust and would be released when her younger sister, Marie, was old enough to marry one of Crawford's two nephews, Henry Crawford.

Together Thérèse and her husband approached the bank and applied for a loan, using the supposed inheritance as collateral. They moved to Paris where they bought an upmarket property in Avenue de la Grande Armée. The Humberts lived a life of luxury, earned themselves a lot of friends and influence and, as the years went by, the lies got bigger and so did the loans. Thérèse opened a salon and was soon mixing with the elite of French society. However, eventually they were forced to take out more and more money to cover the original loans and, although people started to become suspicious, no one could prove that her original story was false.

The whole ruse was centred on a strongbox, which Thérèse kept at their Paris apartment. Inside the box was the alleged final will of millionaire Henry Crawford, naming Thérèse as the sole beneficiary. There was also supposed to be a second will, which left everything to Thérèse's younger sister and Crawford's two American nephews. Thérèse also insisted there was a third document in which the two Crawford boys agreed to give the entire fortune to her while the other two wills were being settled. The fourth fictional document in the strongbox was a deed in which the Crawford boys were supposed to waive their claim to the fortune in return for a payment of six million francs and Marie's hand in marriage.

Thérèse used all this evidence to convince her

financiers to lend her the six million francs to pay off the Crawford nephews, and in return she would inherit over 100 million francs.

In 1883, a French newspaper, *Le Matin*, published an article claiming that Thérèse Humbert was a fraudster. However, her father-in-law, who at the time was the minister of justice, backed Thérèse's story. Over the years, the Humbert's con reached such proportions of perfection that there were even trials at court where sincere lawyers represented the Crawfords and the Humberts. To get over the problem of the two Crawford nephews, Thérèse's own brothers impersonated them, speaking in poor French with even worse American accents.

The Humberts could possibly have continued to get away with their amazing ruse for years to come if it hadn't been for the fact that the judge ordered Thérèse to reveal the address of the Crawfords. Without hesitation she said, '1302 Broadway in New York', speaking out for all to hear. Of course no Crawfords lived at that address and the judge requested they hand over the security box.

The next day, 7 May 1902, the crowds gathered to witness the opening of the box, but the Humberts had already fled the country. When the box was unlocked, it was found to contain an old newspaper, a button and an Italian coin of small denomination. The

Humbert's creditors sued and the scandal rocked the French financial world. The French press printed a list of all the famous people who had been taken for their fortunes, which included the exiled Empress Eugénie, the son of the president of the French Republic and the in-laws of the famous painter Henri Matisse. These, and many other VIPs, embarrassed by the whole affair decided to make themselves scarce.

The Humberts were eventually caught up with in December 1902 in Madrid. Thérèse Humbert was sentenced to five years solitary confinement and hard labour, her husband also received five years, while the two brothers who had masqueraded as the Crawford nephews received two and three years each. It was decided that Marie and Thérèse's father-in-law, Gustave Humbert, were all just victims of the fraud and were allowed to go free.

When Thérèse was eventually released from prison she left France and went to live in the United States. She died in Chicago in 1918 in disgrace and without a penny to her name. However, she will always be remembered for her hoax that fooled an entire society and caused one of France's greatest ever scandals.

PART FOUR

POLITICIANS

BILL CLINTON

The greatest worldwide sex scandal to hit the headlines at the end of the 20th century was undoubtedly that of Bill Clinton, President of the United States. Monica Lewinsky, an intern who was working at the White House during 1995 and 1996, had a sexual relationship with the president during that time, and when this became known, it helped lead to Clinton's impeachment trial. Thus, it was one of the most important scandals of all time, severely affecting the president's reputation, as well as giving Lewinsky a notoriety that is likely to last for the rest of her life.

WHIFF OF A SCANDAL

Monica Lewinsky was a young, hopeful White House intern when she met the president. From California, she had graduated with a psychology degree and moved to Washington, D.C. to work at the White House. She began as an unpaid intern in July 1995, and by November had secured a permanent job there with good prospects. However, in the spring of 1996

Clinton's chief of staff started to noticed that Lewinsky was spending rather too much time in the company of the president. He decided to have her transferred to the Pentagon to try and avoid a scandal, but the president wasn't entirely happy about the arrangement and intervened. He arranged for her to get an important position with top-security clearance as a confidential assistant to the chief Pentagon spokesman, Kenneth Bacon. For this position she would earn $32,700 a year and had travel privileges. Clinton continued to buy Lewinsky lavish gifts and would talk on the phone to her late at night, often engaging in 'sex talk'.

Members of Clinton's staff became suspicious because no intern had ever advanced so quickly up the political ladder. Lewinsky was also given a special pass, which entitled her to enter the White House at night and at weekends, allegedly creeping in away from prying eyes.

However, at the Pentagon things were not going so well for Lewinsky. She couldn't handle her day to day tasks and mismanaged her boss's tight schedule, which resulted in her getting the sack. Clinton immediately stepped in once again and asked a favour of UN Ambassador Bill Richardson, if he would give her a job. Richardson agreed, but then the news of their illicit affair was leaked and the scandal was out.

THE BLUE DRESS

The way the story leaked out was as follows. During 1997 the relationship between the president and Lewinsky continued, even though Lewinsky had left the White House. Lewinsky made friends with a woman, Linda Tripp, when they both worked in the Pentagon's public affairs office. After Lewinsky foolishly revealed to Tripp that she was having a physical relationship with the president, Tripp secretly recorded the telephone conversations between Lewinsky and the president. Tripp also acted as an adviser to Lewinsky, telling her to keep the presents that Clinton had bought her during their affair. She told Lewinsky not to have a blue dress stained with Clinton's semen dry cleaned, so that there would be evidence of what had happened between them, should this be needed for evidence later on.

In the meantime, Clinton was the subject of a court case involving a woman named Paula Jones, who was suing him for sexual harrasment. The case was dismissed, but Clinton paid Jones a large sum to settle the matter out of court. In the process of this, Lewinsky gave evidence denying that she had had a sexual relationship with the president, but Linda Tripp refused to lie under oath in this instance and gave the tapes she had made of the telephone conversations to an independent counsel, Kenneth Starr. Starr later issued a report alleging that Lewinsky and Clinton had had oral sex in the Oval Office and in other rooms at the West Wing of the White House. This rang true in many quarters, since Clinton had also been the subject of another long-running sex scandal involving Gennifer Flowers, a woman from Arkansas who claimed that she had had a 12-year affair with him while he was governor of that state, and had even had a child by him. (The child was apparently given up for adoption.)

THE CIGAR TUBE

Clinton began by denying his affair with Lewinsky, swearing under oath that he had never had 'a sexual affair' ' sexual relations', or a 'sexual relationship' with her. He categorically stated on American national television on 26 January 1998, 'I did not have sexual relations with that woman, Miss Lewinsky'. He later claimed that he did not include oral sex in his definition of 'sexual relations'.

Next, he managed to find a way to argue around his claim, 'There is not a sexual relationship, an improper sexual relationship or any other kind of improper relationship', claiming that this statement was true insofar as, when he made it, the relationship was actually over: as he famously remarked, 'it depends on what the meaning of the word "is" is'.

However, Starr confronted the president with the evidence that he had obtained a blue dress from Lewinsky that had his semen stain on it. Starr also told the president that Lewinsky had described how she and Clinton had conducted their sex play in the Oval Office, with Clinton pushing a cigar tube into her vagina. Faced with this evidence, Clinton backed down and admitted to having misled the court, admitting that he had had an 'inappropriate intimate contact' with Lewinsky. However, he said that he had not committed perjury, because he believed that oral sex was not real sex. He went on to claim that he was passive during these encounters, and that Lewinsky had performed oral sex on him rather than the other way round. When Lewinsky denied this, Clinton's lawyer tried to persuade the court that he had remembered it all differently to her.

SERIOUS AND COMICAL

The Lewinsky affair was finally proved and, at the same time, one of the most serious and comical sex scandals of the Clinton administration made the headlines. Clinton's attempts to evade the truth in the Lewinsky case came at the end of several claims from other women about his sexual conduct over the years, and reinforced the public image of him as a sexually voracious man who was periodically unfaithful to his wife. However, in this case, he had tried, on the face of it, to pervert the course of justice by lying about what had happened between him and the young intern, and as such was suspected of perjury. Steps were taken to impeach him in 1998 by the US House of Representatives, but after a 21-day trial, the Senate did not achieve the two-thirds majority required to convict and remove the president from office under the laws of the Constitution.

Consequently, Clinton remained in office, but his reputation was severely damaged and many felt that he could no longer be trusted. Not only did he appear to have lied under oath, but he had begun a sexual relationship with a young woman (she was only 21 years old at the time) who was half his age, and many regarded this not just as inappropriate, but as immoral, or – at the very least – showing a disregard for his presidential responsibilities.

JOHN MAJOR

John Major, the prime minister of Britain from 1990 to 1997, had a reputation in office of being the 'grey man' of politics. His image was one of a dutiful, somewhat unimaginative man who in his personal life valued his privacy and his family, and amused himself with such innocent activities as playing cricket. However, long after he retired from politics, it was revealed that for four years he had been having a passionate affair with a colleague, and that he was by no means the simple, straightforward man that all had assumed him to be.

CONTROVERSIAL AND OUTSPOKEN

Edwina Currie, the ex-lover who revealed the scandal, had been one of the leading Conservative ministers in Margaret Thatcher's government, along with John Major. Born Edwina Cohen in Liverpool, Lancashire, to an Orthodox Jewish family, she had always been something of a rebel, refusing to take on what she referred to as 'religious mumbo jumbo' of judaism. She was a very bright student, and went on from school to study Philosophy, Politics and Economics at Oxford University, later taking a further degree in Economics in London. For ten years after that she worked as a city councillor in Birmingham, then stood for Parliament in 1983 and was elected.

As a member of parliament, she became well known in the media for her controversial, outspoken views, making a contrast to the careful speeches of her colleagues. In 1986 she reached the peak of her career by becoming a Junior Health Minister in Margaret Thatcher's administration. However, two years later she was forced to resign because she made a tactless remark about eggs, saying that most of the eggs in Britain were affected by salmonella. Whether true or not, this caused a storm, and British farmers pressurised the government to have her sacked.

SPECTACULAR PASSION

She left her post as minister and continued her political work as an MP until she lost her seat in the 1997 General Election. In the years that followed, she became a media star, hosting a radio chat show called *Late Night Currie* and writing a series of raunchy novels, one of which, *A Parliamentary Affair*, was thought to have been based on her own experience. In 1997 her marriage to accountant Ray Currie ended in divorce after 25 years, and she went on to marry John Jones, a retired detective. But it was not until the year 2002 that she published her diaries, which caused a huge scandal, because she admitted for the first time that she had had an affair with the former Prime Minister John Major.

According to the diaries, the affair with 'B', as she called him, had continued for four years, from 1984 to 1988. Her account revealed Major as a passionate lover and she called their sex life 'spectacular'.

'So why did it start?' she began. 'Because I was unhappy with a husband forever slumped snoring in front of the television, not helpful or interested in what I was trying to do . . . Then B came along and he was so nice and so attractive, and so quiet in public that it was a challenge to unearth the real person and to seduce him – easy! And it was unexpectedly, spectacularly good, for such a long time . . .'

The story went on to describe how she fell in love with Major and explained that as both of them were working away from home, they had plenty of time to seek out each other's company. They were also united by a common interest in politics, which neither of their spouses apparently shared. In addition, Currie described Major as kind and courteous to women, which was a rarity in the 'men's club' of Parliament. The two lovers had very different styles – Major was, on the face of it, dull and steady, while Currie was flamboyant and extrovert – but, according to her, that was why they were so attracted to each other. However, in the long run neither felt there was any future to the affair, since they were both married, so eventually they ended it. Afterwards, Currie was very sad, saying in her diaries, 'I didn't expect to love this man, but I do, very much indeed . . . I weep for what I don't have.'

BACK TO BASICS

The political world was astonished by the revelations in Edwina Currie's diaries, and the press had a field day joking about Major's new image, no longer as the 'grey man' of Parliament but as a roving Casanova who had generated such passion from his ex-lover. Major himself responded sheepishly to the furore that followed the publication of the diaries, saying only, 'It is the one event in my life of which I am most ashamed. My wife Norma has known of this matter for many years and has long forgiven me.' But although it seemed like a public relations disaster for Major at the time, in the long term the scandal may have endeared him to the public, because now he seemed rather more human and somewhat less boring than he had done before.

There was a serious side to the scandal, however. During his term as prime minister, Major had initiated a 'Back to Basics' campaign promoting the virtues of traditional family life. This proved extremely unpopular with the public, and was eventually abandoned. But while it was still in operation, several Conservative members of parliament, who had been exposed in the press as having had extramarital affairs, were asked to resign from important governmental positions. In retrospect, considering that Major himself had had a four-year affair with Currie during his own marriage, this smacked of hypocricy, and critics were quick to point out that Major's reputation was tarnished as a result. Also, it was pointed out that if the affair had been revealed at the time it took place, Major might very well not have been asked to become prime minister and form a government in the wake of Thatcher's administration. Instead, the way would have been open to the other main contender, Michael Heseltine, whose policies – particularly regarding Britain's relationship with Europe – were very different. Thus, the course of history might have been changed had the liaison between Major and Currie become known earlier.

MONEY OR REVENGE?

Commentators also speculated as to why Currie had chosen to reveal the affair in her diaries. Some felt that her motive was a financial one – such scandalous revelations would, of course, help to sell her diaries. Others speculated that she had felt deeply scorned when her name did not feature in Major's diaries, given the fact that she had worked closely with him for many years, and that she had published details of the affair in revenge for being ignored. She herself admitted that she had felt hurt that he had failed to mention her, but denied that she had published the story out of revenge.

Whatever her reasons for telling all, the scandal remains one of the most interesting in the history of recent British politics, giving a flavour of life in parliament from a woman's point of view, and casting an altogether new light on the 'grey man' of politics, John Major.

JOHN PROFUMO

The Profumo Affair was perhaps the most memorable scandal of British politics during the 1960s. It concerned a high-ranking Conservative politician, John Profumo, who had an affair with a high-class call girl, Christine Keeler. This liaison apparently lasted only a few weeks, and normally would have been dismissed as a trivial incident, but when rumours began to circulate that Keeler had also been involved with a senior official from the Soviet government, there were fears that national security could had been breached.

BRILLIANT CAREER

John Profumo was the son of a successful barrister, Albert Profumo, who was an aristocrat of Italian origin, but who lived in Britain. Albert held the title of Baron, given to him by the Sardinian royal family, and when he died his son John took over the title.

However, the young Profumo did not use the title in public. John Profumo grew up in the privileged world of the English upper classes, being educated at Harrow, a top private school, and then studying at Oxford University. During World War II, he became a soldier and distinguished himself for his bravery, among other courageous actions helping to organise the D-Day landings in Normandy. He rose to the rank of Brigadier and towards the end of the war, received an OBE for his service to the nation.

In 1940 he stood as a Conservative candidate in the national elections, won a seat and became the youngest member of parliament to do so. With the Labour landslide at the end of the war, he lost his seat, but by the 1950s he was back in power again and was regarded by the Conservative government as one of their greatest assets. Good looking, intelligent, polite and with many contacts in the higher echelons of society, during the decade his career steadily advanced, until in 1959 he became Minister of State for Foreign Affairs. During this time he also married his glamorous wife, actress Valerie Hobson.

By 1961 he had become minister of state for war. He was a very busy, successful man who socialised a great deal, and in this capacity he attended a party at Cliveden, the home of one of his friends, Viscount Astor. It was there that he met Christine Keeler.

Keeler was a beautiful woman, a model, who epitomised the 'swinging sixties' when people of different social backgrounds had begun to mix with each other. Keeler had had a chequered history, having given birth to a baby that lived only a few days after trying to induce an abortion. As well as her modelling career, she also operated as a 'call girl' or prostitute. Her clientele consisted of very high-ranking members of the British upper classes, and it was not long before John Profumo became one of her many lovers.

FALL FROM GRACE

According to Profumo, he ended the relationship only a few weeks after it had begun, but the short liaison was to have a devastating effect, not only on his own career, but that of the Conservative government. The following year, there was a shooting incident in London in which two men known to Keeler were involved. This led to an investigation of Keeler herself, and during this time it was learned that she had had a relationship with Profumo. It then transpired that among Keeler's other lovers was the Senior Naval Attache to the Soviet embassy, a man named Yevgeny Ivanov, and it was this that triggered anxieties that national security might have been breached. Of course, it was highly unlikely that Keeler and her lovers had spent their time discussing the positioning of nuclear installations and suchlike while they were in bed, but the risk was thought to be enough to raise questions in the House of Commons, and eventually, Profumo was challenged about the liaison. Even so, Profumo's personal involvement with Keeler was kept secret, so as to protect his privacy, and the story did not come out until 1963, when a member of the Labour Party, MP George Wigg, started to ask questions in the house about the case.

Initially, Profumo admitted that he knew Ms Keeler, but denied that he had had any sexual involvement with her – or 'impropriety' as he termed it. However, by this time the press had got hold of the story and Harold Macmillan, the then prime minister, became aware that the rumours had to be stopped. Thus, he asked Profumo to explain himself to the House of Commons, hoping that this would help to put the matter to rest. Profumo stood before the house and swore his innocence, but then evidence emerged to show that he had been lying. On June 5 1963 he was forced to stand before the House again and admit what he had done.

For the British politicians, it was the fact that he had lied to his colleagues, rather than the fact that he had been involved in the affair, that rankled. Profumo was forced to quit his job, even though it was demonstrated that his liaison with Keeler had not, in fact, led to any breach of national security. Throughout his ordeal, his wife remained loyal to him, and neither of them ever referred to the matter in public again, even when Keeler published her autobiography and again when the 1989 film *Scandal*, about the affair, was released.

CHARITY WORK

After his fall from grace, Profumo ceased to pursue public life and began working as a volunteer at a local charity, Toynbee Hall, based in the run-down area of London's East End. He did all sorts of menial tasks, including cleaning the toilets there, and slowly won the respect of the local people. His wife also worked for charity and the couple became known for their devotion to a number of charitable causes. During this time, they were lucky enough to be able to live on their inherited wealth.

Eventually, Profumo was asked to become a fundraiser for Tonybee Hall, and agreed reluctantly to do so. He was in a good position to use his many contacts from the past to raise funds for the charity, and began to win the respect of his former colleagues in political circles once more. Lord Longford, another aristocratic social campaigner, praised Profumo as one of the men he admired most in the world. In 1975 he received a CBE for his services to charity, and went to Buckingham Palace to pick up his medal from the queen.

In 1995, when ex-Tory Prime Minister Margaret Thatcher celebrated her 70th birthday, she invited him to a celebration, where he was seated next to the queen, and announced publicly that it was time he was forgiven 'It's time to forget the Keeler business,' she said. 'His has been a very good life.' She also called him, 'one of our national heroes.'

In his later years Profumo rarely appeared in public and was confined to a wheelchair. His last public appearance was at a memorial service for former Conservative Prime Minister Harold Macmillan in 2005. He died a year later, on 9 March 2006, having suffered a major stroke two days earlier.

Today, in view of the many sex scandals that often surround politicians' personal lives, whether in Britain, Europe or the United States, it seems extraordinary that such a minor affair should have been taken so seriously. However, during the 1960s, under a stricter moral climate, and with the paranoia of the Cold War ever present, the reports of Profumo's actions electrified the nation, and led not only to the destruction of his reputation, but to the demise of the Conservative government of the day.

LORD LAMBTON

Lord Lambton was a British aristocrat who resigned from Parliament in 1973 because of a scandal involving his liaison with prostitutes. At the time, he was regarded as a brilliant and ambitious politician in the government of Edward Heath.

A LIFE OF LUXURY

Antony Claud Frederick Lambton was born into an extremely rich aristocratic family and before 1970, as the Sixth Earl of Durham, was known as Viscount Lambton. As was the custom, he renounced his peerage to enter the House of Commons as a Conservative member of parliament, but insisted on continuing to use his title, thus becoming involved in a legal battle. He grew up in luxury on family estates in Ireland, and was educated at the prestigious Harrow School, an elitist boarding school for boys near London. During World War II, he served as a soldier, but was invalided out and went on to do war work in a factory. In 1921 he married Belinda Blew-Jones, a fellow aristocrat, and the couple went on to have one son and five daughters.

In 1945 Lambton stood for parliament, but it was not until 1951, after serving on Durham City Council, that he gained a seat as a Conservative member of parliament. In 1970 he was made a parliamentary under-secretary of state for defence. In the same year, his father died and he inherited his father's title, but according to the rules of Parliament, had to give it up if he was to continue as a member of parliament and government minister. However, after disclaiming the title, he insisted on continuing to be addressed as 'Lord Lambton' in the House of Commons, which caused a great deal of controversy. Lambton became completely obsessive about the issue, which earned him more than a few enemies in the House, and helped to confirm the stereotypes of snobbery and arrogance that are so often associated with the British upper classes.

SMOKING CANNABIS WITH NAKED GIRLS

Perhaps partly because of his arrogant stance, there were those in the media who wished to bring him down, and in 1973 they got their chance. Under the name Lucas, Lambton visited a prostitute, Norma Levy, a beautiful dark-haired young woman whose looks were similar to that of Christine Keeler, who had been involved in the Profumo scandal. Lambton's real identity became known to the prostitute when, in typically careless style, he handed her a personal cheque. Together with her husband, Norma Levy decided to capitalise on the discovery and take incriminating photographs of what took place on his next visit. They concealed a tape recorder inside a teddy bear, and Mr Levy hid behind a two-way mirror so that he could take photographs of their famous client. When Lambton came to the house on his next visit, he was photographed smoking cannabis with Norma and another prostitute, the three of them naked in bed together.

THE SCANDAL IS REVEALED

When Lambton left, unaware of what had happened, Mr Levy tried to sell the photographs to the tabloids. Instead, they were handed in to the police. Then one of the more sensationalist tabloids, *The News of the World*, printed the story and Lambton's secret was out. As soon as this happened, Lambton decided to resign, writing to the prime minister and to his own constituency. He issued a statement to the press saying: 'My own feelings may be imagined but I have no excuses whatsoever to make. I behaved with credulous stupidity and consequently let down those I most wished to please – the prime minister, the Conservative Party, my electorate, who have given me 22 years of loyalty and my family.' He emphasised that he had never discussed any aspect of his job with the prostitutes, which given that he had been engaged for most of the time in recreational activities with the two of them, was not hard to believe. Further humiliation followed when he appeared in court on drugs charges. He pleaded guilty to possession of cannabis and amphetamine tablets and was fined £300.

After the revelation, an enquiry was held to see whether there had been any breach of security as a result of the liaisons, since Lambton was a junior minister in the defence department. However, Lambton assured the court that he had not taken his red state boxes of government papers when he attended his rendezvous with the prostitutes. Since it was clear to everyone that this would have been a rather unlikely thing to do in the circumstances, the enquiry was satisfied that no breach of security had occurred.

Nevertheless, Lampton had to go, especially as after the incident he made matters worse by telling police that he used prostitutes because he felt a 'sense of futility' in his job as a junior minister. He also claimed that a battle to continue using an aristocratic title had made him obsessive, and that gardening and sex with prostitutes, among other 'frantic activities' had helped him to allay his obsession. Later, in his retirement, he made the simple, perhaps more truthful, statement in an interview with television host Robin Day, that he had visited prostitutes because 'people sometimes like variety. It's as simple as that'.

After his downfall, Lambton retired from the political scene to a large villa called Cetinale in Tucany, Italy, where he lived until his death, surrounded by wealthy British expatriates. He and his wife separated and he lived with his mistress, Claire Ward. He seldom returned to Britain, except to attend parties in London, or to go shooting on his estate. Instead, he devoted himself to gardening, reading and entertaining, which he did in style, becoming known as the 'King of Chiantishire'. He was famous for his sharp tongue, writing acerbic book reviews for a right-wing British newspaper, and gossiping about his many guests. During the 1980s he wrote short stories, novels and a two-volume study of the Mountbatten family, which drew widespread criticism for its unflattering portrait of Earl Mountbatten. In his later years he continued to write, entertain and garden at Cetinale, until his death in December 2006.

MARK FOLEY

Mark Foley was a Republican member of the United States House of Representatives and a campaigner against child abuse. In September 2006 he was forced to resign after it emerged that he had sent sexually explicit e-mails to teenage boys who had formerly worked as Congressional pages. The scandal rocked the American media, particularly because Foley had been vociferous in his condemnation of child abuse and exploitation.

GAY RUMOURS

Mark Adam Foley was born in Newton, Massachusetts, the son of a police officer. At the age of three he moved with his father, mother and four siblings to Lake Worth, Florida, and later attended high school and college there. As a young man he started a restaurant with his mother and then moved on to become a real estate broker. He began to serve as chairman for a variety of enterprises, including a hospital, and by the age of 23 was a member of Lake Worth City Council. He set his sights on a political career, but it was not until 1990 that he was finally elected to the Florida House of Representatives. Two years later he was a member of the Florida Senate. It seemed that his political ambitions were well on the way to being achieved.

However, there were some who questioned his personal life, in particular the fact that he was not married and was rumoured to be gay. A number of articles and commentaries had appeared in the alternative press and on-line speculating that he was gay. The rumours continued to circulate as Foley made a bid to enter the US Senate, and later it was reported by the mainstream press that the fact that Foley was gay was an open secret in the political world.

CHILD PORNOGRAPHY CAMPAIGN

In 1994 Foley was elected to the US House as a Republican. Two years later he was re-elected with a larger share of the vote, and after that his popularity grew. By 2003 he was in the running to replace Bob Graham at the Senate, but the rumours continued to thwart his career. He had become known as a campaigner against child pornography, serving on a committee concerned with missing and exploited children. He particularly focussed on child pornography, pointing out that there were websites on the Internet featuring suggestive images of pre-teen children, and advocating that these should be outlawed, since, in his words, they were 'nothing more than a fix for paedophiles'.

Foley drew up a bill to forbid the use of such images, but it proved unworkable since it would have banned many types of ordinary commercial photography involving children. He also wrote to the governor of Florida about a local teenage nudist programme that he disapproved of. He was responsible for changes in sex offender laws, which were supported by TV shows, victims' rights groups and children's groups. His legislation became part of the Adam Walsh Child Protection and Safety Act of 2006, signed by President Bush. In addition he pioneered the use of FBI fingerprint background checks in hiring staff for volunteer youth organisations.

SUGGESTIVE E-MAIL MESSAGES

In many ways Foley's stance was one of a puritanical, right-wing Republican who stood for old-fashioned values. For example, he supported the death penalty, strict sentences for violent crimes and was against abortion. For that reason, it was all the more damaging to his career when stories that he was gay, bisexual or living with a male lover, were published in the *New York Times* and *New York Press*, both alternative papers. Foley denounced the rumours as 'revolting' and stated that his sexual orientation was not important. However, as many noted, he did not deny them. Shortly afterwards, he withdrew his candidacy, saying that his father's serious illness had changed his priorities.

A scandal broke in 2006 when it was reported on ABC News that the previous year Foley had sent suggestive e-mail messages to a former Congressional page. According to the report, Foley requested a photograph of the boy and asked him what he would like for his birthday. He also told the page that he had been for a long bicycle ride and was about to go to the gym. When the matter was reported, Foley's office responded that the boy had asked for a recommendation and that, in such cases, former employees were often asked for photographs for the purposes of identification.

However, another page then came forward and reported that Foley had sent him sexually explicit messages by e-mail. These messages were much more direct, and mentioned sexual organs and acts in a lewd way. This time Foley could find no excuse for his behaviour, and accordingly resigned from office. In a statement he said, 'I am deeply sorry, and I apologise for letting down my family and the people of Florida I have had the privilege to represent.'

SECRET ALCOHOLIC

But the scandal was by no means over. One by one, more pages came forward alleging Foley's inappropriate conduct, which appeared to have gone on for more than a decade. It emerged that Foley had already been warned about his behaviour in 2005 by a House clerk and a house republican. Foley countered the claims, insisting that he was not a paedophile, and had not had any sexual contact with a young person. He explained the e-mails by saying that he was an alcoholic and had sent the messages while drunk. He issued a statement that he was checking himself in to a rehabilitation clinic. He also let it be known, through his lawyer, that he had been molested by a church minister between the ages of 13 and 15, and added, finally, that he was a homosexual.

The scandal provoked a furore in Washington, and there were calls for Foley's Republican bosses such as Speaker of the House Dennis Hastert to resign. The affair did their careers a certain amount of damage, but after Foley's resignation the matter was dropped.

In 2006 a man named Anthony Mercieca identified himself as a former Catholic priest who had had a relationship with Foley while he was a teenager. He said that the liaision had taken place in Fort Worth, while Foley was serving as an alter boy. The priest, who was now retired and living on the island of Malta, told how he and Foley had taken naked saunas together, but said that no actual sexual activity had taken place.

JIM WEST

Jim West was Mayor of Spokane, Washington, when he was involved in a sex scandal in 2005. He was accused of sexually abusing two young boys during the 1970s, and also of luring teenage boys into his office as interns. One of the most shocking aspects of the scandal was that he had campaigned forcefully against gay rights, yet he himself had engaged in gay sex for many years in his private life.

CHILD SEXUAL ABUSE

James Elton West had grown up in Spokane County, Washington, attending high school there. In 1978 he graduated from Gonzaga University with a degree in Criminal Justice and went on to serve in the US army. As a Republican, he joined the Washington Legislature, and worked hard to further his career. Many respected his commitment to his job, although some found his style abrasive. Nevertheless, his career flourished and he became mayor of the city. As Senate majority leader, he supported or introduced a great deal of anti-gay legislation, and in 1995 was involved in the impeachment of the governor, Mike Lowry, when a scandal regarding Lowry's alleged sexual harassment broke. However, ten years later it was West who was at the centre of a bigger, more serious scandal involving the sexual abuse of minors.

According to several reports, when West was a Boy Scout leader in the 1970s and 1980s, he had sexually abused two young boys. Later, as mayor, he corresponded on the Internet, under the name 'Right-BiGuy', using his position to lure teenage boys into sexual relationships with him. He was discovered to be using the Gay.com website to do this, and when confronted with the accusation that he had been trawling for sex on the Internet, admitted that this was what he had been doing. However, he continued to deny that he had ever had sex with minors.

CHILD WITNESSED SUICIDE

In June 2005 the Spokane Republican Party called for West to resign. A commission was set up to enquire into the allegations against him, and the FBI was called in to consider whether West had actually broken any laws, or gone against any of his policies.

For example, he proposed a bill outlawing sexual activities between any young people aged below eighteen, yet as it later emerged, he himself had been sexually involved with teenage boys, and – it was alleged – had even had sex with underage boys. In addition, West had also tried to have all gay and lesbians teachers and carers banned from working in educational and social institutions, even though he himself was gay, or bisexual. He later said that he regretted voting for these laws, but explained his hypocritical stance, and the gap between his public face and his private behavior, by saying, 'If someone hires you to paint their house red, you paint it red, even if you think it would look better green'. However, his plea for leniency was rejected and he was asked to stand down, and was officially stripped of his duties on 6 December 2005. Later, he was diagnosed with colon cancer, and after undergoing several operations, died on 22 July 2006. Two months later the FBI took away West's computer to analyse it, but on 16 February 2007 he was cleared of all the charges. He left office and became ill with colon cancer, but according to some reports, shortly before he died on 22 July 2006, he was considering returning to office.

MORE ALLEGATIONS

The darkest part of the story emerged in recent years, when two men came forward alleging serious sexual abuse at the hands of West and another leading Spokane figure, the county sheriff's deputy, David Hahn. West was friendly with Hahn, who was revealed as a paedophile, and committed suicide as a result in 1981. At the time both men were working with young boys in their capacity as scout leaders, and were members of an organisation called Morning Star Boys Ranch.

The men, Robert Galliher and Michael Grant, both in their 30s, alleged that during their childhood West and Hahn had sexually abused them. On some occasions they fondled them and forced them to have oral sex, while on others they sodomised them. One of the most horrifying aspects of the story was that when it was discovered that Hahn was a paedophile, he took Grant into his bedroom and pointed a gun at his head, then turned it on himself and blew his brains out in front of the boy, who ran away and hid.

SODOMY AND ORAL SEX

This happened, according to Grant, when he was very young, at the age of about seven or eight. Hahn is said to have picked him up from time to time in his patrol car, offering him a lift home. However, instead, Hahn regularly sexually abused him. On one occasion Hahn took the boy to his apartment, where he called West to join them. The boy was taken into the bathroom, and one by one, the men sodomised him.

Hahn had been forcing his attentions on another young boy, Robert Galliher. Like Grant, Galliher came from a poor family and from a young age spent a good deal of time out on the streets with his friends. Hahn befriended the Galliher family, and young Robert and his brother Brett were impressed by his sports car, which was equipped with an early version of the mobile phone. Hahn regularly took the boys on outings – separately, of course – to the gym and to his apartment. He then introduced Robert to West, leaving them alone together. He claims that West forced him to engage in oral sex, threatening him if he told anybody what had happened. On some occasions the men gave Robert marijuana to smoke, although they did not partake themselves.

TRAUMATIZING EXPERIENCES

Sadly for both these men, who were naturally trauma-tized by their experiences, the crimes committed by Hahn against them did not come to light for many years. After Hahn's suicide, the records of complaints against him were destroyed and the case was closed. It was only later that the men felt able to come forward. Up to that time they had been too frightened to make these disclosures against the mayor, fearing that his powerful position might cause them to be put in jail or otherwise punished. Both men had had a history of drug abuse and spells in jail, and therefore felt themselves in a weak position to criticise the powers that be.

What later emerged was that there had been a huge cover-up of Hahn and West's activities. In addition, another man, George E. Robey, who was a scout leader and a friend of the two men, was also alleged to have sexually abused boys in his care. Like Hahn, he killed himself, but there were no records to show that he was the subject of an investigation. Galliher also alleged that before West died, he visited him in prison and told him not to talk about the past. West had threatened 'severe consequences' if anything untoward came to light.

CRUEL AND DISTURBING

Until his dying day, West never admitted to the crime of having sex with under-age boys. He said that he had no idea his friend Hahn was a paedophile, and denied that there was ever any sexual abuse at the boy scout camps he ran.

The Hollywood film actress Marilyn Monroe, originally Norma Jean Baker, whose life was full of scandal.

Chuck Berry, one of the founding fathers of rock'n'roll, at the 50th Annual BMI Pop Awards at the Regent Beverly Wilshire Hotel in Beverly Hills, California on Tuesday, 14 May 2002. Some of his antics revealed an extremely unpleasant streak in his nature – especially his relationships with women.

c.1903: *Thérèse Daurignac, better known as Madame Humbert, perpetrated large scale fraud on the strength of a bogus inheritance from an imaginary millionaire. The scandal nearly destroyed the Third Reich and ruined the lives of thousands of her creditors.*

Lord Lambton, MP for Northumberland, Berwick-upon-Tweed, seated at his typewriter in November 1958. He was regarded as a brilliant and ambitious politician but was forced to resign following a scandal involving his liaison with prostitutes.

Evangelist preacher Jimmy Swaggart confessed his misdeeds to his congregation, breaking down in tears at the height of his sermon.

Supreme Court Justice Clarence Thomas listens to US President George W. Bush speak at the the Federalist Society's 25th annual gala in November 2007. His name was associated with a scandal that saw Thomas accused of sexual harassment.

Russian monk Gregory Rasputin (1871–1916) who was advisor to Russian Empress Alexandra, wife of Nicholas II. Their close relationship caused a scandal and led to his ultimate murder.

Diego Maradona of Argentina during a match against Brazil in Buenos Aires, Argentina in 1981, before he ruined his life and career with drugs and booze.

'I ran scout camps for five years,' he said. 'I had 1,300 kids a year come through the scout camp ... and I taught a lot of kids how to swim.' Because of his position, he was believed, and it is only now that the truth is beginning to come out.

According to the Galliher boys' mother, Marlene Traynor, there was never a formal investigation into either Hahn or West's activities, even though she reported the sexual abuse of her children to the police in the 1980s. The police paid for some counselling for the children, but never followed up the claim. When Hahn committed suicide, Traynor was horrified to find that Hahn was given an official funeral. 'He was given a bloody hero's funeral,' she said. 'It's like he died in the line of duty.'

Today, the true story of the activities of David Hahn, Jim West and others in the boy scout camps of the 1970s and 1980s is only just beginning to emerge. But it seems clear that the allegations now coming forward point to a form of child sexual abuse that was far more cruel and disturbing than the inappropriate sexual relationships West formed through gay Internet websites in the 1990s. And, as many have pointed out, it is only when the real facts of the case are discovered that the victims who suffered so much at the hands of West and his friends can begin to rebuild their lives.

TED KENNEDY

Edward Moore Kennedy, brother of John F. Kennedy, is a prominent US Senator today, and at one time was a contender for president of the USA. However, a major scandal erupted in 1972, involving an accident on Chappaquiddick Island and, in the wake of the adverse publicity from this, his chances of running for the presidency were dashed.

BROTHERS ASSASSINATED

The youngest of nine children born to Joseph Kennedy and his wife Rose, Edward 'Teddy' Kennedy grew up in the privileged atmosphere of a prominent, wealthy Irish-American family. He attended prestigious schools and was educated at Harvard; however, in May 1951 he was expelled from the university for cheating – ironically, during an ethics exam. He later went on to study law, and during his years as a student, helped to manage his brother John's political career.

In 1960 John Kennedy was elected president of the United States. His younger brother Robert was appointed attorney general, and became the president's closest advisor. Edward also became a powerful figure, and the three brothers dominated the American political landscape until John was assassinated in 1963. When Robert was assassinated in 1968, it seemed that their younger brother Edward would be a popular choice for president, and that another Kennedy in the White House would help to heal the wounds of the past. However, because of the scandal at Chappaquiddick, that was not to be.

MARRIED MEN

The scandal involved Ted Kennedy and a young woman called Mary Jo Kopechne, who was 28 years old at the time of her death. Since graduating from college, Mary Jo had worked in Washington, initially for Senator George Smathers and then for Robert Kennedy. After the death of John Kennedy, Robert Kennedy ran for president and Mary Jo, along with other young female colleagues, worked hard on the campaign, earning the nickname, 'the boiler room girls'. Sadly, after his assassination they had to close down the offices. As a way of thanking them for their hard work, Ted invited them all down for the weekend to Martha's Vineyard, the playground of the elite. There, on 18 July 1969 they watched a yachting race at Edgartown, and then went on to a small party held in their honour on the island of Chappaquiddick.

There were six girls in all: Mary Jo Kopechne, Susan Tannenbaum, Maryellen Lyons, Ann Lyons, Rosemary Keough and Esther Newburgh. Ted invited five of his male friends along to make up the party: US Attorney Paul Markham, Joe Gargan (Kennedy's cousin, who was also his lawyer), Charles Tretter, Raymond La Rosa and John Crimmins. The men were all married, but none of their wives attended. Joe Gargan rented the cottage where the party was held, and John Crimmins supplied the drinks. As later transpired, he brought three half gallons of vodka, four fifths of scotch, two bottles of rum and two cases of beer. All this for 12 people, some of whom were not drinking.

CAR CRASHED OVER BRIDGE

At around 11.15 p.m., Kennedy offered to take Mary Jo Kopechne back to the ferry, which would take her to Edgartown. According to his account, he lost control on the drive back and, instead of turning left to the ferry road, he took a right turn and found himself on a road that led unexpectedly to a narrow bridge. Not knowing the way, he made a mistake and crashed the car over the side of the bridge. The car fell into the water and turned over. Kennedy then told how he had found himself in the water, and had looked around to find Mary Jo, but had been unable to see her. Fearing for his life in the strong current, he left the car where it was, and crawled out of the river. Suffering from shock and concussion, he managed to get back to the cottage, where he asked Gargan and Markham for help. The three of them went back to the river and tried to dive down into the water to open the car and get Mary Jo out, but they failed in their efforts. Then Kennedy left the scene, returned to the ferry landing and swam his way over to the mainland, where he returned to his hotel.

It was only in the morning that he called the police. He explained the delay by saying that he had been in a state of shock, and had only come to his senses when he woke up. Kennedy also maintained that he had not been drunk at the time he was driving, although many knew that he was a heavy drinker. However, because of his powerful position, the police accepted his explanation, and he was taken to court and charged only with the offence of failing to stay at the scene and report an accident he had caused. The law called for a mandatory jail sentence for this crime, but Kennedy managed to get off with a two months' suspended sentence.

Not surprisingly, a scandal broke out when the story came to light. Why had Kennedy been driving this young woman home by herself, late at night, taking her in the wrong direction to an isolated part of the island? Was he having an affair with her? Or worse, had he tried to get her drunk at the party and then take her out to have sex with her? Nobody knew, but the circumstances looked suspicious.

SUFFOCATED TO DEATH

Then new evidence emerged. Christopher 'Huck' Look, a local sheriff, had come upon the car after midnight, parked near the road junction with a man and woman inside. When he appeared, the driver apparently panicked and drove the car off in the direction of the dirt road. In addition, the question was raised as to why, when the car crashed into the river, Kennedy had not sought assistance from the house owners nearby, why he had swum back to the mainland and why he had failed to report the incident until persuaded to do so by Gargan and Markham? According to Gargan's later testimony, Kennedy had tried to cover up the accident and his part in it by suggesting that Kopechne had been in the car alone.

The body of Kopechne was recovered, trapped in the car, by diver John Farrar. It emerged that she had suffocated, rather than drowned, to death, as she had been trapped in an air pocket. It was estimated that she could have lived for up to two hours after the accident, which indicated that had Kennedy got help earlier, she might well have lived.

No one but Kennedy knows exactly what happened that night on Chappaquiddick, but many suspect that he valued his career more than Kopechne's life and tried to cover up the incident. Whether or not this is true, the affair certainly cost him his chance of the presidency, although in later years he became a successful senator.

CECIL PARKINSON

Cecil Parkinson caused a political scandal in Britain during the regime of the Thatcher government in the 1980s, when it came to light that his former secretary Sara Keays was pregnant with his child.

Despite his upper-class demeanour, Cecil Parkinson came from a working-class background. The son of a railway worker, he was a bright child and worked hard at school, eventually gaining a scholarship to Cambridge University. He chose to go into politics, and in 1970, he was elected as a member of parliament. He was a favourite with party leader Margaret Thatcher, and when her government came to power in 1979 he was made a junior minister. His career flourished, and two years later he became chairman of the Conservative Party and paymaster general, which meant that he was part of the Cabinet. He was also given an official title, Chancellor of the Suchy of Lancaster. After the 1983 election, he became a leading minister in the government, as

Secretary of State for Trade and Industry. A tremendously successful politician, who was married with three daughters, it seemed that he had achieved everything he could wish for.

A BROKEN MAN

However, during the same year, a huge scandal broke. For 12 years, Parkinson had been having an affair with his secretary, Sara Keays. According to Keays, the relationship had carried on because Parkinson continually promised her that he would leave his wife and marry her. According to her, he proposed marriage on at least two occasions. Eventually Ms Keays became pregnant, prompting speculation that she had done so to force the issue, which she denied. Whatever the truth of the matter, Ms Keays published a statement in *The Times* newspaper publicly criticising Mr Parkinson and 'setting the record straight' about the relationship between the two of them.

In her statement, Keays said, 'My baby was conceived in a long-standing, loving relationship which I allowed to continue because I believed in our eventual marriage'. She felt that it was wrong for her to remain silent in the circumstances because it would cast doubt on her reputation, and she felt that her child ought to know who its father was. She perceived it as a fundamental right for a child to know this, and many agreed with her.

Margaret Thatcher initially supported Parkinson, but in response to the scandal he offered his resignation, which she felt advisable to accept. In a statement to the press, made through his lawyer, he admitted the affair but made no other comment. Those who knew him reported that he did not entirely accept Ms Keays' version of the event, and was a 'broken man' as the result of what appeared to be the end of his political career.

When the child, Flora, was born, a long-running, bitter dispute between Keays and Parkinson started over maintenance payments. To make matters more difficult, the child, Flora, had to undergo a major operation when she was four years old, and as a result suffered learning difficulties. She also suffers from Asperger's syndrome, a neurobiological disorder which is characterised by difficulties in social interaction. Naturally, the press were fascinated in the very public battle between her parents, which was exacerbated by the problems that Keays now faced in bringing up her daughter. As a result, Parkinson gained a series of court orders forbidding the press to discuss Flora. These rulings were so strict that she was not allowed to appear in school photographs or perform in school plays. However, when she turned

18, the court injunction expired, and Flora then appeared in the press and on television to tell her side of the story.

The court injunction, which had begun as an attempt to protect the child, now seemed to have emerged as an attempt to protect Parkinson. Speaking on a television documentary, Flora described how she had never met her father, saying, 'I would like to meet my daddy, because I haven't been given the chance to see him yet'.

In a radio interview Keays gave vent to her feelings about the unfairness of what had happened. Flora had been born with epilepsy, and as a result had to have the right frontal lobe of her brain removed when she was four. Sara had devoted her life to looking after her daughter, educating her at home and encouraging her in sports such as trampolining, horse riding and ballet. She had also travelled the world looking for experts who could help Flora when she was diagnosed with Asperger's syndrome, a form of autism. Yet because of the injunction, nobody knew about the struggles they were going through. Keays said, 'What the judge effectively did was to say, it's okay for everybody to know about all the lies that have been uttered about her mother . . . but nobody can know about Flora.'

What especially angered Keays was that, in a very short time, the episode was forgotten and Parkinson was back in action as a career politician. By 1987 he was secretary of state for energy and two years later, transport minister. When Margaret Thatcher resigned, he resigned with her and received a title, Baron Parkinson of Carnforth. He went on a TV satire show about current affairs, and was thought to have performed well, although the injunction prevented anybody referring directly to the scandal that had taken place.

In 1997 the leader of the Conservative Party, William Hague, made Parkinson party chairman once more. According to Keays, at this time Flora had entered secondary school and was mercilessly bullied as a result. But over the years, she had realised that the Conservative Party were even prepared to sacrifice the happiness and well-being of herself and her child in order to protect the career of one of their most illustrious members.

The Parkinson scandal, though many Conservative politicians and supporters would prefer to forget it, remains one of the most fascinating of recent times in Britain. It brings up many serious issues to do with the responsibility of fathers to their children, as well as the rights of unmarried mothers. Today, Keays still feels that she has been badly treated, both by the establishment and by Parkinson. When news of the affair between her and Parkinson first broke in the

1980s, she was vilified by many women, who saw her as a threat to the institution of marriage.

Although some have criticised the belligerent tone of Keays' complaints against her former lover, it is clear that she has been a devoted mother to her daughter, who today is flourishing despite her many setbacks in life. Even Parkinson's eldest daughter, Mary, who has a history of drug abuse and other problems, has paid tribute to her father's former mistress, saying that she has done 'a terrific job'.

STROM THURMOND

James Strom Thurmond was a high-profile American politician who at one time was governor of South Carolina, and also became a senator. In 1948 he ran for president of the United States, largely on a policy of maintaining segregation between black and white people. However, it later transpired that as a young man, he had fathered a black child by a maid working in his parents' home. This threatened to bring down his political career, but in the end he remained in office as senator until the age of 100, becoming the oldest senator ever to do so at the time (later, his record was broken by Senator Robert C. Byrd).

FILIBUSTER AGAINST CIVIL RIGHTS

Thurmond was born on 5 December 1902 in Edgefield, South Carolina. His parents were John William Thurmond, a lawyer, and Eleanor Gertrude Strom Thurmond. He was educated at local public schools and went on to study horticulture at Clemson University. In 1923 he gained his degree and became a farmer, teacher and athletic coach. By 1929 he had risen to the position of Edgefield county superintendent of education. He then read law and became the town and county attorney of the district. His career in the judiciary prospered, and before long be became a judge, leaving for a short while to serve in the army during World War II. On his return, he ran for governor of South Carolina, and was elected in 1946. He later took office as a senator. A passionate advocate of segregation, he was the originator of the 1956 Southern Manifesto, which campaigned against the Supreme Court desegregation ruling that had been passed that year.

In 1957 Thurmond continued his campaign of opposition to desegregation in the South by mounting a filibuster against the civil rights bill. He spoke for just over 24 hours, winning the record for the longest filibuster in Senate history, and became known as one of the most prominent spokesmen against the ideal of equal rights for black and white people in the USA. However, what most of the public did not know was that Thurmond himself had had a sexual relationship with a black woman, and was the father of a mixed-race child. It was not until after his death that the fact became public knowledge, prompting criticism from many quarters that his views had been hypocritical.

THE FAMILY SECRET

Thurmond's daughter, Essie May Washington-Williams was born to an African-American maid, Carrie 'Tunch' Butler on 12 October 1925. At the time, Butler was only 16 years old. Thurmond was 22. When their daughter Essie May was born, Carrie moved away from her home town and the situation was hushed up for fear that it would ruin Thurmond's burgeoning political career. However, Thurmond continued to stay in touch with the mother of his oldest child, even when he himself married. He helped pay for his daughter's upkeep and education, and even continued the payments when she was an adult.

As an infant, Essie May was fostered briefly by one of her mother's sisters, from whom she derived her name. As a young girl, she was raised in Pennsylvania by her Aunt Mary (her mother's sister) and her Uncle John, whom she called Mother and Father, while Carrie continued to work. It was only when she was 16 that Essie May's biological mother told her that her real father was the famous politician Strom Thurmond. Carrie took Essie May to meet her father in 1941. Her father arranged financial help so that

Essie May could attend South Carolina State University, where she graduated with a degree in business. Essie May later moved to California, where she married and raised four children before going on to work in education.

DEVOUT SEGREGATIONIST

While Essie May was growing up, Thurmond went on to marry his first wife, Jean Crouch, who died of cancer. He married his second wife, Nancy Janice Moore, when he was 66 years old, in 1968. She was a beauty queen of only 23 at the time. The couple had four children: Nancy, James, Juliana and Paul. Thurmond and his wife later separated, but never divorced.

It was only when Thurmond died that Essie May came forward and admitted that she was the daughter of one of the most well-known senators in the United States. Up to that time, she said, she had kept silent 'out of love and respect for her father'. The Thurmond family then publicly acknowledged her parentage, and his staff and close friends said that they had long suspected this to be the case, since Essie May had had frequent access to her father over the years.

Interestingly, during his lifetime Thurmond never denied the relationship when challenged, even though the scandal could have destroyed his career.

On 11 October 1972 the *Edgefield Advertiser*, a small local newspaper in the town where he was born, bore the headline 'Senator Thurmond is unprincipled – with colored offspring – while parading as a devout segregationist'. However, the story provided no details, and when he was asked to say more the Senator brushed aside the question.

WIDESPREAD HYPOCRISY

The fact that the scandal did not have an adverse affect on his career shows how widespread the hypocrisy was that allowed a white politician to argue for strict segregation while having sexual relations, and even children, with a black person. Although Thurmond called black people 'niggers' and dedicated much of his life to trying to block their aspirations for equality, at the same time he was helping his daughter through college. Also, during the 1970s, once the civil rights bill had been established, he endorsed racial integration more quickly than many other senators. He was also noted for employing black members of staff, and for making the birthday of Martin Luther King Jr a federal holiday. Not only this, he enrolled his white daughter in an integrated public school.

In conclusion, it seems that the experience of fathering a black daughter caused Thurmond to change some of the racist views he espoused in his youth, although he never acknowledged this publicly. It would be fair to say that Thurmond was controlled by views at the time about segregation. Consider, if you will, what would have caused a major scandal. For example, Thurmond actually confessing that he loved Carrie Butler or wanting to marry her. Claiming that he wanted to live as Essie Mae's father and not just her benefactor. At the time racism was based on domination – ironically a man could have sex with women below his class, just so long as he married his 'own kind'.

GARY CONDIT

Gary Condit was a Democrat who served in the House of Representatives from 1989 to 2003, representing the district of the San Joaquin Valley in California. In 2001 he was involved in a major scandal when an intern whom he described as 'a friend', Chandra Levy, went missing.

'A GOOD EXAMPLE'

Condit was born in Woodland Junction, Oklahoma, on 21 April 1948. His father was a Free Will Baptist minister. (The Free Will church is based on an idea of atonement and follows a theology close to Calvinism. It lays a great deal of emphasis on local independent churches, and is strongest in rural communities in America.) The Condit family, which included Gary's two brothers and a sister, went to church four times a week. Other than that, there was little else to do in Woodland Junction, which consisted mainly of a school, a church and a country store. At the age of 14, Condit and his family moved to Tulsa, where his father had the opportunity to preach in a larger church. Condit went to Nathan Hale High School where he met his future wife, Carolyn Berry. The pair were married on 18 January 1967, when they were both aged 18. A few months afterwards their son Chad was born. In the same year Condit's father moved to California in search of better prospects. Gary followed him there, with his wife and child, and lived in the San Joaquin Valley. He gained a degree from California State University, and after a short stint in a public relations firm was elected to the local city council. He began to carve out a career for himself as a politician and became mayor of the town of Ceres, before being elected to the California State Assembly on the campaign theme of 'A Good Example'. As it turned out, in his personal life Gary was anything but.

In the assembly Condit became a member of the so-called 'Gang of Five', a group of 'Blue Dog' (moderate or conservative) Democrats. They openly challenged the leadership of the Asembly's speaker, Willie Brown, but were unable to dislodge him. Although he became unpopular among the Democratic leadership, at home he was revered as a hero, the 'boy made good'. He made a public show of not drinking or smoking and leading a righteous family life, but those around him knew him as a flamboyant socialiser with an eye for the ladies.

SECRET AFFAIR

With the election of President George W. Bush to office, Condit's political fortunes looked set to improve. Bush wanted to build a bipartisan relationship with the 'Blue Dog' Democrats, and it looked as though Condit was in the right place at the right time to advance his career. However, it was exactly at this point on 30 April 2001, when Bush made a speech to mark his 100th day in office that Gary Condit's life began to unravel.

On 11 May the *Washington Post* published a report on the disappearance of a young woman, Chandra Levy. From a conservative Jewish family in Modesto, California, Levy had earned a degree in journalism at San Francisco State University, and was pursuing a career in politics as an intern in the Bureau of Federal Prisons which meant moving to Washington, D.C. On 1 May 2001, police announced that she had gone missing. Police investigated and a number of suspects were interviewed, including Gary Condit. It was reported on a Washington TV news station that a California congressman had been interviewed about her disappearance, and it later transpired that she and Condit were known to each other. Levy's parents contacted Condit, asking for help in tracing her. Condit responded by pledging $10,000 in reward money. He confirmed that he had known her and described her as 'a great person and a good friend'. However, more questions were asked as to what exactly the relationship between a man in his 50s and a woman in her 20s was, but Condit continued to maintain that they were just good friends.

LIES AND DECEIT

In early July a flight attendant named Anne Marie Smith alleged that she had an affair with Gary Condit that lasted nearly a year. She said that Condit had asked her to sign an affidavit denying the affair, and told her not to talk to the FBI about Chandra Levy's disappearance. Condit denied that this had happened, but did not deny that he had had an affair with Smith. Then Levy's aunt, Linda Zamsky, issued a statement to the effect that Levy had told her she was having an affair with Condit. Faced with this allegation, Condit admitted that this was the case. He agreed to let investigators search his apartment, but before they arrived he was seen throwing out a gift box he had received from another woman. By now his reputation was at an all-time low. His efforts to cover up his infidelity had led his detractors to suspect that he had had something to do with Levy's disappearance; there were even claims that he may have ordered her killing to cover up the affair. There was no evidence to show that this was the case, but his lies to the police did not help his cause and seriously damaged his reputation. As Dick Thornburgh, former US attorney general, said: 'Sooner or later, the truth is going to come out. And I think unfortunately all congressman Condit has done here is to create an impression that he is unwilling to co-operate with authorities, which in turn leads to a suspicion of some kind of culpability.'

Many media pundits felt that Condit's career was now over. However, it was also noted that President Bill Clinton had survived the Lewinsky scandal, and that after an absence Condit might well return to office. He was very well liked in his local district, and many refused to believe that he could have been involved in Levy's death. However, when he ran for re-election he lost and left Congress in January 2003.

BODY FOUND

On May 22 Chief Charles Ramsey of the Columbia Police announced that remains matching Levy's dental records had been found in Rock Creek Park by a man walking his dog. The police declared the death a homicide, and interviewed a man who had been imprisoned for assaulting two women in the park. The man, a Salvadoran national named Ingmar Guandique, denied committing the murder and subsequently passed a polygraph test.

Currently, the Levy homicide has not been solved, although the FBI have connected it with another homicide, that of Joyce Chiang, an attorney. Chiang lived only four blocks away from Levy's apartment building, and her belongings were found in park land, before her body was washed up in a river nearby. As both women were in their 20s, dark-haired and petite, the theory has been advanced that they were killed by the same person. To date, however, both cases remain unsolved.

In recent years Gary Condit has continued to attract controversy. In February 2005 he opened an ice cream franchise with his wife and children in Glendale, Arizona, but later the franchise was revoked, with the claim that the Condits owed around $14,000. There were also disputes regarding Condit's congressional financing, and claims that his children, Chad and Cadee, had received payments that were not due to them. For example, they had been paid sums for 'no discernable work', and had been commissioned to make a documentary about their father, despite the fact that neither of them had any experience as film makers. Thus, scandal and controversy continue to surround Gary Condit, even though at present he is out of office.

PART FIVE

RELIGIOUS SCANDALS

THE SPANISH INQUISITION

The Spanish Inquisition took place between the years 1478 and 1834. Inquisitions were used during the decline of the Roman Empire and were run by religious authorities to try and weed out non-believers. However, their methods were scandalous and the Spanish Inquisition was one of the worst on record.

Spain was under a constant strain from the numerous religious organisations – Catholicism, Islam, Protestantism and Judaism – all of whom had different beliefs. In addition to this, Spain had been oppressed by Islamic control for 800 years and it was only in recent years that it had been liberated, although not entirely as Islam was still in control in Granada up until 1492.

Following the success of the Crusades, Spain needed to find a way to unify its fortified nation, and the marriage in 1469 of royal cousins Ferdinand of

Aragon and Isabella of Castile eventually brought stability. They chose Catholicism as the religion for their country and asked permission of the pope, Sixtus IV, in 1478 to begin the Inquisition in an attempt to purify the people of Spain.

Ferdinand and Isabella began their purification by driving out the Jews, Protestants and other non-believers of the Catholic faith. The main threat to their Inquisition was the *conversos* (a converted) a Jew or Muslim who had falsely converted to Catholicism but who secretly practised his or her former religion. The job of the Inquisition was also, and perhaps more importantly, to clear the name of the people who had been falsely accused, but who had generally been converted.

Although religion was one of the most predominant reasons for the start of the Spanish Inquisition, it would be fair to say that the Jews and Christians already hated each other before its onset. The Christians were angry because the Jews had crucified Christ, and the Jews were angry because the Christians had changed the Jewish beliefs and called it Christianity. In the end it was the Christians that got their revenge, and they did this by murdering Jews and calling it the Inquisition. At the time the Spaniards considered the Inquisition to be a major triumph for Catholicism, but the costs were high in the terms of lives lost.

Of course, religion was not the only reason for the Inquisition there were strong political undertones as well. Spain used the Inquisition to protect their precious monarchy. Ferdinand and Isabella were aware of the tensions building up between the Jews and the Christians and feared that it could lead to riots, massing killing and possibly a religious civil war. By using the Inquisition they believed they would be able to calm the stormy waters and secure their positions in the monarchy.

The Spanish government and its religious officials, who wanted to maintain a purity of blood, had to find ways of preventing marriage between the different religious groups and they achieved their goal once again through the Inquisition. In addition Government officials also used the Inquisition to gain governmental positions that were held by Jews. They had tried before to get the Jews out of office but had failed, so they supported the Inquisition in every way. They started to spread rumours that the Jews were the reason for any misfortunes that fell upon Spain, which turned out to be a brilliant plan because the public then wanted them killed. This left the way open for the Christians to fill their positions.

Another possible reason behind the start of the Inquisition was the need for money. Spain was suffering economically from the effects of war and they needed to replenish their funds. The Inquisition gave them the excuse to kill thousands of Jews and then take their possessions to refill the government coffers. It was well known that the Jewish community had accumulated a lot of wealth at that time.

THE INQUISITORS

The inquisitors themselves believed that they were saving the Jews from the hideous fate of being delivered to the Underworld. In their distorted belief they felt because the Jews were dying at the hands of one of God's own children, they would gain the wisdom and knowledge from this person and therefore be allowed to enter Heaven. Although today it is hard for us to comprehend this belief, the inquisitors were raised purely on a religious education and could not reason beyond this belief.

The ruling for the judges of the Inquisition was that they had to be at least 40 years old, have a flawless repution, be renowned for their virtue and wisdom, masters of theology, or doctors or licentiates of canon law, and they must obey the normal ecclesiastical rules and regulations.

The Inquisition was run by using a procedure set up by the Inquisitor-General, by establishing local tribunals. Any accused heretics had to face the tribunal.

They were given the chance to confess their heresy against the Catholic Church, and were also encouraged to name other heretics in return for leniancy. If they were prepared to admit their wrongs and turned in other heretics, they were either released or given a minimal prison sentence. However, if they were not prepared to admit their heresy or indict others, they would be publicly killed or imprisoned for the rest of their life. The Spanish Inquisition turned into a reign of terror.

TOMÁS DE TORQUEMADA

In 1483 Dominican Tomás de Torquemada became the first Inquisitor General of Spain and confessor to Isabella of Spain, and he turned out to be one of the most evil men in the history of the Inquisition. He was the person who was responsible for establishing the rules and procedures and for creating the various branches of the Inquisition all over Spain. He remained the leader for the next 15 years and is believed to have been responsible for the execution of over 2,000 Spaniards.

There is no doubt that Torquemada's dedication to his appointed task has become legendary, and in 1492 he persuaded Ferdinand and Isabella to expel all the Jews from Spain who were unwilling to convert to Christianity. Spain soon gained the reputation of becoming one of the most intolerant countries in Europe and 160,000 Jews were forced to leave their homes. Ten years later the same demands were made of the Spanish Muslims, and soon the Inquisition spread its wings to Latin America, Portugal and the Spanish Netherlands.

After Granada and the remaining followers of Spanish Islam fell in 1492 to the armies of Ferdinand and Isabella, Torquemada then had to decide how he was going to deal with the Moors. The Moors were not large in number but they were a highly influential Jewish community that had flourished in Spain. Although it is uncertain how much influence the Muslims and Jews had had on the Moors, they were still expelled by the thousands, including many who were not guilty of any offence.

In the first ten years the Inquisition is known to have tried and punished thousands of people, including many *conversos*. Those people who were judged to be heretics were executed, often by burning them at the stake. Those Jews that were ordered to leave Spain, emigrated to North Africa, the Ottoman Empire and other parts of Europe.

Later in the Spanish Inquisition, the Inquisitors sought to discipline people who were suspected of practising Protestantism.

METHODS OF TORTURE

After those on trial had been found allegedly 'guilty', they were marched back to the cells and then brought before the examiners. The examiners were shrouded in secrecy wearing black hoods that covered their faces. The guilty person was made to sit before a table covered in a black cloth and dimly lit by candles. He was then asked if he or she was guilty and although the person had no idea what they had done, the inquisitor delighted in making the prisoner confess by various methods of torture.

One horrifying method was something they called 'the Silence of God', which involved a wedge-shaped piece of wood being placed in the person's mouth which that be screwed to open wider and wider until the jaw virtually became dislocated. After hours of this torture the prisoner would be asked again, 'Are you guilty?' If they were still reluctant to confess, the inquisitor would heat a pair of branding irons up in front of their eyes. This usually had the desired effect and they were thrown into the cells to contemplate their fate.

The following day, the prisoner would be asked the same question, but by this time to avoid further punishment they would confess to anything. However, Torquemada had already preempted the prisoner's reaction and would arrange for them to go back for more of the same torture. As a tally as to how many days the prisoner had been tortured they would lose a finger daily.

Other forms of torture included forcing confessions by placing a thick piece of cloth over the prisoner's head. Then a bucket of water was poured over their head and the weight of the cloth would slowly asphyxiate the victim. However, just before the victim gasped his or her last breath, the cloth would be removed so that he or she could feel the benefit of the next cruel torture.

The accused would have his thumbs tied behind his back and then he would be hung up by a rope until he was just suspended by his two digits.

And so the days went on with a new torture devised for each day. Red hot pincers, teeth tearing, head screw and so on. The very last resort was the act of evisceration. The abdomen was slit open and the entrails removed, followed by a pair of hot irons pushed into the accused's body. This operation required great skill, because it was considered a major sin if the prisoner died while in the hands of the inquisitor. They had to ensure that their prisoner had enough life left in him to be aware of his final execution. This always took place on a Holy day and to most death was a welcome end.

THE AFTERMATH

Although the Spaniards considered the Inquisition to be a major success it was a disaster in terms of economy. Many of Spain's economically important citizens had been expelled from the major cities, depriving the crown of a much-needed tax revenue. The Church, with royal approval, censored many books and prohibited students to study abroad for fear of bringing Protestant ideas back into Spain. This had the effect of excommunicating Spain from other intellectual developments in Europe. This had a roll-on effect, which made it harder for Spain to catch up with the rest of Europe in later centuries.

Torquemada was hated by many. Several attempts were made on his life and he retaliated by sending his inquisitors out on the streets to round up anyone who had the audacity to walk about in daylight. Of course he got away with it because he was allegedly 'saving people's souls'. It has been estimated that Torquemada may have tortured or killed as many as 20,000 people.

The Spanish Inquisition's reign of terror was finally suppressed in 1834. It is an example of the Church's violent and corrupt past and has been compared with the scandals connected with the Crusades.

MOUNTAIN MEADOWS MASSACRE

The early history of the Church of Jesus Christ of Latter-day Saints (LDS) is certainly fascinating but also reveals some quite shocking facts. The Mormons, as the followers of the church were known, insisted that their faith was the only true Christian church and that other groups had deviated from the true teachings. This belief and many others caused strained relationships with other Christian organisations, which often ended in extreme violence.

In November 1999 the LDS made a rather disturbing discovery while they were restoring a monument to the victims of a gruesome massacre that took place in 1857 in south-west Utah. Members working on the restoration uncovered the bones of at least 29 people, who were pioneering men, women and children that were among those killed in a bloodbath incited by religious fervour. The discovery was embarrassing to the Church because the bodies had originally been buried in haste a year and a half after the dreadful massacre by federal troops.

Right from the beginning, the LDS was at odds with the federal government and its members were frequently persecuted for their unorthodox beliefs. One of the most disturbing and tragic events that took place in the history of the Mormons took place on 11 September 1857, and became known as the Mountain Meadows massacre. Even today the massacre has remained a topic of controversy, historians still struggle to understand why this event took place and it has left the Church with a feeling of guilt.

THE BUILD UP

The first Mormons settled in Salt Lake City in 1847. They were the first wave of pioneering members of the LDS who had been driven out of Nauvoo in Illinois by angry mobs. Over the next couple of years the remainder of the members reached the valley and the Great Salt Lake City was built, under the direction of a man named Brigham Young.

By 1850 Utah was established as a US territory, with Brigham Young as its first governor. Scandals arose about the behaviour of some of the Mormons and, rather than face up to their own failings, they started to rebel against federal authority. When the news reached Washington, there was uproar and they demanded that something had to be done and the president, James Buchanan, ordered federal troops to advance on the area.

In the summer of 1857 roughly 1,500 United States troops were marching towards Salt Lake Valley. News of the approaching army spread fast and preparations were made to defend themselves. The Mormons were still reeling from having been forced to leave their homes and this time they were determined they would not be driven away again. This conflict, known as the Utah War, was resolved peacefully, but it was the Baker-Fancher emigrants that were caught up in the forthcoming massacre.

HEADING FOR TROUBLE

The Baker-Fancher wagon train consisted of approximately 120–140 people who were heading for California from Arkansas and Missouri. They were a group of men, women and children who were led by John T. Baker and Alexander Fancher, bringing with them a plentiful supply of cattle, horses and mules.

The wagon train arrived in Salt Lake City at the end of July 1857 and set up camp just outside the city on the Jordan River. Their arrival did not give rise to any concern and they were advised to circumnavigate the city by circling round the northern edge on their way to California. However, they changed their route when they reached Bear River and went round the southern side. There were no reports of any problems until the Baker-Fancher wagon reached Fillmore which was about 241 km (150 miles) south of Salt Lake City.

Apparently at this point in their journey there were rumours going round that the emigrants had threatened violence against the Mormons and that they had poisoned the water in their springs, which resulted in the death of some local Paiute Indians. It was common knowledge that the emigrants had come from the Arkansas region, where earlier in the year a Mormon apostle, Parley Pratt, had been murdered. It was also thought that some of the members of the Baker-Fancher train had participated in Pratt's murder and that they had bragged about it after the event. Of course, these were only rumours, but whatever the truth of the matter the presence of the train in the area did nothing to alleviate the tensions that were already present.

MAKING PLANS

The Baker-Fancher train set up camp at a place called Mountain Meadows, unaware that some of the residents of Cedar City had decided that some type of action was needed against them. Cedar City was the last place on the route to California where the emigrants could stock up on supplies, but the essential goods were not available in the town and the local miller was trying to charge exorbitant prices to grind just a small amount of grain. Weeks of hardship, drought and frustration caused the situation to get out of hand and it is claimed that one of the emigrants took a gun and killed the miller, Joseph Smith. Fancher was fuming and rebuked the men for their action. Although the town marshal attempted to arrest some of the men as they tried to leave town, he was forced to back down, but the residents of Cedar City were not prepared to let the matter rest. They contacted the local militia and asked them to follow the men and arrest the offenders. However, the militia leaders had decided against direct interference with the train because of the federal troops that were heading their way. They suggested that the Mormons collected their supplies together because they would need these if they had to flee into the mountains when the troops arrived.

Meanwhile a meeting was held in Cedar City with William Dane, the district militia commander, and the Mormons pursued the matter of arresting the offending members of the wagon train. Dane denied their request and said: 'Words are but wind – they injure no one; but if they [the emigrants] commit acts of villence against citizens inform me by express, and such measures will be adopted as will insure tranquillity.'

Annoyed that no one was prepared to help them, the leaders of Cedar City decided to formulate their own plan. If they couldn't use the militia to arrest the men, then perhaps they could persuade the local Paiute Indians to intervene by killing some of the men and stealing their cattle.

They planned the attack to take place on a part of the track that narrowed as it ran past the Santa Clara River canyon, just a few kilometres outside of the Mountain Meadows camp. This area came under the jurisdiction of Fort Harmony, which was controlled by Major John D. Lee. The Cedar City mayor and Major Isaac Haught went to discuss the planned attack with Lee. They talked late into the night concerning what to do about the emigrants, during which time Lee told Haight that he thought the Paiutes would 'kill all the party, women and children, as well as the men' if they were pushed to attack. Haight agreed with Lee and the two of them decided that they would lay all the blame of an attack at the feet of the Paiute Indians.

When the Paiutes were first told of the plan, they were reluctant to take part because they had lived in peace for many years. Although they had been known to kill the odd emigrant to obtain food, they had not made any large-scale attacks for a long time. However, using plunder as a lure and assuring them that the approaching troops would kill as many Paiutes as Mormons, they eventually agreed.

On Sunday 6 September Haight returned to Cedar City and held a meeting with a council of local leaders who held church, civic and various other military positions. When he told them what was planned, they met the news with stunned resistance, which sparked off a very heated debate. When everything calmed down, the council leaders asked Haight if he had informed the president, Brigham Young, of his plans, and when he told them he hadn't they suggested that he sent an express rider with a letter explaining the situation and what he felt should be done.

THE FIRST ATTACK

The following day, before Haight had even had a chance to send the letter to Young, Lee and the Paiutes made a surprise attack on the camp at Mountain Meadows, instead of at the planned location in the Santa Clara canyon. Although several of the emigrants were killed, they managed to fight off their attackers and forced them to retreat. Aware that their assailants would probably return the emigrants quickly took evasive action. They formed their wagons into a tight circle and by doing this they created a barrier and survived a further two attacks from Lee and the Paiutes.

When the Cedar City militia heard about this premature attack on the train, they decided to intervene to try and alleviate a volatile situation, but instead they made the matter worse. When they spotted two emigrant men riding outside of the corral, they fired on them, killing one of them. The second man managed to get back to the camp and told his companions that his friend had just been killed by a white man not a Paiute Indian.

This left the Mormons in a very delicate position. Not only were the emigrants now aware that they were involved in the attack, but they also knew that the military commander would soon be informed that they had blatantly disobeyed his orders. A letter was quickly despatched to Brigham Young about what had happened, and the news that both white men and Indians had attacked the emigrants was not well received. If the surviving emigrants were allowed to continue their journey into California, the news that they had been attacked by Mormons would spread quickly. If the approaching army got wind of what had happened, retaliatory action was certain. Added to that, the fact that other emigrants were heading towards Mountain Meadows, Young and the Cedar City leaders were well aware that the situation could quickly become explosive.

DISOBEYING ORDERS

On 9 September Haight with two militia captains once again went to see Dame to ask permission to enlist the help of the militia. But Dame said that he felt the emigrants should be allowed to continue their journey in peace. When the meeting was over, Haight took Dame to one side and told him what had happened and that the emigrants were now aware the the Mormons were involved in the original attack in which some of the members of the train had been killed. Dame, now free from the restrictions of the other council members, changed his mind and tragically gave in to Haight's original request.

Armed with this information, Haight returned to Cedar City and immediately called out about 30 militiamen, who joined those already waiting outside the emigrant corral at Mountain Meadows. Those who had hated the vigilante force that had driven them out of their home towns were about to embark on the same behaviour – but this time on a much more serious scale.

THE MASSACRE

In a last ditch effort to save the situation, on 11 September Lee rode to the emigrant camp carrying a white flag. He pleaded with them to accept their terms and that they would be accompanied by militia past the Indians and back to Cedar City. However, in return they must leave their possessions behind and surrender their weapons. The emigrants were suspicious and put their heads together to try and work out what action to take. They had already been pinned in their corral for several days, many of their people were injured and dying, and they didn't have enough ammunition to hold off another attack.

Putting faith in Lee, the emigrants agreed to his terms. He told the first two wagons to leave carrying the youngest children and the injured, followed by the women and other children on foot. The men and older boys left last, each one escorted by an armed militiaman. They travelled about 1.5 km (1 mile) and then following a prearranged signal, the militia turned and shot the emigrant standing next to him. At the same time the Panuite Indians came out from their hiding places and attacked the women and children. The children and the injured lying in the front two wagons were also killed, until nearly every one of the emigrants was dead.

TOO LATE, TOO LATE

When Brigham Young's express letter of reply reached Cedar City, the massacre had already taken place. He told the Mormons that the federal troops would not be able to reach the area before winter and 'So you see that the Lord has answered our prayers and again averted the blow designed for our heads'.

In the letter he continued:

> *In regard to emigration trains passing through our settlements, we must not interfere with them until they are first notified to keep away. You must not meddle with them. The Indians we expect will do as they please but you should try and preserve good feelings with them. There are no other trains going south that I know of. If those who are there will leave let them go in peace. While we should be on the alert, on hand and always ready we should also possess ourselves in patience, preserving ourselves and our property ever remembering that God rules.*

[Brigham Young to Isaac C. Haight, 10 September 1857, Letterpress Copybook 3:827–28, Brigham Young Office Files, Church Archives]

When Haight read Young's letter he wept like a child and all he could say was, 'Too late, too late!'

THE OUTCOME

Of the original Baker-Fancher party only 17 people survived, and all of these were children who were considered to be too young to remember what had happened. These children were adopted by local families, but were returned to family members in Arkansas when government officials intervened in 1859. The children themselves and other family members were deeply affected by the massacre and even one and a half centuries later it still remains a painful subject.

Isaac Haight and John Lee were excommunited from the Church and in 1874, a grand jury indicted nine men for their part in the massacre. Although most of them were eventually arrested, it was only Lee who stood trial and was executed for his part.

Family members of the men who masterminded the attack suffered as well, as neighbours ostracised them or put curses on them. The Paiutes also suffered for their part and the massacre left an indelible blot on the history of the region. Although it is obvious today that there were great efforts to cover up the massacre, no one is really sure just how involved the higher Church leaders were in trying to hide the atrocity. Whatever the answer, the discovery of the bones in 1999, complicated an already controversial subject. The discovery has once again stirred up deep emotions in the descendants of both the victims and the villains.

A reburial of the bodies was attended by hundreds of descendants of the victims and survivors of the Mountain Meadows massacre, as well as descendants of the Mormon militia. There was a definite tension in the air with thoughts of reconciliation, but feelings still run very deep.

JACK HYLES

Jack Hyles was a leading figure in the Baptist church, pastoring the First Baptist Church of Hammond in Hammond, Indiana. His literal interpretation of the Bible often put him at odds with his fellow Christians, but that was nothing compared to the scandal that broke about his private life in the late 1980s. For a man who was supposed to stand as a shining example to his followers, his behaviour has been described as 'a clear violation of the Scriptures'.

A LIFE IN THE MINISTRY

Jack Frasure Hyles was born on 25 September 1926 in Italy, Texas, a rather run-down area south of Dallas. His early years were tough, by his own admission, but by the age of 18 he was drafted into the US army and served as a paratrooper with the 82nd Airborne Division. During World War II he met and married Beverly, and as soon as the war was over he entered the East Texas Baptist University to pursue his dream of entering the ministry. After graduation Hyles started to preach at several small Texas churches, and through his popularity the congregation grew rapidly.

In 1959 Hyles moved to Hammond, Indiana, and took the position as pastor to the First Baptist Church of Hammond. When he first arrived the church had a congregation of around 700, but several people soon started to leave because they didn't like the new pastor's style of preaching. Unperturbed, Hyles soon led the church into an independent status and his congregation gradually escalated to around 20,000.

In 1972 Jack Hyles founded the Hyles-Anderson College with financial assistance from Russell Anderson, which specialised in the training of Baptist ministers and Christian schoolteachers.

One of the most notable achievements of Jack Hyles was his church bus ministry. Its purpose was to reach the 'lost souls' who weren't able to get to his church, and soon his buses were penetrating all the surrounding communities. Boys, girls, mums and dads all came to hear Hyles preach as a result of hearing the gospel while riding on his church buses.

He became known as 'Brother Hyles' and received many accolades during his 50 years in the ministry, but he has also been the subject of much controversy and criticism regarding his and his family's un–Christian behaviour.

ALLEGATIONS

In May 1989, Victor Nischik, a former deacon of the First Baptist Church, , made allegations against Hyles. He accused him of being a 'cult leader' and claimed that he had been having an affair with his wife, Jennie, for many years. Jennie was Hyles' assistant. Nischik, who was an accountant for the church, also accused Hyles of questionable financial dealings. He is believed to have given Jennie over $100,000 over 20-years in addition to her own salary.

Despite Hyles denying all the allegations, Nischik claimed that he had alienated his wife from her family. He also said that even with this knowledge, Hyles continued to keep Jennie in his employ and have close and intimate contact with her in his offices behind locked doors. Nischik also claimed that Hyles took Jennie on long car rides, often staying in hotels overnight without either of their spouses being present.

Jack Hyles apparently had plenty of opportunities to try and clear his name, and yet he repeatedly refused to meet those who accused him face to face. Hyles' response to the allegations made by Nischik was to expose the man as being a womaniser and a homosexual who had no right to condemn others.

As if that scandal wasn't enough, there was also a lot of moral allegations being spread about the behaviour of Hyles's son, David. It was claimed that despite the fact that he knew his son was a womaniser, he actually recommended that he be given his own pulpit to preach from at Miller Road Baptist Church, allegedly using his own position to further his son's ministry. By doing this, he deliberately allowed a man who had problems loose on a congregation, which resulted in the near destruction of the church. It is believed that David became involved with at least 19 women from the congregation.

David Hyles was also under scrutiny for the death of baby Brent Stevens while in the care of Brenda Stevens and David himself. After his divorce from his first wife, David went to live with Brenda and her child. Rumours were rife that Brenda had posed for pornographic pictures in *Adam* and Chicago Swingers magazines, allegedly for an advertisement for group sex. After David married Brenda ,Brent, Brenda's 17-month-old son by a previous marriage, was found battered to death at their home. At the coroner's inquest, Brenda failed to turn up, while David pleaded the Fifth Amendment. (The Fifth Amendment gives all citizens accused of major crimes the right to have their cases contemplated by a grand jury before being brought to trial.)

David and Brenda had a son together and called him Jack David Hyles, but Brenda ran him over with the family car when he was just five years old and killed him. She claimed that her son had fallen out of the car and she couldn't avoid running him over. In June 2003 David Hyles was kicked out of the Pinellas Park Baptist Church in the Florida Keys, this time over a sex scandal involving nine other women. Despite all these problems, David Hyles still continues to make speeches in churches regarding the growth of Sunday Schools and their importance in achieving youth awareness.

Even with all the scandal surrounding the Hyles family, their followers refused to believe what was being said about them. Robert L. Sumner, a Christian author, Baptist pastor, evangelist and editor of the fundamentalist newspaper called *The Biblical Evangelist* was vilified when he broke the code of silence and published what he knew about the sordid events. One of the congregation even went as far as to say, 'If you criticise my preacher I'll ripe your face off!' That was the incredible power that Jack Hyles had over his flock.

ANOTHER SCANDAL

In March 1993 the First Baptist Church of Hammond was the subject of yet another scandal. A. V. Ballenger, who was a deacon and one of the bus drivers for the

First Baptish Church of Hammond, was accused of molesting a seven-year-old girl in 1991 during a Sunday school class. Possibly the most damaging of these witnesses was Ballenger's own 17-year-old niece, who said that he had touched her private areas while she lay feigning sleep in a bed at her uncle's house. She claimed that she would often spend nights at his house as she was the same age as Ballenger's own daughter. Along with his niece there were three other witnesses when the case was brought to trial, two of whom were women who had claimed to have been fondled by Ballenger. One was a 21-year-old student at Indiana University, who said she had visited Ballenger's home a number of times when she was much younger, because her own mother and Mrs Ballenger were close friends. Another witness was a 20-year-old woman from the Columbia Center public housing project in Hammond, who told how she used to ride the bus to the First Baptist Sunday School. Ballenger was the bus driver, and on more than one occasion she found herself alone with him on the bus and he would run his hand inside her dress and fondle her private areas. All three of the victims said they had not reported the incidents when they were younger because they were scared what people would think of them and they doubted anyone would believe them anyway.

Although Ballenger tried to indicate that the witnesses were all 'crazy' and didn't know what they were saying, he was convicted in March 1993 and sentenced to five years in jail.

Jack Hyles, who of course testified on behalf of Ballenger, defiantly tried to declare the outcome of the trial as null and void, claiming that the courts had no jurisdiction in matters of the church. Ironically, Hyles spoke to the girls' parents and told them, 'Deacon Ballenger just likes little girls!'

SUED FOR NEGLIGENCE

As if Jack Hyles and his church had not been condemned enough, on 3 October 1997 they were once again the subject of a scandal in Hyles' church. Hyles and his church were sued by the attorney of a mentally disabled woman and her sister for negligence with respect to sexual assaults that are alleged to have taken place over a six-year period. Hyles was accused of simply standing by while the woman was raped by two or three males. At the time another church member had also watched without taking any action to protect her. Apparently this was not the first time that the matter had been reported to the police, but no criminal charges were filed on either occasion.

Jack Hyles died on 6 February 2001, aged 74, from complications following heart surgery. Despite all the scandals surrounding his years with the church, he is still remembered fondly and is often referred to as 'their pope'. He is survived by his wife, their four children, his sister, 11 grandchildren and four great-grandchildren.

What did Jack Hyles say about his alleged wrong-doings? His response was that sin does not need to be repented of, only forgotten saying, 'We don't even have a right to remember our sins.' [Hebrews 10:17]

JIMMY SWAGGART AND JIM BAKKER

In the late 1980s two of the largest figures in TV evangelism were destroyed due to sex scandals. The two men concerned were Jimmy Swaggart and Jim Bakker, both of whom were very popular in the Christian Broadcasting Network which broadcast TV programs with a large, and loyal following.

JIMMY SWAGGART

Jimmy Lee Swaggart was born on 15 March 1935 in Louisiana. Swaggart was the cousin of two famous recording artists, Jerry Lee Lewis and Mickey Gilley, and Swaggart himself loved to sing and play the piano. His parents were both Pentecostal evangelists, and from an early age the young Swaggart would preach on street corners and lead congregations in singing. In 1952, when Swaggart was just 17, he married Frances Anderson and they had one son, Donnie, who also became a minister.

Swaggart became a full-time preacher in 1958, and spent his early years travelling around spreading the word. In 1960 he started to record some of his gospel music, but he also found another easy way of reaching people – through Christian-themed radio stations. By 1969 Swaggart had his own radio programme called *The Camp Meeting Hour*, which was aired over several different radio stations throughout the Bible Belt in the United States.

From radio Swaggart advanced to television and, under his established ministry the Assemblies of God, he quickly became the most popular television preacher in the United States. The *Jimmy Swaggart Telecast* was regularly watched by as many as two million people. In fact, there seemed to be no end to Swaggart's popularity. In addition to his television broadcasts he had his Jimmy Swaggart Ministry headquarters in Baton Rouge, Louisiana, and 4,000 followers at his Family Worship Center. He also had a printing and mailing production plant, a television production company, a recording studio and his own Bible College. However, Swaggart's world was soon to crumble beneath his feet, but not before he spilled the beans about a rival evangelist, Marvin Gorman.

HYPOCRITICAL BEHAVIOUR

In 1986 Swaggart discovered that fellow Assemblies of God minister, Marvin Gorman, was having an affair with one of his congregation. The following year, Swaggart released fire and brimstone on another rival evangelist, Jim Bakker, regarding his misconduct. Swaggart dug the knife even deeper by appearing on the *Larry King Show* and describing Bakker as a 'cancer in the body of Christ'.

Gorman was incensed by Swaggart's revelations and decided to retaliate. He hired a private detective to follow Swaggart. This paid off when the detective found Swaggart in a motel in Louisiana with a prostitute by the name of Debra Murphree and managed to take photographs of them in an embarrassing situation. Before showing the photographs to the officials from the Assemblies of God, Gorman decided to give Swaggart the chance to come clean. He went to see him and showed him the incriminating photographs, but Swaggart refused to be blackmailed. Gorman went straight to the officials and showed them the evidence, and Swaggart was suspended from broadcasting his television programme for a period of three months.

The following Sunday, Swaggart appeared before a congregation of 7000 people at Baton Rouge. In a truly dramatic act befitting that of an accomplished actor, he broke down in tears and confessed his 'moral failure' without giving details of his indiscretions. 'I have sinned against you and I beg your forgiveness,' he sobbed from the pulpit. Of course his confession was even more scandalous since he himself had already denounced the behaviour of his fellow evangelists, knowing full well that he was not exactly 'squeaky clean'.

Four days later, Debra Murphree appeared on a television programme in New Orleans, stating that Swaggart was a regular customer, although they never actually engaged in the sexual act. He liked to pay her to take her clothes off while he simply watched.

Swaggart, who felt he was far too important to heed the ruling of the officials, decided to broadcast his programme as usual. He said, 'If I do not return to the pulpit this weekend, millions of people will go to hell!' The officials, believing that he was not fully repentant by disobeying their ruling, immediately defrocked him, removing both his credentials and ministerial licence.

CAUGHT AGAIN

On 11 October 1991 Swaggart was caught in yet another tryst with prostitute Rosemary Garcia. The couple were pulled over by highway police in California for driving down the wrong side of the road. When the police questioned Garcia, she told them that she had been propositioned by Swaggart, who had pulled over to her side of the road.

'He asked me for sex. I mean, that's why he stopped me. That's what I do. I'm a prostitute,' Garcia told them. However, this time instead of being repentant, Swaggart told his congregation quite blatantly, 'The Lord told me it's flat none of your business!'

AFTERMATH

Directly after the latest scandal, Swaggart's son, Donnie, told his father's followers that he would be temporarily stepping down as head of the Jimmy Swaggart Ministries, as he needed time to 'heal'. Although the ministry's revenue was greatly reduced following the scandal, Swaggart returned to preaching and he and his son still continue to broadcast to 30 different countries.

JIM BAKKER

James Orsen Bakker was born on 2 January 1939 in Muskegon, Michigan. Like, Swaggart, he was a minister with the Assemblies of God with his then-wife, Tammy Faye Bakker. Their career in the Christian Broadcasting Network began in 1966, when the Bakkers joined Pat Robertson, but their audience at the time barely reached into the thousands. However, through their enthusiasm the Bakkers managed to build the show's popularity and using a variety show format, made *The 700 Club* one of the most successful and longest-running televised evangelist programmes ever.

Taking their success with them, the Bakkers left for California in the mid-1970s and soon built a name for themselves with their very popular show *The PTL Club*. By the early 1980s the Bakkers' empire was growing rapidly with their own theme park, Heritage USA, and a satellite system to distribute their network 24 hours a day. Their revenue was enormous and their lifestyle was one of greed, glitz and pure shamelessness, topping it all with 'his and hers' gold Rolls Royces.

THE EMPIRE FALLS

In March 1987 it came to light that Bakker had had a sordid affair with a former model, actress and church secretary, Jessica Hahn. Apparently, Jim had paid her $265,000 of the ministry's money to keep quiet about the affair, and that he had allegedly raped her. To add to the scandal it was known that homosexuality was also rampant within the PTL studio, with a leading evangelist, John Wesley Fletcher being caught in the act of giving oral sex to a man in a room at Bakker's own mansion. It was also alleged that Bakker had been seen naked with three of his male staff in the steam room at his house, and that they had been fondling one another. Whatever the truth about Bakker's homosexual activities, the Hahn scandal was enough to start his empire crumbling.

When the scandal broke, the media started to question his lavish lifestyle and excessive spending. It was eventually disclosed that Bakker had actually defrauded his 'flock' out of $158 million by overselling the shares in his religious theme park. Some of the money had been used to satisfy his own pleasures and in 1989, Bakker was convicted of fraud, tax evasion and racketeering. Bakker was sentenced to 45 years in federal prison.

In 1992 the couple were divorced at the request of Tammy Faye,, just after a court commuted his sentence to 18 years. However, after serving only five years of his sentence, Bakker was released in 1993 for good behaviour.

A NEW START

When he was released on parole Bakker had expected people to 'spit on him' but instead, and to his surprise, he was welcomed back into the flock with open arms. In fact, Billy Graham bought him a house and a car and helped him start a new life for himself. When Bakker addressed a Christian leadership conference in 1995, he received a standing ovation from 10,000 clergymen.

In 2003 Bakker started broadcasting again in his daily *Jim Bakker Show* in Missouri, accompanied by his new wife, Lori Bakker. It appears once again people are only too prepared to turn a blind eye to behaviour that is not very befitting to one of the Lord's preachers. For a man with so many loyal followers, it was surprising to learn in his own book, *I Was Wrong*, that the first time he read the Bible from cover to cover was during his term of incarceration.

As for Jessica Hahn – she took the money and ran. Her first stop was to a plastic surgeon to become a 'born again' woman with a new nose, teeth and breast enlargement. She also netted a neat one-million-dollar deal with *Playboy* for a spread and video called *Thunder and Mud*, which has been described as a female mud-wrestling tournament hosted by Jessica Hahn.

SCANDAL IN THE ROMAN CATHOLIC CHURCH

The second half of the 20th century has seen the Roman Catholic Church rocked by a succession of child sexual abuse scandals allegedly committed by members of the clergy. The cases involved schools or orphanages where children were under the care of Catholic religious orders. Some of the allegations have led to successful prosecution, while others are thought to have been successfully covered up. Whatever the outcome, the scandal is one of the biggest challenges that the current pope, Benedict XVI, has had to deal with.

BRENDAN SMYTH

One of the worst examples of a clergyman using his links with children to facilitate sex abuse occurred in

Ireland. The priest in question was Father Brendan Smyth. Smyth was a Catholic priest who abused his position to obtain access to children. It is believed that over a period of 40 years Smyth managed to rape literally hundreds of children in the parishes of Belfast, Dublin and the United States.

Originally from Northern Ireland, Smyth joined the Norbertine Catholic religious order, which was founded in 1120 by St Norbert of Xanten. Smyth joined the order, also known as the Premonstratensians, in 1945 and it is believed they were aware of his dubious sexual activities as early as the late 1940s. However, they failed to report him to the police, and instead moved him from parish to parish whenever the allegations reached dangerous proportions. It appears that at no time were there warnings issued regarding Smyth's history of sexual abuse so that he was kept away from children. Instead he was free to continually molest for the next 40 years.

When Smyth was finally arrested in 1994, it not only led to the collapse of the Fianna Fáil (Labour coalition government) but it also did an immense amount of damage to the credibility of the Catholic Church in Ireland. When Smyth died in prison in 1997, the Norbertines covered his grave in concrete for fear of it being vandalised. In 2005 one of his victims succeeded in having the word 'Reverend' removed from his gravestone – not a very fitting title for a paedophile priest. The Smyth case continues to haunt both the Church and the state to this very day, as it was the first of the high-profile cases against a priest for abusing children.

JOHN GEOGHAN

Another key figure in the Roman Catholic sex abuse scandal is that of John Geoghan, who probably stands out as one of the worst cases in the recent history of the Church. His case not only shook the foundations of the archdiocese in Boston, Massachusetts, USA, but also led to the resignation of the archbishop emeritus of Boston, Bernard Francis Law. His case became the catalyst for revelations of other clergy abuse and Church cover-ups. It forced the hands of the archdiocese into releasing damaging documents that showed the Church's obsession with avoiding scandal and trying to protect its own reputation.

Geoghan was ordained in 1962 after graduating from the Cardinal O'Connell Seminary. He was assigned his own parish, Blessed Sacrament in Saugus, but had to be constantly moved to a new parish as each new allegation emerged. He was eventually treated for his paedophile urges and went to live in a residence for retired priests.

To many of the single mothers in his parish, Geoghan was nothing more than the kindly priest who shook their hand at the end of a service. He also offered to help them get their children ready for bed, offering to bath them, read them a bedtime story and then tuck them up for the night. Little did they realise that the outwardly friendly man was actually fondling their children through their nightclothes.

When the scandal started to come out, as many as 150 people came forward, claiming they had been either fondled or raped by Geoghan. Geoghan was accused of sexual abuse on more than 130 people over a period of around 30 years. He was defrocked by the church in 1998 and found guilty in January 2002 of indecent assault and battery for grabbing the bottom of a ten-year-old boy in a swimming pool at a club for boys and girls in Waltham in 1991. He was sentenced to ten years in prison.

The Boston archdiocese was forced to make settlements amounting to $10 million with 86 of Geoghan's victims, because there was evidence that it had transferred the man from parish to parish despite warnings of his behaviour. As a result of the Geoghan case, it also came to light that the archdiocese had displayed a similar pattern with other priests whenever sexual allegations were made. More than a dozen civil suits are believed to be still pending.

During his time in prison, due to the nature of his crime, Geoghan was allegedly subjected to abuse by some of the guards. One inmate wrote a letter to prisoner rights lawyers saying that he had actually witnessed guards at the Concord prison abuse Geoghan, including defecating in his bed and destroying his property.

Geoghan met a grisly end while in protective custody on 23 August 2003. He was trapped in his cell at the Souza-Baranowski Correctional Center in Massachusetts, and then strangled and stomped to death by fellow inmate, Joseph Druce. Druce was in prison for murdering a man after he had allegedly made a sexual pass at him after the man picked him up while hitchhiking. That in itself caused a scandal because many felt the two men should never have been allowed to share the same cell.

EAMON CASEY

Compared to the severity of the other sexual abuse cases that came to light, the scandal regarding the former Bishop of Kerry, Dr Eamon Casey, seems quite trivial in proportion. However, at the time it was considered to be a major scandal, as Casey was a prominent and outspoken figure in the Roman Catholic Church in Ireland.

Casey was ordained as a priest for the Diocese of Kerry on 17 June 1951 and appointed Bishop of Kerry in July 1969. He became well-known for his work with Irish emigrants in Britain and for taking sides with the staff of the Dunnes Store (a supermarket and clothing retail chain in the Republic of Ireland). In 1984 they were involved in a lockout when they refused to sell goods that had come from South Africa famous at the time for its apartheid.

However, Bishop Casey was forced to resign his post in May 1992 when it was revealed that he had had a longstanding sexual relationship with an American divorcee by the name of Annie Murphy. They had had a son, Peter, who was born in 1974. It was also alleged that he misappropriated Church funds by using them to pay his maintenance obligations to Murphy. After his resignation, Casey went to work as a missionary in Ecuador, and it is believed that some of his clergy friends repaid the Church funds on his behalf. The resignation of Bishop Casey is thought to be a determining factor in the hierarchy of the Roman Catholic Church, because it started to lose its considerable influence over the sociology and politics of the Republic of Ireland.

In 2005, Casey was under scrutiny again when a woman, a native of Limerick living in the United Kingdom, made allegations against the bishop about incidents that had happened 30 years earlier. However, a tribunal said that the allegations could not be proved and the director of public prosecutions decided in August 2006 not to bring charges.

After his self-imposed exile, Casey returned to the United Kingdom and accepted the offer of a curate's position in Haywards Heath, East Sussex. All too aware of the furore that his scandal had caused in the past, Casey kept his head down and, apart from a ban for drink-driving, his time there was peaceful.

Casey returned to Ireland in February 2006 and now lives in Shanaglish, a small village near Gort, County Galway. Although the scandal regarding Bishop Casey seems small-fry compared to the atrocities committed by hundreds of other clergy, it has to be said that his relationship with Annie Murphy was prohibited by church doctrine. Added to that his behaviour was that of a hypocrite, because his duties included speaking against illicit sex – that is sex between unmarried people.

<u>ANDREW MADDEN</u>

The story of Andrew Madden is one of victim, not villain, and shows just what a devastating effect sexual abuse can have on an adolescent. Andrew Madden always dreamed of one day becoming a priest, but his love of the Catholic Church was soon destroyed when he became the subject of sexual abuse. Madden was a choir boy in Father Ivan Payne's parish, and it was the start of realising his dream. He loved to go behind the scenes in a busy parish church and help Payne on the alter in front of all the parishioners. He was excited that one day he would be standing there saying Mass himself. However, one day his excitement turned to terror, when Madden was molested by his favourite priest. The abuse lasted for three years until Madden was 15 years old.

The impact the abuse had on the young boy was devastating and lasted well into his adult life. Too frightened to talk about what had happened, he lost his direction in life. He started to drink and found it impossible to have a loving relationship. In the early 1990s, drained by constant bouts of paralysing fear and anxiety, he plucked up the courage and threatened to take legal action. The Church, desperate to cover up the scandal, paid Madden IR£27,500 and forced him to sign a letter of confidentiality. Believing that this would shut him up, the matter was pushed under the carpet.

However, eventually Madden had the strength to go public and the story broke in *The Sunday Times* in September 2003. The reaction by the Church was complete denial, accusing the newspaper of lying and saying 'That boy doesn't know what he is saying'. When Madden heard about their reaction, still fragile about the whole situation, he broke down in tears. However, his desire to pursue justice on the matter was unbreakable and he took the next major step. He went to the garda, revealed the priest's identity and showed them the document giving details of the Church's sordid transaction.

Although the process was slow, the priest was eventually charged with sexual abuse, not just of Madden, but of several other boys as well. Payne served four and a half years of a six-year prison sentence and was freed in 2002. The investigation into Payne had opened the floodgates and dozens of abuse cases came to light, many having taken place in Church institutions.

Needless to say, as with many of the other paedophile cases, the Church helped the villain by instigating a cover-up. As soon as the abuse came to light they moved Payne to a different parish and gave him a job inside the Archbishop's own house, counselling married couples. Even after he was jailed Payne continued to receive visits from his superiors, and after his release he was given a luxury Dublin flat and a weekly allowance, condoning his perverse crime.

DONALD KIMBALL

The last case covered in this section is that of Donald Kimball, who was a charismatic young priest from California who had his own radio ministry, which he directed towards young people. The innovative and award-winning show blended popular music with Bible teachings, making him very popular with local teenagers. However, Kimball used this popularity to his advantage and lured teenage girls into having sex with him.

Abuse allegations first came to light in 1997, when a lawsuit was filed against Kimball by four different people, including a brother and sister who said they had both been molested by the priest. Criminal charges were filed in 2000 and Pope John Paul II formerly defrocked Kimball.

When the case went to court in 2002 Kimball was acquitted of raping a 14-year-old girl in 1977, even though the woman testified at his trial saying that she had been raped behind the altar of a Santa Rosa church. She also added that Kimball had later paid for an abortion. The conviction of molesting a 13-year-old girl in 1981 was, however, upheld, after the girl gave evidence against Kimball, saying that she had been molested in his room at Healdsburg rectory. However, this conviction was overturned the following year when the United States Supreme Court overturned a law in California that extended the statute of limitations involving sex crimes involving children.

The Church settled the plaintiff's civil suits by paying them about $120,000 each. Kimball later served a prison sentence, not for sexual abuse, but for attacking a photographer for *The San Francisco Chronicle* in the courthouse during his child molesting trial.

Kimball's body was found at around 6.00 a.m. in September 2006, at the home of a friend, but the Sonoma County Sheriff claimed that there were no signs of criminal activity, although an autopsy would reveal more. Donald Kimball was 62 years old at the time of his death.

VATICAN SCANDAL

In 2003 the Vatican itself was subject to an enormous scandal. A 40-year-old confidential document was uncovered from the secret Vatican archive, which gave damning evidence regarding cases of sexual abuse involving the Catholic Church. The document itself was 69 pages long and bore the seal of Pope John XXIII. It had been sent to every bishop in the world with instructions outlining a policy of 'strictest' secrecy in dealing with allegations of sexual abuse. It also threatened anyone who spoke out on the subject with excommunication. The document also called for any victims who made a complaint to Church officials to take an oath of secrecy. It also stated that the document should be 'diligently stored in the secret archives of the Curia [Vatican] as strictly confidential'. The document was written in 1962 by Cardinal Alfredo Ottaviani and focuses entirely on the crimes of assault that it describes as: 'worst crime . . . sexual assault committed by a priest . . . attempted by him with youths of either sex or with brute animals.' Bishops were instructed to pursue any such cases 'in the most secretive way, restrained by a perpetual silence (including the alleged victim)'.

The document was uncovered by a Texan lawyer, Daniel Shea, when he was working on behalf of victims of abuse in the United States. He immediately handed it over to the US authorities and asked them to launch a federal investigation into the alleged 'cover-up'.

The exposure of this document will hopefully free the victims from their silent and private shame into which they have been forced, and it will hopefully bring the priests and religious figures concerned into public shame for their totally un-Christian behaviour.

PART SIX

JUDGES
AND
TEACHERS

CLARENCE THOMAS

You may have never even heard of Clarence Thomas – he is the only the second African-American to serve in the United States' Supreme Court and possibly their most conservative member. His life has been riddled by many contradictions and has been reviled by many people for his opposition to government programmes that are intended to help minorities. If you have heard the name, then it was probably associated with a scandal that saw Thomas accused of sexual harassment of a former colleague.

PAVING THE WAY

Clarence Thomas was born on 23 June 1948, in Pin Point, a small domain of around 500 inhabitants in Georgia, USA. Pin Point was named after the plantation that once stood on the land, and was given to the former slaves when it was divided up after the American Civil War. The inhabitants of Pin Point worked hard to earn a meagre living doing manual labour on a dirty, marsh-ridden area that possessed neither roads nor sewers.

Thomas was the second child and first son of Leola Williams and M. C. Thomas. Thomas never really got to know his father, though, because he abandoned the family when Thomas was just two years old and his mother was expecting her third child. Leola managed to hold her family together by taking a job as a housemaid, aided by handouts from the local Baptist church.

When Thomas was seven he and his brother were sent to live with their grandfather, Myers Anderson, who lived in Savannah. This was the result of a stressful time for his mother, because their wooden house had burnt to the ground just before she was about to remarry. Life with his grandfather had a profound influence on the young Thomas. Not only were the standards of living far higher than he was used to, but Anderson also believed in a good education followed by hard work.

Anderson was a fervent believer of the Catholic faith, a loyal Democrat and also an active member of the National Association for the Advancement of Colored People (NAACP). It was a time when African-Americans were browbeaten, being forced to ride on the back of buses, banned from most restaurants and had little prospects of a decent job. Anderson decided if he was to get anywhere in the world and beat racism he would need to work for himself. He successfully built up a business by delivering wood, coal, ice and heating oil from the back of a pick-up truck. As a result of his flourishing business, Anderson was not only able to provide his grandsons with a comfortable home, but he also enrolled them in an all-black grammar school which was run by white nuns, St Benedict on the Moor.

Anderson was a fair and loving man, but impressed on the two boys the importance of working hard at school if they wanted to achieve a reasonable standard of living. The nuns themselves were hard taskmasters who pushed their students to achieve their greatest potentials. After school the boys weren't allowed to go home and put their feet up. They worked for their grandfather helping him deliver fuel.

In later life Thomas often recalled his grandfather's words of wisdom: '. . . school, discipline, hard work and right from wrong were of the highest priority'.

If Thomas had any spare time he liked to go to the local Carnegie library, further from home than the one in Savannah, but blacks weren't allowed in there. After two years at the grammar school, Thomas moved to a Catholic boarding school just outside Savannah, not because he had problems but because his grandfather was pushing him towards priesthood. Thomas was the only African-American in his class at St John Vianney Minor Seminary, and for the first time felt the brunt of severe racism. He was excluded from social activities by his classmates and constantly ridiculed because of his skin colour. However, Thomas persevered and eventually graduated with admirable grades.

The next rung on the ladder towards becoming a priest was enrolment in the Immaculate Conception Seminary in Missouri. However, racism was rife and he left after only a short while, saying that he could not stay in a school that didn't practise what it preached. The final straw came when one of the students cheered at the news of Martin Luther King Jr's murder.

Thomas worked with his grandfather for a while and then in 1968, enrolled in Holy Cross, a Jesuit college in Worcester, Massachusetts. It was here that Thomas felt truly comfortable with his colour. Not only had the college started an ambitious black recruitment programme in the wake of King's death, but he also helped form the Black Student Union. In the union's second year, the members decided it would be a good idea if all the members lived together in one dormitory, but Thomas was the sole dissenter, believing that everyone should profit from associating with the white majority. After much pressure Thomas gave in but said that he wanted his white roommate from the previous year to come and live with him. During his time at Holy Cross, Thomas was an avid supporter of the Black Panther Party, which was an African-American organisation set up to promote civil rights and self-defence. Because of this support he urged a student walkout in protest against investments in South Africa.

In 1971 Thomas graduated ninth in his class and achieved an honours degree in English. The day after his graduation, Thomas married his girlfriend, Kathy Ambush, a student at a Catholic woman's college not far from Holy Cross.

Thomas had decided that he wanted to pursue a career in law, and was accepted at Yale University Law School under its 'affirmative action programme', which was aimed at increasing the representation of women and minorities in areas of education from which they have previously been excluded. However, Thomas didn't want to feel privileged because of his race, and did everything possible not to draw attention to himself. While at Yale, Kathy gave birth to his only child, a son that they named Jamal. To prove his abilities not just to himself but to his superiors as well, Thomas decided to specialise in tax and anti-trust law and when he graduated he was highly sought after by firms who suggested he should do *pro bono* (for the public good) work. However, Thomas took this as an insult and decided to return to Missouri, where he took a position in the offices of Attorney General John Danforth. Danforth was a young Republican and quickly became Thomas's political mentor. As the only African-American in the office, Thomas requested that he be allowed to work on taxes cases not civil rights.

In 1977 Danforth was elected to the Senate and Thomas decided to take a job in the private sector, working in the pesticide and agricultural department of the Monsanto Company, a St. Louis business that specialised in chemicals. His job there was mainly getting pesticides through government registration. This job lasted about two years when Thomas decided to head for Washington to work for Danforth once again, but this time as his legislative aide. As before he avoided any racist issues at work, but on the other side of the coin decided to join the black conservative movement, which felt that preferential treatment towards African-Americans did more harm than good. Thomas believed that the only way that African-Americans could make their way in the world was by helping themselves.

When Thomas attended a conference of black conservatives in 1980, the *Washington Post* wrote an article about him which was brought to the attention of President Ronald Reagan. The president offered him a job as the assistant secretary for civil rights in his department of education. Thomas decided to accept the job and was quickly promoted to head of the Equal Employment Opportunity Commission (EEOC). However, Thomas had a tough time in this position, which concentrated on laws against discrimination in the workplace. The Reagan administration found he was too independent-minded, but Thomas gradually bought them round to his way of thinking and made a lot of changes.

These changes in the EEOC, however, angered many of the civil rights groups, on top of this he had personal problems which made things difficult for Thomas. His grandfather died in 1983 and the following year divorced his wife, although he managed to keep custody of his son. Two years later he met the woman who was to become his second wife, Virginia Lamp, who was a senior aide to Republican Dick Armey.

THE US COURTS AND A SCANDAL

No one was really surprised, due to his success in the government offices, when Thomas was appointed a judge on the US Court of Appeals for the District of

Columbia in 1990. When Thurgood Marshall – the first African-American to be appointed to the Supreme Court – retired in 1991, the new president, George Bush, decided to elevate Thomas to the Supreme Court. This nomination, however, met with strong opposition from the minority groups who opposed Thomas's conservative views on civil rights. He withstood many days of questioning from the Judiciary Committee, but they were unable to shake him on his views.

Just when his nomination looked as though it would be passed, a sensational scandal broke which looked as though it was about to ruin his career. The press had leaked information about an FBI report which had been shown to the Judiciary Committee, alleging that Thomas had sexually harassed a former employee at the EEOC, Professor Anita Hill. Hill, now a professor at the University of Oklahoma College of Law, was brought in for questioning by the Committee. Amid a flurry of controversy, the hearing was reopened and the nation was transfixed as the case was relayed via television network. Hill, who was also an African-American and a Yale Law School graduate, outlined her allegations in full detail. Thomas categorically denied the charges and said the whole ordeal was 'a high-tech lynching for uppity blacks'.

After a long and drawn-out hearing, the Committee failed to uncover any positive proof of Hill's allegations and in the end the Senate voted 52 against 48 to confirm Thomas's nomination into the Supreme Court. At the age of 43, Thomas is the youngest member of the court and is known for his habit of listening rather than asking questions, something which he said he developed as a young boy.

JUDGE DALLAS POWERS

Judge Dallas Powers and his wife, Joyce, have lived in Warren County, Ohio, since 1964. They have two children and three grandchildren and were a well-respected and popular family. Powers has a Bachelor of Science Degree from the University of Dayton and a Degree of Juris Doctor from Chase College of Law. Powers also served as a first lieutenant in the United States Army, finally being discharged in May 1968.

Powers is a member of the Ohio Bar Association, American Bar Association, Warren County Bar Association and The Ohio Association of County and Municipal Court Judges and was the first elected judge of the Warren County Court in November 1988. He has given a lot of support to education and children's recreational activities and so it was a huge scandal when this upstanding citizen was accused of public indecency in the courthouse.

Together with his former probation officer, 34-year-old Libbie Sexton, Powers was accused of 13 felonies and three misdemeanour charges of sexual indecency. Powers also faced charges of theft, involving more than $5,000 in regular and overtime hours which he authorised for Sexton from December 2001 to November 2004.

Powers' troubles started on 30 August 2004, when a court employee walked into the judge's office and found him and and Sexton engaged in a sexual act. The employee reported the incident to another part-time judge and Powers was questioned over the indiscretion. Powers claimed that everyone knew about the affair and added, 'The complaints didn't come because of the affair. It was because of the preferential treatment. The other employees didn't like that when there was overtime Sexton got it or that she wore what she wanted at work'.

MORE ALLEGATIONS

Once the investigation got underway, more allegations started to come out of the woodwork. Sexual harassment and discrimination charges arose against the judge who, now in his 70s, had had a career that spanned over 27 years. There was even a civil suit that alleged Powers trained courtroom cameras at some of the female attorneys to 'observe their physiques'. Several of the employees at the court said they had actually witnessed sexual activity between Powers and Sexton on more than one occasion.

Powers' lawyer advised him to stay away from the courthouse until the dust had started to settle, but after stewing over the situation over the Christmas period, he decided to return to work. However, instead of keeping his head down he foolishly sacked three members of the probation department for insubordination. This action incensed much of the staff at the court and further accusations followed.

DETAILS OF ALLEGATIONS

In September 2004 another sexual misconduct complaint was made against the judge. One of the Warren Court employees, Terry Smith alleged that Powers had been discriminating against her in favour of a junior deputy clerk by the name of Libbie Gerondale. She had been hired by Powers in December 2001, causing Smith to have to take time off from work because of stress. Smith was head county court clerk and, although she would normally be present when Powers hired junior clerks, on this occasion he told her that her presence wasn't required.

Smith claims that it was common knowledge that Powers was having a sexual relationship with 34-year-old Gerondale, and said that she knew that there was something going on right from the start. Smith went on to say that there was a certain standard of clothing that was permissible at the courts, and that she had had to warn miss Gerondale on several occasions about wearing short skirts and low-cut blouses.

Smith said she then became aware of the amount of overtime that Gerondale was clocking up, far more than any of the other clerks, and eventually Powers decided to assign Gerondale to another supervisor, taking away Smith's powers over her. In his own defence Powers said he took this action because there was a certain amount of friction between the two women. When Smith approached Powers again and complained about the preferential treatment that Gerondale was getting, he demoted Smith and took away many of her statutory duties.

Smith's complaints against Powers were taken seriously and became part of a much larger investigation. When another woman levied a sexual harassment complaint against Powers, it prompted county officials to start interviewing all court employees. The latest accusation meant that almost one-third of the court's 17 female employees have made complaints against the judge.

One woman alleged that Powers had fondled her and pressurised her into sexual contact in his court chambers. Another said that Powers was discriminating against the women who were not prepared to provide him with sexual favours.

As the investigation progressed, it was disturbing that there were so many allegations but they had taken so long to come out. Court employees told the investigators that Powers' behaviour had disturbed them, but many felt too intimidated to complain. Several people said that his general manner and demeanour led people to be afraid of him. It wasn't until one woman was brave enough to speak out that the others were prepared to give witness as well.

THE OUTCOME

Judge Dallas Powers was the first Ohio judge to be prosecuted with sex crimes in his own courtroom. In a deal with prosecutors, Powers agreed to plead guilty to two misdemeanours – lesser crimes of intimidation and showing preference to a public employee – but denied the counts of public indencency. He was told he would have to serve three years' probation and could not hold a public office for seven years. Already in his 70s, Powers has now retired, bringing an end to his 27 years as a United States judge.

DEBRA LAFAVE

Debra Lafave was a beautiful, 23-year-old female teacher who admitted to having sex with one of her under-age pupils. Although she certainly wasn't the first teacher – or indeed the last – to be caught for such an illicit liaison, her story became an international scandal.

THE FULL STORY

To perhaps try and understand why Lafave acted the way she did, it is necessary to dig deep into her past. For it is here that we find a trauma that affected her so badly, it was something she said she could never recover from. Debra Beasley was born on 28 August 1980 in Tampa, Florida, and had an older sister, Angie, whom she adored. However, as a young child Debra suffered from many insecurities – phobias, panic attacks and obsessions – all which marred her adolescent life. When she was in the eighth grade and just 13 years old, Debra was raped in school. She was forced into a lavatory and the boy began to rape her until a teacher came in and stopped him. Debra was too frightened to tell the teacher that she had not been a willing participant and ironically, the boy was not just a fellow schoolmate, but one of her boyfriends. She became to believe that men were always the dominant one in a sexual relationship and that the woman had to please them.

By the age of 15, Debra had developed an eating disorder and was starting to rely on drink to try and make her life bearable. She also attempted to commit suicide twice, once by taking an overdose of pills and secondly by slitting her wrists. The main problem was that Debra was stunningly beautiful and she was like a magnet to men. Many of her friends said that she ought to become a model and by the age of 18, she worked for a magazine called *Makes and Models*.

Despite her beauty, Debra also had brains and wanted to achieve more in her life and went to study English at the University of South Florida, with the goal of becoming a teacher. Although she managed to stop drinking, Debra still suffered from spells of depression and was forced to take antidepressants, which after a spell failed to have any effect.

The years before Debra graduated she was devastated by the news that her sister had been killed in a car accident. Debra still feels today that if Angie had been around she would never have committed the stupid act that would change her future. Despite all her problems, Debra managed to graduate and took a job as an eighth grade reading teacher at the Greco Middle School in a Tampa suburb.

Her first year went well, she was a popular teacher and added to that she also married Owen Lafave, a man she had been dating for five years. The relationship was going well, they were best friends, they did everything together, but it was still marred by Debra's bouts of severe depression. Like many sufferers of bipolar disorder (which she was later diagnosed with), Debra had her spells of extreme highs and extreme lows, but for the most part Owen coped with his wife's illness, but the drinking started to get him down.

MEETING THE BOY

Debra was aware that her looks got her a lot of attention, but she didn't realise the effect she was having on one 14-year-old boy. One of Debra's friends used to coach the school football team and on occasion she would go along as extra support. One of the boys starting making himself known to Debra, just doing silly things like waving and saying 'Hi' every time he saw her.

The friendship started to get out of hand when Debra chaperoned a field trip to Sea World in 2004 and the boy in question was in her group. Owen was also on the trip and, although nothing untoward took place, Debra and the young boy started to talk and became friends.

After the trip the friendship started to spiral out of control. Debra was a very delicate individual and the young boy started to become flirtatious. Although in her heart she knew she was the role model to this young boy, somehow she crossed a line that should never have been crossed.

In spring 2004 the 23-year-old professional seemed to transform into an out-of-control adolescent. She started smoking, listening to rap music and also dressed in a very provocative way, which didn't go unnoticed by her fellow teachers. Although her husband and some of her colleagues made a few comments, Debra just shrugged it off. During this period she was spending more and more time with the 14-year-old boy, one of her students, and he was becoming more and more flirtatious with each meeting. Instead of being a responsible teacher, Debra drew the boy closer and closer into her confidence without his parents' knowledge. She started driving the boy to and from basketball games and she admitted later on that as her attraction for the boy grew, her mental state started to deteriorate.

At the time, Debra could not see that she was doing anything wrong – after all nothing had actually happened. But then she took the next step – a very dangerous step – she kissed him. Her attraction for the boy turned into a full-blown crush.

A week or so after the kiss in the classroom, just as the summer holidays were about to start, the boy was staying with his cousin in Ocala, about 160 km (100 miles) away from Tampa. On 3 June Debra became desperate to see the boy and, while Owen was out at work, she decided to drive to Ocala to see him. She picked up the boy and his cousin and drove them all the way back to her flat. She ordered pizza for them all, rented a movie and, while his cousin watched the television, Debra took the boy upstairs to her bedroom and they engaged in oral sex.

SUSPICIONS

Although they had been married for less than a year, Owen was starting to become suspicious and suspected his wife of having an affair. He even told his mother that he thought Debra was being unfaithful, but at the time never dreamt that it was with one of her own students.

Debra was becoming more and more reckless with each day and ten days later, on June 14, she invited the boy to help her clean the classroom. She crossed the unforgivable line and had sex with the boy at the school. From there Debra could no longer contain her lust for the boy and the following day she drove him to Ocala to see his cousin. They picked his cousin up from his house and then to his shock, Debra handed him the car keys (despite the fact that he was only 15) and told him to drive. Meanwhile, in the back of the car she had sex with her student. Not even worrying about whether the boy's cousin would tell anyone, Debra then took the boys out for a smoothie and then shopping. She was captured on a security camera wearing a very brief sundress, supposedly unaware that she was doing anything wrong.

THE NEWS SPREADS

The news that Debra was hanging around with young boys spread like wildfire. She was seen in the shopping centre by the mother of one of the cousin's friends. She in turn told the cousin's mother, who then asked the boy's mother if she was aware that her son was hanging around with his beautiful teacher. Debra tried to appease the situation by calling the boy's mother, unaware that she had already confronted her son and he had told her just how far they had gone. The police had already been informed and detectives went to interview the boy, who confirmed his story. They decided the best way to trap the teacher was to get the boy to phone her while they listened in. He asked Debra if she had enjoyed herself the day before, to which she replied she had. The detectives then asked the boy to call again, but this time to invite her over to his house. While on the phone Debra made the boy promise that his mother wasn't at home.

Debra arrived at the appointed time on 21 June 2004, but instead of the boy waiting for her, as she stepped out of her car she was surrounded by police. She couldn't comprehend at first what she had done, but then when they told her she was being arrested for lewd and lascivious behaviour with a 14-year-old boy, the severity of the situation sank in.

The boy was asked personal details about Debra to prove that she had indeed been his sex partner, while Debra was forced to have an embarrassing internal examination. Not only could Debra now face up to 30 years in jail but she had to come to terms that her career was in ruins and her marriage was over.

GOING TO TRIAL

According to three psychiatrists who were hired by the defence, it was confirmed that Debra was suffering from a bipolar disorder, which may have explained her rather erratic behaviour. It is known that women who suffer from this disorder often experience hypersexuality.

The preliminary hearing took nearly two years in which time Owen divorced her, Debra's pictures appeared everywhere and she became engaged to a childhood sweetheart by the name of Andrew Beck. In November 2005 Debra's laywer managed to make a plea bargain with the prosecutors and said that Debra would plead guilty to 'lewd and lascivious battery' if she was given house arrest instead of a prison sentence. However, the judge rejected the plea bargain and demanded that it went to trial.

With the fear of a prison sentence looming over her head, Debra prepared herself for the worst. Then, quite out of a blue, the boy's mother told the prosecutors that she wanted to drop all charges. They felt it wasn't worth putting their boy through the ordeal of testifying in court. With the media following Debra Lafave wherever she went, they also felt it wouldn't be long before their son's face and name were all over the papers. For once the media intensity had done Debra a favour.

Debra could not believe that she had been let off so lightly and immediately phoned her fiancé to tell him the news, breaking down in sheer relief. At a news conference later that day she said:

The past two years have been hard for all parties involved. I pray with all my heart that the young man and his family will be able to move on with their lives.

Debra is now on controlled medication to try and fight her bipolar illness, and under the terms of her plea agreement was put on house arrest for three years and then on intensive probation for a further seven. She is only allowed to leave home to go to work and for essential errands. However, worse, far worse, she is a registered sex offender who will never be allowed to work with children or live within close proximity to a school. She wears an electronic ankle bracelet and every single movement of her life is tracked.

Many people still feel that she should be in prison for her crime against an adolescent, but others feel that deep down she is a good and kind person who was a victim of her own distorted mind. She currently works as a waitress and, unable to profit from her crime, can never write her story for others to learn of her struggle with illness.

AMY GEHRING

The case of Amy Gehring has raised a lot of questions, and there has been considerable debate as to how this 26-year-old supply teacher was ever allowed to teach in the first place. Although Gehring was cleared of indecently assaulting two schoolboys whom she was accused of having sex with, she did openly admit that she had had sex with a 16-year-old pupil at another school where she previously worked.

Amy Gehring grew up on a farm in a small hamlet in Ontario, Canada. She graduated from the University of Western Ontario, but never pursued a teaching position in her homeland. She came to the United Kingdom in 2000 on a working holiday visa, at a time when supply teachers were in great demand due to staff shortages.

Concerns regarding her professional conduct first came to light in October 2000. She was suspended by the agency that had employed her, TimePlan, amid claims that she had kissed one of her pupils and invited another boy back to her flat, where she had sex with him.

TimePlan had a meeting with child protection officers on 12 October, and they were advised not to send Gehring to another school while they carried out their investigation. However, on 23 October the agency were told by the police that no charges were being brought against Miss Gehring and that the matter had been dropped. When TimePlan spoke with Gehring, she categorically denied that anything untoward had taken place.

Before placing Gehring in another assignment, the agency spoke with the police and the Child Protection Unit (CPU) to see whether they thought it was advisable to send their client to an all-girls' school. After a lot of consideration – and to be on the safe side – they decided that they would just send Gehring on one-day placements to stand in for absent teachers.

However, after just one day at a comprehensive school in Surrey on 1 November 2000, she was accused again of entering into sexually inappropriate relationships with some pupils. She was interviewed by the police and the CPU as part of their enquiries and warned about her future behaviour. They also wrote to TimePlan saying that they believed that Miss Gehring could not be trusted and was more than likely to target young male pupils if placed on any further assignments. Despite these warnings, Gehring was given several other short placements before returning to the comprensive school in question for the remainder of the term.

MORE SCANDAL

On 5 January 2001 playground gossip was rife and TimePlan were once again informed by parents about alleged assaults taking place at the school by Gehring. It was claimed that she had had sex with a boy in an alley close to the school. Then she had attended a private party being held by some of the pupils on New Year's Eve, where she allegedly got very drunk on Malibu and Barcardi Breezers and supposedly had sex with two other boys.

This time the matter was not dropped and the case went to trial. In her own defence, Gehring said, 'I put myself into situations I shouldn't have at parties because I became close to them [the pupils]. Looking back, I feel quite stupid for all of the things that I did. I was away from my family in a different country and I was spending most of my time with them. I became one of the kids basically'. She also admitted that she had got so drunk at the party that she couldn't even remember if she had had sex or not! Although she did add that she had gone to the doctor the next day to get the morning after pill just to be on the safe side.

The morning after the party, Gehring sent text messages to one of the boys asking him, 'Did we have sex last night? I can't remember. Please don't think bad of me. Oh my God, I'm so sorry'.

Gehring's defence lawyer put it to the jury that it was possible it was just a case of two teenage boys having just too much testosterone, complicated by a lot of gossip, rumours and innuendos.

One of the boys admitted in evidence that he had been offered a lot of money by a newspaper to give his story. He said he had had sex with Gehring in broad daylight in an alley near the school and that she had also performed oral sex on him in a toilet at the party on New Year's Eve.

Another 15-year-old boy also gave evidence that he had had sex with Gehring in a downstairs toilet at the same party.

The jury was directed by the judge to find Miss Gehring 'not guilty' of a further charge against another boy, as the alleged incident did not constitute indecent assault because the boy supposedly insti-gated the sex. The jury failed to reach a verdict after deliberating for 10 hours and 15 minutes and in February 2002, Guildford Crown Court cleared Miss Gehring of all charges.

RETURN TO CANADA

Amy Gehring returned to her homeland but, although having been cleared of having sex with under-age schoolboys in Britain, she had to face disciplinary charges in her native Canada. She was accused of seven counts of professional misconduct relating to her behaviour back in the United Kingdom. She was found guilty of seven counts of professional misconduct, including abusing students 'physically, sexually, verbally, psychologically or emotionally' and banned from teaching in Canada for at least ten years.

The tribunal said Miss Gehring had failed to uphold the profession's standards and that she had behaved in a 'disgraceful, dishonourable and unprofessional' way. Gehring, who was not actually present at the hearing, said that she had no plans to pursue a career in teaching.

Gehring's case made MPs question the regulations regarding supply teachers and it has also highlighted the United Kingdom's rather out-of-date laws regarding 'adult-child' sex. The law, dating back to 1956, prohibits a man from having sex with a girl aged 15 or under, but does not prevent a woman from having sex with a boy of 15. If an adult woman does have sex with a boy of 14 or 15 she can, just like Gehring, only be charged with 'indecent assault'.

PART SEVEN

GOVERNMENT SCANDAL

J. Edgar Hoover

The Federal Bureau of Investigation, better known as the FBI, has for many years held secret files on some of the most villainous criminal minds of the 20th century. However, perhaps one of the most intriguing scandals to come out of this major law enforcement agency is that of its own ruler, J. Edgar Hoover. It wasn't until his death in 1972 that details came out that perhaps the man who spent his lifetime fighting against crime wasn't quite so squeaky clean himself. Hoover stood for everything that was decent and his solid principles made him the ideal head of the FBI, a position which lasted for 48 years. And yet, if the stories are to be believed, Hoover was steeped in corruption. Perhaps what the public saw was indeed an amazing charade to cover up his more underhand activities. Was it really true that Hoover wore dresses with lace stockings and high heels, and a black curly wig and make-up? Was he really being blackmailed by the Mafia?

RISING UP THE RANKS

The 1920s saw the United States riddled with law-breakers, particularly as it was a time when it was illegal to either make or consume alcohol. The distillation and distribution of alcohol became very big business and gangs started to compete for supremacy. As a result, violence and corruption was everywhere and the Mafia were soon taking a stronghold on the major cities of the United States.

The United States had no national police force at this time to try and deal with a situation of such magnitude, and Congress chose an unknown professional bureaucrat by the name of J. Edgar Hoover to head the newly formed FBI. Although funds were scarce and its agents did not have much authority in its early days, Hoover soon turned the department into the world-famous and internationally acclaimed institution that is now recognised all over the world. Hoover's 'G-men', as they were known, soon became national heroes as they captured some of the most notorious criminals – John Dillinger and Machine Gun Kelly – to name just two.

Hoover quickly introduced a new set of standards for his agents. Not only did they need to have a college degree but he also insisted on a very high personal moral and dress code. He was a strict disciplinarian and demanded personal loyalty from anyone who worked for him. Within three years the FBI had the best fingerprinting techniques in the country, the best trained agents and the best record for fighting crime.

HOOVER'S BEST FRIEND

When Clyde Tolson originally applied to join the FBI, his application was turned down. However, he tried again the following year, 1928, and this time his application form was spotted by Hoover. Tolson was hired and was quickly promoted through the ranks and, after only three years he was appointed assistant director of the up-and-coming law enforcement agency.

Tolson and Hoover became close – or perhaps it is fair to say very close – friends and over the next 40 years were constant companions. They were like siamese twins – they rode to and from work together, ate lunches together and even went on holiday together – in fact there was hardly a time when they were seen apart. When rumours reached Hoover that people were calling him a homosexual, he lost his temper and started to hunt down the individuals who had dared to intimate such a thing. Little did he realise that behind his back some of his FBI employees had labelled the two men 'J. Edna and Mother Tolson'. Hoover made it his duty to try and find the people who had started the rumours and he used his agents as musclemen. They visited the suspects in their homes and threatened them if they didn't stop spreading slanderous remarks about Hoover.

Although today there is nothing scandalous about being a homosexual, in the 1920s it wasn't accepted in the same way. Added to this, Hoover was outspoken on his views about homosexuality and often referred to them as 'queers' and 'fairies'. This was extremely hypocritical, especially as there were rumours that he loved to dress in women's clothing. Hoover is alleged to have paid off anyone, including gangsters, who obtained any embarrassing pictures of the other, rather sordid, side to his life.

When Hoover died in May 1972, he left virtually his entire estate to his companion, Tolson, and he also took hold of Hoover's secret files. Most of Hoover's personal effects were destroyed, in accordance with his wishes, and so if there was any evidence of a sexual relationship between the two men, this secret information died with them.

HOOVER AND THE MAFIA

For many years Hoover refused to believe that there was such a powerful crime syndicate as the Mafia, even though there was a mountain of evidence proving this fact. Because of his denial and his lack of action against them, the Mafia began to spread their wings even more until they controlled many of the major cities across the United States. Some have intimated that Hoover refused to crack down on organised crime because he was being blackmailed by the Mafia for his secret life as a homosexual. It is believed that the powerful Mafia boss, Meyer Lansky, was in possession of incriminating photographs and had put considerable pressure on the FBI boss.

Hoover's war on organised crime didn't really get going until 1933 when a wave of crime swept over parts of the United States, turning names like John Dillinger, 'Machine Gun' Kelly, 'Pretty Boy' Floyd and 'Baby Face' Nelson into heroes. Hoover was not happy with the glorification that these gangsters were receiving and he saw it as a challenge. The FBI was Hoover's life and he defended it like it was his own progeny. This was another reason behind his lack of action against the mobsters in previous years, because he feared failure. When Hoover did eventually send his agents against the Mafia hardmen, the media and public loved it. At last the FBI was receiving recognition and taking on a new image.

Hoover's war on the gangsters was always conducted with two main criteria on his mind –

success for his FBI men, but also veneration for none other than J. Edgar Hoover himself. The publicity served a double purpose, because not only did it boost his reputation but it also kept the media from snooping into other areas of his life that weren't quite so above board. With his notoriety reaching its peak, Hoover was living the life of luxury, befitting that of a king. He used his own agents to keep his house spick and span and a string of bullet-proof cars to drive him wherever he wanted to go. He also used some of his agents to place enormous bets for him at racetracks across the United States, at the same time swearing them to secrecy about his gambling habits.

HOOVER AND JFK

Hoover had built up dossiers on anyone of importance – judges, movie stars and politicians were all too scared to put a foot wrong for fear of recrimination. When John F. Kennedy came to power in the 1960s, it was hoped that he would retire Hoover and replace him with a less corrupt individual. However, Hoover had got his hooks in first and used Kennedy for his own political leverage. Kennedy knew better than to mess with Hoover – after all his own file was probably one of the thickest and most incriminating of all. Hoover didn't approve of Kennedy's liberal views and his plans for civil rights, so from the onset of his presidency Kennedy was a target and the incriminating evidence mounted.

The file started back at the beginning of World War II when Kennedy had a romance with 28-year-old Inga Arvad, who was suspected of being a Nazi sympathiser. After that he copiously gathered every snippet of dirt on Kennedy, delineating numerous liaisons with women and campaign contributions from Mafia bosses. Although Hoover was always outwardly polite to Kennedy, behind his back he attempted to smear his reputation as much as he could.

Throughout his presidency Kennedy and his brother Robert, were constantly reminded about the secret files held by Hoover. They often received memos containing a piece of damning information about a member of the family, reminding the Kennedys that the director of the FBI needed to be treated with respect.

A NEW ATTORNEY GENERAL

Although there was no love lost between the Kennedys and Hoover, there was never any direct confrontation. Hoover had always been allowed to govern the FBI without any interference, but the situation changed drastically after Robert Kennedy was appointed as Hoover's new boss. For the first time

Hoover was forced to deal directly with the President, but this time through the office of the attorney general. Robert Kennedy made it obvious that Hoover was his subordinate and even went as far as placing a direct phone line between his and Hoover's office. Hoover knew he was close to the age of retirement and therefore did not directly wish to challenge Robert Kennedy and risk a premature end to his very illustrious career.

Even though Hoover did not relish the appointment of Robert Kennedy, his agents were overjoyed. Here was a man who believed in fighting organised crime, and for the first time they could challenge the power of the Mafia but with the backing of the Justice Department. They had never been happy about Hoover's reluctance to accept the severity of the Mafia situation. It appeared that Kennedy understood the true nature of the gangsters and realised how it affected the United States as a whole, and begrudgingly Hoover had to go along with it.

If news of an indiscretion got into the hands of the press, Hoover used this to his own advantage by going to the Kennedys and bringing the offending article to their attention. This was done to save face and pretend that he was trying to protect them, when all the time he was stockpiling every adulterous act they committed. When Hoover learned that President Kennedy had had several illicit liaisons with a woman called

Judith Campbell Exner he used this information to try and intimidate the president. Hoover had heard rumours that Exner was a close friend of two high-profile Mafia bosses, Johnny Rosselli and Sam Giancana, and he became concerned that the Mafia would use this connection to gain influence over the president. Hoover also felt this was the perfect opportunity to make Kennedy aware that he knew all about his affairs. He arranged a meeting with the president and although there is no evidence of what was actually said, it is thought that he would have advised Kennedy about how dangerous the liaison was with a woman who also befriended the Mafia. Hoover certainly knew how to use subtle blackmail.

The icing on the cake was when Hoover discovered that both brothers had had an affair with the famous Hollywood actress Marilyn Monroe. He used this information to his advantage, not only allowing him to continue his role as head of the FBI but also without any further interruption from either of the Kennedys.

Hoover stayed in his job for another ten years after both Robert and John Kennedy had been assassinated. With his friend Lyndon Johnson being appointed to the presidency, Hoover no longer had a threat hanging over his head and he was free to run the FBI the way he wanted. There is no doubt that under his rule the FBI became one of the world's most effective and formidable law enforcement organisations.

THE LEGACY

Hoover died peacefully in his sleep on 1 May 1972. It sent a shockwave throughout the government of the United States as hundreds of officials, including President Nixon, desperately tried to find Hoover's secret files that could seriously damage all their reputations and possibly careers. What they didn't know was that Hoover had ordered the destruction of many of his secret dossiers, but the ones that were remaining caused a sensational scandal as some of the secrets of America's most powerful men and women were revealed.

The people who knew Hoover throughout his life are divided in their judgements about him. Some have described him as a patriotic and dedicated servant to his country, while others say he used his power and influence to his own advantage. As head of the FBI Hoover saw himself above reproach and seemed prepared to do almost anything to remain with his first true love – as head of the FBI.

THE FALL OF
PRESIDENT NIXON

To most people the name 'Watergate' is associated with the fall of President Nixon, but do you really know the details behind the scandal that rocked the very foundations of the Whitehouse? It all started in June 1972 in Washington, D.C. with a burglary at an office complex at the Watergate Hotel. Five people broke into the Democratic National Committee (DNC) headquarters in the Watergate with the intention of bugging their telephones. The men were a group of anti-Castro Cuban refugees called 'The Plumbers', which was made up mainly of former FBI and CIA agents. The break-in resulted in one of the largest scandals to hit the United States government.

REASONS BEHIND THE BREAK-IN

In the early 1970s the United States was still feeling the effects of their role in the Vietnam war. This war was the longest military conflict in US history, and one which claimed the lives of more than 58,000 Americans. It was a military struggle fought in Vietnam from 1959 until 1975, involving the North Vietnamese and the National Liberation Front against the United States and the South Vietnamese. At the end of the war many people had changed their views concerning the validity of the war, and one of these people was a man called Daniel Ellsberg. Ellsberg was a former defence department analyst and his feelings were so strong about the conflict that he decided to turn over a secret report written by the Pentagon to the *New York Times*. Needless to say the paper was delighted to have such classified information and immediately started to publish what it called the 'Pengaton Papers'. President Nixon and many other government officials were furious that such information had been leaked to the press and took legal action. However, when this failed Nixon decided he needed to turn somewhere else for help.

'THE PLUMBERS'

The 'Plumbers' were a specialised, clandestine group formed by the Whitehouse with the express job of 'fixing leaks'. Nixon summoned the 'Plumbers' and gave them the name of their next target – Daniel

Ellsberg. The reasoning behind this action was that if it wasn't possible to stop the paper publishing the documents, then the next best thing would be to discredit the man who had provided the information. The group's first job was to break into the office of Ellsburg's psychiatrist to see if they could dig up any dirt. The 'Plumbers' were persistent in their goal and Nixon soon rewarded them with another undertaking.

On 17 June 1972 the group broke into the DNC headquarters to find out what they were up to and to bug their offices. However, this time a security officer saw the men break into the offices and alerted the police; the men were apprehended before they could complete their mission.

Under interrogation, insights about the background of the burglars started to come to light, much to the embarrassment of Nixon and his government. It turned out that one of the men used to be a Republican Party security aide, while another was found to have a cheque worth $25,000 intended for Nixon's re-election campaign. In fact, it soon became evident that all three of the 'Plumbers' were on the payroll of the Committee to Re-elect the President.

Despite this evidence, Nixon went on to win the presidential election in one of the largest landslide victories in history. However, following his re-election, the repercussions from the burglary at Watergate started to spread like a tidal wave. As the connection between the 'Plumbers' and the Whitehouse became public knowledge, several members of Nixon's staff were forced to resign, including Whitehouse Chief Counsel, John Dean. Rumours were rife and many people were convinced that Nixon himself was involved in the scandal. In May 1973 the Senate opened a hearing about the break-in and, under pressure, Nixon appointed Archibald Cox as special prosecutor.

THE INVESTIGATION

As the investigation got under way, damning evidence against Nixon came to the fore. John Dean was the first former Whitehouse staff member to admit that he had had discussions with Nixon on the best way to cover up the Watergate affair. As if that wasn't bad enough, the hearings also revealed that Nixon had a highly developed taping system put in place within the Oval offices, which had taped all of his conversations. When the Senate committee heard about the tapes they immediately demanded that Nixon handed them over. Nixon visibly squirmed, using every excuse he could think of why he shouldn't let the hearing have the tapes.

The United States held its breath while the Senate

and Nixon came head to head. Nixon, still trying to avoid handing over the tapes, said that one of them had an 18-minute gap on it and that it would be better if he sent in a [heavily edited] transcript of the conversations, as opposed to the actual tapes. However, the Senate continued to put pressure on Nixon to release the tapes and, when he continued to refuse, the House of Representatives voted to impeach him. Realising that he was being pushed into a corner, Nixon decided to take evasive action.

On 20 October 1973 Nixon was forced into committing what afterwards became known as the 'Saturday Night Massacre'. The 'massacre' was a pivotal event in the Watergate scandal and one that eventually led to the resignation of Nixon. Archibald Cox, the special prosecutor, had been persistently trying to gain access to the Watergate tapes, but with no success. On Saturday 20 October, Cox told Nixon that he could not longer comply with the deal he had worked out with the Senate to turn over only summaries of the tapes. He told Nixon that he would continue to make every effort to get access to the tapes, but in response Nixon requested that Attorney General Elliott Richardson fired Cox from the investigation. However, Richardson refused and Nixon demanded the attorney general's resignation. The next person Nixon called on was Deputy Attorney General William Ruckelshaus, asking him to fire Cox. Ruckelshaus also refused to buckle under pressure and Nixon fired him as well.

Eventually Nixon found a man who was prepared to do his bidding – Solicitor General Robert Bork – who stepped in as acting attorney general after Richardson and Ruckelshaus had been fired. Bork complied with Nixon's order and fired Cox, but the resulting backlash forced Nixon to have a new special prosecutor appointed – Leon Jaworski. However, this also backfired as Jaworski himself starting putting pressure on Nixon to hand over the tapes. Nixon's answer to this was to abolish the Office of the Special Prosecutor. News of all the firings broke at 8.25 p.m., the same evening that the Whitehouse released a statement.

As soon as news of the 'massacre' broke it led many people to conclude that Nixon had to be covering up damning information that only the tapes could reveal. The Senate continued to push for the tapes to be handed over and when the matter was eventually passed over to the Supreme Court in July 1974, Nixon quickly resigned as president to avoid impeachment. The repercussions from the Watergate scandal have been enormous. It was an exceptionally complex affair and one that is full of intrigue and underhand backroom deals. It was a major scandal that exposed some dirty politics taking place in the Whitehouse under Nixon's reign.

EUGENE TALMADGE

A disturbing revelation came to light after files were released regarding the lynching of two black couples in Georgia, even though the event took place more than 60 years ago. It is believed that a former three-term governor, Eugene Talmadge, may have sanctioned the murders in an effort to sway rural white voters during a particularly tough election campaign. The murders took place on 25 July 1946 on Moore's Ford Bridge in Wallon County, Georgia. The four victims were George and Mae Murray Dorsey and Roger and Dorothy Malcom, all workers on a share-cropper plantation.

The murders were promptly investigated by the FBI, but little progress was made and the case was never solved. In 2001 Roy Barnes, the then-governor, reopened the case and released 3725 pages from the old police files to the Associated Press under the Freedom of Information Act. Although Barnes felt there was enough information to finally have a trial, the main problem he faced was the fact that virtually every witness who could testify against the surviving suspects were now dead.

A CONTROVERSIAL GOVERNOR

Eugene Talmadge was a United States Democratic Party politician who served as governor of the US state of Georgia from 1933 to 1937 and again from 1941 to 1943. Although he was re-elected to another term in 1946, he died shortly before taking office. Talmadge was beginning to lose the popular vote, however, due to his virulent rascism and outspoken opposition to President Franklin Roosevelt. Talmadge was vehemently opposed to black civil rights and in 1941 tried to fire two university system administrators, because they had been outspoken about integrated public schools. When the Board of Regents refused to comply with his wishes, Talmadge reacted by sacking them all and replacing them with people who were more in tune with his 'line of thinking'.

Talmadge was also accused of having connections with the Ku Klux Klan, allegedly using them during elections to try and stop African-Americans from voting in Georgia. Talmadge was elected as Governor of Georgia following a campaign of terror by the Ku Klux Klan, and on the eve of the election fiery crosses burned outside the courthouses of Georgia. Notices signed 'KKK' were pinned to the churches frequented by African-Americans, with a warning, 'The first nigger who votes in Georgia will be a dead one.'

Other warnings were issued either by mail or by dropping propaganda literature from aeroplanes over predominantly African-American areas. On the day of the actual election, literally thousands of African-Americans woke to find miniature coffins on their front doorsteps. Many people took the warnings seriously and Talmadge was elected governor of Georgia.

Bit by bit, Talmadge succeeded in taking control of various state departments by any means possible, often using extremely forceful tactics. To secure his position, he fired the original staff and replaced them with his own supporters. Talmadge did not approve of President Roosevelt and his regime and by 1934 the split between the two men was a deep chasm. Despite Roosevelt promoting the candidacy of Claude Pittman for the governor's position, Talmadge had a landslide win, getting twice as many votes as Pittmann. Following his victory Talmadge took to the road openly criticising Roosevelt and promoting his own candidacy for president. However, his bid for presidency failed and he settled for fighting against Roosevelt's New Deal in Georgia. In 1936 Talmadge was out of politics for a while, but in 1938 he was re-elected and once again he was allowed to assume dictorial powers in Georgia.

FBI SUSPICIONS

Talmadge came under the watchful eye of the FBI in 1946 when he made a visit to the north Georgia town of Monroe a couple of days before the election. It was also the day after a particularly nasty racial attack had taken place, in which a black sharecropper had stabbed and severely wounded a white farmer. The sharecropper was one of the four people who was later lynched on Moore's Ford Bridge.

J. Edgar Hoover, the director of the FBI at that time, received a report regarding Talmadge. It stated that the governor had met with the brother of the stabbed farmer, George Hester. Allegedly he had offered the man, and any of his friends, immunity if they wished to 'take care of the negroes'.

The investigation into Talmadge started in the months before his death in December 1946, and yet it appears he was never even interviewed on the subject. The death of the two couples took place after a particularly stormy period in the run-up to the elections, making it appear to be politically motivated.

There were also rumours going around that an army veteran by the name of George Dorsey had been secretly dating a white woman – this was something that was strictly taboo in the South at that time, an area that was renowned for its segregation. The white population in Monroe were enraged with Roger Malcom, who had been put in prison after stabbing the white farmer, Barney Hester. For some reason a local white farmer by the name of Loy Harrison paid $600 in bail so that Malcom could be freed and then offered him and his wife a lift home, together with another black couple, George and Mae Murray Dorsey. When they reached Moore's Ford Bridge, Harrison claimed that the car was suddenly surrounded by a mob of around 30 people. They pulled the two couples out of the car, dragged them along a dusty trail and then tied them to some trees. Then they fired three volleys, leaving the four bodies slumped in the dirt. Dorothy Malcom was seven months pregnant at the time.

President Truman was outraged and immediately sent FBI agents to Monroe to investigate the murders. However, on arrival the agents found that the local community – black and white alike – had clammed up and were not prepared to talk. Even Harrison told the agents that he was unable to identify any of the men that had attacked his car. The black families, who often shared their land with white sharecroppers, were petrified when approached by the FBI for fear of recrimination. One man even fled into the cotton fields and had to be chased. When the agents caught him he said he had been threatened into silence.

The FBI eventually pinned it down to a possible 55 suspects, including George Hester, but no one was ever arrested because they just didn't have enough proof or witnesses. The FBI gave up on the case and it remained in cold storage until 1991, when a man called Clinton Adams came forward as a witness. He claimed to have seen the lynching when he was just a young boy of ten. He said he had been hiding behind some bushes close to Moore's Ford Bridge and had seen the whole incident. Although the FBI decided to re-open the file, they felt it would probably lead to a dead end because most of the suspects would probably already be dead. Although the case file is not officially closed, it will probably never be proved whether Eugene Talmadge was behind the lynching, although from his track record it looks highly probable.

KEEPING IT IN THE FAMILY

Unlike his father, Herman Talmadge – who also served as governor for Georgia – received notoriety as part of the Senate committee that investigated the Watergate scandal. However, his own problems were contributary to his own downfall in 1980, when he was defeated for re-election. One of his main problems was an alcohol addiction, which spiralled out of control following the death of his son, Bobby, who drowned in 1975. Added to this, and far more destructive to his career, were the allegations of financial misconduct. Herman was charged with accepting more than $43,000 for fabricated expenses. At the time the Talmadges were going through a bitter divorce and his wife, Betty, took pleasure in testifying against her husband before the Senate Ethics Committee.

His reputation was tarnished enough to lose him the general election against Republican Mack Mattingly, after which he more or less retired from the public eye. His health declined in the late 1990s and he died at his home in Hampton, Georgia, on 21 March 2002 at the age of 88.

PART EIGHT

ARISTOCRATIC SCANDALS

RASPUTIN AND THE ROMANOVS

The story regarding the Romanovs really begins in the year 1868, the year that the heir to the Russian throne was born – Nicholas II. For many years Russia had been in a state of upheaval and in the year 1881, Nicholas had the traumatic experience of seeing his beloved grandfather, Alexander II, assassinated right before his very eyes. His carriage was bombed by a group of revolutionaries called the People's Will, and Alexander II was carried unconscious to the Winter Palace in St Petersburg, where family members, including 13-year-old Nicholas, could do nothing except watch him die.

Alexander III had been a liberal tsar, but frightened by his father's death, he became a stern ruler believing in autocracy. Despite seeing his father's oppression of the minorities, especially the Jews, Nicholas grew up to be a shy, gentle and kind young man.

Nicholas met the love of his life when he was 16

years old – Princess Alix of Hesse-Dharmdst. They were first acquainted in 1884 at the wedding of Alix's older sister Ella, who was marrying Nicholas's uncle Sergei. Although Alix was only 12 years old, it was love at first sight when she saw the handsome 16-year-old Nicholas, and it was a meeting neither of them would forget.

Alix, unlike Nicholas, had not had a very happy childhood. Her older brother Freddie died when Alix was just a baby. He was only two years old himself and suffering from haemophilia, so when he fell from a two-storey window he literally bled to death. Alix's mother was Princess Alice, the daughter of Queen Victoria of England. She became very depressed after the death of her son and died herself prematurely at the age of 35 of diptheria, along with Alix's younger sister. After her mother's death, Alix went to live with her adoring grandmother.

Neither Victoria nor the tsar were keen on the relationship between Alix and Nicholas, but when his son continually turned down all other potential wives, Alexander eventually gave in and the couple became engaged in 1894.

Nicholas was not expected to take over the throne for many years, but his father died unexpectedly when Nicholas was only 23. Nicholas was not ready for the position and claimed, 'I am not prepared to be a tsar. I never wanted to become one' and turned to Alix for support. The very next day, Alix converted to Russian Orthodox, and Nicholas made his first decree, proclaiming her new name – Alexandra Feodorovna. One week after his father's funeral, Alexandra and Nicholas were married.

Nicholas and Alexandra enjoyed many happy years of marriage and had four daughters, Olga, Tatiana, Marie and Anastasia. Despite their happiness, the couple still longed for a son, an heir to the Russian throne, and their prayers were finally answered in 1904 with the birth of Alexsei. They were elated, but this joy was to be short-lived, as tragedy struck. Alexsei started bleeding profusely from the naval and Nicholas and Alexandra had to face the truth – he had picked up the haemophilia gene. With her son's life hanging by a thread, Alexandra became fanatical about her religion and turned to a peasant by the name of Gregormo Efimovich Rasputin for help.

RASPUTIN – THE 'MAD MONK'

Rasputin was born in 1869 in Prokovskoe, Siberia, to a peasant family. Despite attending school he was illiterate and chose to join a monastery as soon as he became of age. However, his life in the cloisters was soon blighted when he found the pleasures of the opposite sex and was forced to leave the monastery in disgrace. Rasputin started travelling as a so-called 'faith healer', claiming that he had special powers which enabled him to cure the sick. He lived off the funds given to him by his satisfied customers.

Despite his rather scruffy appearance, Rasputin had a sort of magnetic charm, and it wasn't long before he caught the attention of certain members of the Russian aristocracy. To the tsar and his family, Rasputin was a hero, a holy man and hopefully their son's saviour. They believed he was the only person who could stop Alexsei's bleeding. However, the remainder of Russia saw Rasputin's darker, more sinister side. Out of sight of the royal family Rasputin's behaviour was wild, but in front of Nicholas and his wife his actions were beyond reproach.

Miraculously, the first time the tsar called on Rasputin for help, he was able to stem the bleeding and, as a result, became their hero. He was permitted to socialise in royal circles and was soon showing a powerful influence over Alexandra. Nicholas was not happy with the power Rasputin held over his wife, but scared that his son's health would suffer if he sent the man away, he decided to try and ignore the situation.

As the first storm clouds of World War I loomed over Russia, Nicholas went to the front to take command of his troops against the Germans. Nicholas left his wife in charge of the government, but this was an unwise move as, being German, her subjects felt they were unable to trust her. Rasputin became Alexandra's adviser, which further alienated her with the Russians, and it wasn't long before rumours were spreading that the couple were having an affair. Alexandra truly believed that her son would only remain healthy if Rasputin was around, so she kept him closely by her side, which had a devastating effect. With the government starting to crumble in 1916, a band of conspirators, including several members of the imperial family, decided that something had to be done.

THE DEATH OF RASPUTIN

Using Rasputin's love of women as a lure, the band of conspirators lured him to the Youssoupov palace on the night of 16 December 1916. A splendid banquet had been laid on for Rasputin and the other guests, and the monk was offered some pastries, which he was told had been specially prepared for his benefit. Indeed, they were special – they were laced with lethal amounts of cyanide. Rasputin was delighted and tucked into the pastries with relish. However, the poison, which was supposed to work immediately, didn't seem to be having any effect on the monk. As he laughed and flirted with the women, his assassins became impatient and one of them took a pistol out of his robes and shot him in the back. Rasputin slumped to the floor and, under the impression that he was dead, the conspirators went off to celebrate.

After about an hour, one of the royal party, Prince Felix, went back to make sure that Rasputin was well and truly dead. As he touched the body he noticed that it was still warm, although it showed no other signs of life. As he turned to walk away, however, Rasputin rose to his feet and attempted to strangle the prince. Felix managed to escape the monk's grip and ran off to tell his friends that Rasputin was very much alive.

Rasputin ran across the courtyard after him yelling, 'Felix, Felix, I'll tell everything to the tsarina'. However, before he could finish his sentence he was shot in the back and again in the head. His assailant then struck him with a blow to the head just to make sure that this time Rasputin was dead. When they found that Rasputin was still breathing, the assassins bound his body and threw him into the Neva River, where he died from drowning.

Although Rasputin was dead, the damage that had been done to the image of the imperial family was irreparable. When Nicholas returned from war he was furious that Felix and his conspirators had killed Rasputin and forced them to become exiles. As the

Bolsheviks became more and more powerful, Nicholas's position as tsar became increasingly tenuous and on 17 March 1917, he was forced to abdicate in favour of his brother, Michael Romanov.

CAPTIVITY AND EXECUTION

After a short period of house arrest in Tsarskoe Selo, the imperial family were moved to Tobolsk in Siberia. Their treatment by the guards was appalling; they were rude and threatening and never allowed the young sisters to lock their bedroom doors. It was hoped that the Romanovs would soon be able to escape to England, but their hopes were quelled when King George V, Nicholas's own first cousin, refused to give the family refuge.

The family were later transferred to Ipatiev House in the Russian city of Ekaterinburg. They stayed there for 78 days, but their last day was 16 July 1918. Late in the night the family were woken and told to get dressed. They were led down to the cellar, where they were made to stand in two rows – Nicholas, Alexandra, their four daughters and their faithful servants Dr Botkine, lady-in-waiting Anna Demidova, their cook Kharitonof and footman Troup. Then the men opened fire and the cellar became a scene of chaos and bloodshed.

The assassins did their utmost to destroy the last remains of the royal family and their servants. They threw their bodies down a mine shaft and dropped grenades on top of them. They later removed the bodies from the shaft and either burnt them or doused them with acid. What was left of the corpses were thrown into a pit and buried. For many years the location of the grave was kept a well-guarded secret, for fear of recrimination from the Soviet government. Rumours quickly spread that perhaps one, if not more, of the children had actually survived.

One day after taking power in 1991, the Russian president Boris Yeltsin retrieved the remains and the long identification process began. DNA experts from Russia, Britain and the United States worked for ten years and came to the conclusion that the bones belonged to Nicholas, his wife Alexandra, Olga, Tatiana, Anastasia and their four servants. Only nine of the 11 bodies were ever found and those missing are believed to be Alexsei and either Marie or Anastasia.

ANNA ANDERSON

In the years following the murders of the Romanovs, several people came out of the woodwork claiming to be the missing daughter, Anastasia. The most documented case was that of Anna Anderson. In

February 1920 a woman jumped off a bridge in Berlin. She survived and was taken to a local mental institution, where she refused to give any details of her identity. It wasn't until 18 months later that she claimed to be the Grand Duchess Anastasia. She explained that she had survived the execution because the bayonet the assassin had used on her was blunt. She said one of the soldiers had seen that she was still alive and had rescued her, taking her with him to Romania.

Many people believed that Anderson was an imposter, but Prince Sigismund, a childhood friend of Anastasia, was convinced by many of the answers she gave him. When she was finally released from the hospital in 1922, Anderson lived off the charity of many of her supporters. This annoyed Anastasia's uncle, Grand Duke Ernst of Hesse, who was determined to prove that she was a fraud. Using his own money he backed an investigation to try and prove that Anderson was a Polish factory worker, Franziska Schanzkowska, who had disappeared just before Anderson herself surfaced. His claim was never proved.

In 1938 Anderson decided to take her case to the German court to try and prove her identity and therefore claim her rightful inheritance. The case dragged on until 1970, at which time the court finally ruled that she had not positively proved that she was

Anastasia. The matter was finally put to rest when Anderson died of pneumonia in 1984 and was cremated at her own request.

THE MONTAGU AFFAIR

During the 1940s and 1950s life was made very difficult for gay men and women on both sides of the Atlantic. In America, McCarthy's domestic witch-hunts set out to expose any opposition to the cold war. Anyone who did not fit his straight-laced all-American ideal was therefore seen as dangerous and subversive. Gay men, lesbians, bisexuals and transgendered persons came under this category. They were publicly outed and consequently fired from jobs, redlisted and alienated by their communities in a widespread attack which became known as the 'Lavender Scare'.

INSTITUTIONALISED BIGOTRY

Life was no easier for gay men in the UK. The British establishment was virulently anti-homosexual and the government openly pursued and upheld anti-gay legislation. The British Home Secretary, Sir David Maxwell Fyfe, even promised the public 'a new drive against male vice. . . that would rid England of this plague'.

If a high-ranking politician made such a bigoted statement today, they'd find themselves under caution for inciting hate-crimes! In those days, however, it was completely illegal for men to engage in sexual relations with one another, and a conviction meant a criminal record as well as a prison sentence. Each year up to 1,000 men were locked up in Britain's prisons and policemen routinely roamed the streets as agent provocateurs, posing as gay men in order to lure unsuspecting individuals into soliciting sex from them. They also tapped telephone lines and made searches without the appropriate warrants.

THE DASHING LORD MONTAGU

Edward Douglas Scott Montagu, the third Baron Montagu of Beaulieu was born on 20 October 1926. He inherited his title at the tender age of two when his father was tragically killed in an accident. As a fully-fledged member of the English aristocracy and a direct descendant of King James I, his early life was one of old-fashioned privilege, wealth and respectability. He brushed shoulders with royalty and attended the best public schools that England and it's colonies had to offer, including Broadstairs in Canada, Eton and New College Oxford. But Edward Montagu was a little different from a lot of other boys. He knew from an early age that he was bisexual and he had privately come to terms with the fact. However, it was not until he arrived at Oxford University that he met other gay and bisexual young men.

LIVING THE HIGH-LIFE

As an Oxford graduate and the youngest member of the House of Lords, it did not take long for the elegant and eligible bachelor to become the toast of London town. At 28 years old Montagu was young, attractive, wealthy and titled with an exciting career in public relations and a 'natural affinity for the life of a bon vivant'. He had also fallen in love and become engaged to an American actress and socialite Ann Gage. Things were going swimmingly, but then controversy struck.

A VERY BRITISH SCANDAL

Baron Montagu had lent a portion of his land to a scout troop, when he had his camera stolen. A minor episode in anyone's life. That is unless you happen to be a well known public figure and your camera contains photographs of nubile and partially clothed young men frolicking in the surf! The police were called to investigate the theft, but Montagu was transformed from victim to criminal when a 14-year-old member of the scout troop made an accusation of assault against him. He was tried and eventually cleared – but the authorities were determined to bring him down.

Edward, his cousin; Michael Pitt-Rivers and his friend Peter Wildeblood were soon charged with 'inciting certain male persons to commit serious offences with male persons', the same offence that Oscar Wilde was famously charged with in 1895.

WILD BY NAME, WILD BY NATURE

Peter Wildeblood, a diplomatic correspondent for the *Daily Mail*, met Edward Montagu whilst he was working for a London Personal Relations firm. Montagu later described him as 'a very amusing person, with a good sense of humour, a worthwhile person to spend time with'. However, Wildeblood was also a dangerous person to know because he was openly gay.

In the summer of 1953, Wildeblood borrowed Montagu's beach hut for a holiday. He threw a party on his first night there and invited Montagu and some of his house guests from Beaulieu. The prosecution claimed that Lord Montagu, Pitt-Rivers and Wildeblood encouraged the party to develop into a male orgy. The trial would become a *cause célèbre* which so horrified the British establishment that it changed the course of British history, not to mention the lives of millions of gay men and women, forever.

THE SENSATIONAL TRIAL

The chief witnesses at the trial were RAF servicemen Edward McNally and John Reynolds, who had been present at the beach hut party. The director of public prosecutions had promised them that they would not face prosecution so long as they testified against Pitt-Rivers, Wildeblood and Montagu. The RAF boys admitted in court to dancing together and engaging in 'abandoned behaviour' at the beach hut that evening. McNally also produced love letters that were written to him by Peter Wildeblood, and the letters were read aloud in court. In response, Wildeblood caused a sensation by publicly admitting his homosexuality, but claimed that the evening in question was actually extremely dull and that no such activity took place.

The trial began on 15 March 1954 in the Great Hall of Winchester Castle. It lasted for eight days and although Montagu denied the charges, all three men were convicted and sent to prison. Pitt-Rivers and Wildeblood each got 18 months and Montagu received a 12-month prison sentence.

The police feared a violent reaction outside the courtroom and so they kept the young men behind after sentencing for several hours. When the men were finally brought out, they were greeted by cheering crowds. Public opinion had reached a tipping point. Far from stirring-up public hatred, the trial had inspired sympathy for Montagu, Wildeblood and Pitt-Rivers. They were perceived by many, not as dangerous and corrupting homosexuals, but as victims of a Macarthy-esque witch hunt.

THE WOLFENDEN REPORT

It was as a result of this change in public opinion that the government set up the committee on homosexual offences and prostitution, chaired by Sir John Wolfenden. On 4 September 1957, the Wolfenden report was published. It's primary recommendation was that consensual sex between adult men in private should not be illegal. It took ten years, but eventually homosexuality was decriminalised in Britain. From then on thousands of gay men and women could get on with their lives, free from the threat of prosecution.

THE HOUSE OF WINDSOR

Royalty has always been awash with scandal, which is made all the worse by their high profile and the intense media and public interest. However, it must be said that the House of Windsor does seem to have had more than its fair share of improprieties. The current queen, Elizabeth II, has had to cope with a lot of criticism, and yet she has proved to be a stoical figure who still retains the respect of her people. The behaviour of some of the younger members of her family has often evoked criticism of the monarchy and, at times, brought them close to collapse. Of course, scandal was not confined to the reign of the current queen – royals have long been known for their philandering ways and extravagant lifestyles.

PRINCE OF WALES AND THE ACTRESS

Albert Edward, the Prince of Wales and son of Queen Victoria, and his close circle of friends became known as the 'Marlborough Set' and were considered to be the crowning point of London society. They were the elite and anyone of importance dreamt of being accepted into the prince's circle of friends. Lillie Langtry was the wife of a wealthy merchant, Edward Langtry, who gradually climbed the social ladder by inventing herself as an actress and an entrepreneur. She was intelligent, humorous and fascinated both men and women with her outstanding beauty and was admired by people from all walks of life. Lillie was a highly controversial figure, who had a string of affairs and left many men with a broken heart.

It was inevitable that the prince – 'Bertie' as he was known by his friends – should hear about Lillie and he told his confidantes that he would love to meet the woman with the famous violet eyes. A discreet dinner party was arranged at the home of Sir Allen Young. Some of his closer friends advised against such a meeting as Lillie was married and Bertie himself was married to Princess Alexandra of Denmark, and indeed had five children with her. Despite this fact he refused to give up his bachelor lifestyle and insisted that the meeting went ahead.

Lillie was placed next to the prince while her husband had no choice but to sit at the other end of the dining table. She was overawed at meeting the prince for the first time and it took Lillie quite a while to relax and found it difficult to get the words out. She was impressed by his sense of humour and the kindness he showed her, and it soon became obvious that Bertie was infatuated with the woman with the witty tongue and stunning face.

Not long after the first meeting, the prince and Lillie were seen out riding together in Hyde Park and, although this wasn't an unusual occurrence, on this occasion the prince had become completely infatuated with his companion. It soon became obvious to both Lillie's husband and the princess that the prince and Lillie were having an affair, and yet they both chose to accept the fact gracefully. This gave way to a period of blissful liaisons between 1877 and 1878, when they were both given the time to enjoy each other's company. Bertie was so obsessed with Lillie that he even had a house specially built in Bournemouth, where they could share intimate time together.

Lillie would only have to ask and the prince would oblige and so, when she requested to have an audience with the queen, Bertie arranged a meeting. Although it is suggested that Victoria was somewhat frosty towards Lillie, it did open new doors with regards to her social life. She was invited to all the finest gatherings and soon her close circle of friends included such notable people as Oscar Wilde and the painter Whistler, both of whom helped her climb the ladder of fame. However, the spell was soon broken when the cost of Lillie's high life was affecting the Langtry's financial status. Lillie's simple black dresses had been replaced by expensive haute couture and although Bertie had always been generous with his gifts, he had never given his lover money. Then came another stumbling block – the arrival of another stunning woman in London. Sarah Bernhardt was a French stage actress who had made her fame in Europe in the 1870s. The prince greeted Sarah with great enthusiasm and was soon under her charms, Lillie had quickly fallen from favour.

As soon as the rumours started spreading that the affair between Lillie and the prince was starting to lose its sparkle, the creditors moved in on the Langtrys. In October 1880 Edward Langtry was declared bankrupt. Lillie was heartbroken and embarrassed and sought solace in the arms of Bertie's younger cousin, Prince Louis of Battenberg. It wasn't long before Lillie discovered that she was expecting the young prince's child and immediately the royal house closed its ranks and sent Louis off to serve in the navy.

Lillie was moved away from London to try and avoid a major scandal and she rented a cottage outside St Helier on the island of Jersey. With Edward away on his travels, Lillie hoped that she could go through her pregnancy without attracting too much attention, but in such a small community it was impossible to keep it a secret. Although Bertie had not seen Lillie for many months, when he heard the news that she was pregnant he quickly came to her aid. He sent two men from Buckingham Palace to accompany her to Paris, where she stayed in an apartment belonging to one of the prince's closest friends.

Lillie gave birth to Jeanne-Marie in March 1881, and after a brief spell at playing 'mum' she decided that she missed the bright lights of London and placed her daughter in the care of her own mother in Bournemouth. With no money and a husband who was permanently away, Lillie had to find a way of earning a living and, at the suggestion of Oscar Wilde, she tried her hand at acting. It wasn't long before she was back on her feet and an accomplished actress.

Although the real father of Lillie's child was never revealed, when her husband eventually found out from a newspaper article that his wife had had a baby in San Francisco, he fell to pieces and had to be committed to a mental asylum.

EDWARD AND MRS SIMPSON

Although Bertie's affair with Lillie Langtry did nothing to threaten the monarchy, when Edward

VIII had an affair with an American divorcee, his infatuation cost him the crown.

Bessie Wallis Warfield always dreamed of becoming a debutante, but the bright lights of London's socialites always seemed to elude her. She grabbed the first opportunity to escape her hometown of Baltimore by marrying a naval pilot, Earl Winfield Spencer, but it was a disaster from the start. Wallis was unable to put up with her husband's moods ,which were exacerbated by a drink problem, and so after a short while she found herself a single woman once more.

Wallis married again in 1928 to a man named Ernest Simpson, who headed the London office of his wealthy family's shipping business. At last Wallis was to get to live in London and quickly became a hit on the social circuit. She became the hostess with the mostest and entertained lords, ladies, dukes and duchesses, all of whom she charmed with her amazing confidence.

The dinner party that was to change her life took place in December 1930. It was hosted by Wallis Simpson in her own home and her illustrious guests were Benjamin Thaw (first secretary of the US embassy in London), his wife Consuelo and her sister Thelma, Viscountess of Furness. Lady Furness was not only stunningly beautiful, but she was also the subject of a well-kept secret. She was the mistress of the Prince of Wales, the future king of England. Wallis, Thelma and Consuelo became close friends and Wallis was soon privy to the intimacies of Thelma's life.

Wallis, despite her popularity, had never met the Prince of Wales and she told her friends that she would love to meet him. Her wish came true when she eventually met him at a house party held by his mistress in Melton Mowbray, Leicestershire. As soon as she set eyes on Edward, Wallis was charmed and she knew if she could woo him, it would take her to the next level in her social life. Using intimate knowledge she had learned from Thelma, Wallis started to use her charms and seduce the most eligible bachelor in the world.

Soon the Simpsons became regular guests at the prince's country retreat, and Edward was also a frequent visitor to the Simpsons's home. Unaware that her so-called 'friend' had designs on her lover, Thelma confided in Wallis that she was off to the United States and asked her if she would look after the prince while she was away. And look after him she certainly did – by the time Thelma returned from her trip Edward and Wallis were already lovers.

Edward was not a particularly strong man and he loved the strength he found in Wallis. Wallis, in return, doted on the prince, realising that with him she had reached her pinnacle of social status. The prince threw all caution to the wind and started to display his mistress quite openly in public, while the press tried their hardest to keep the news under wraps to avoid a scandal. By January 1936 Edward had become king and his love for Wallis was something that he was not prepared to give up. The Simpson marriage cracked under the strain of the royal affair and Wallis sought for divorce.

Shortly before the death of his father, Edward had spoken to the prime minister, Stanley Baldwin, informing him of Wallis's intention to seek a divorce from her husband. As head of the Church of England, Edward was forbidden from marrying a divorced woman and Baldwin was horrified. It was one thing to turn a blind eye to the king's affair with a married woman, but with a divorcee it was a completely different ball game. Baldwin begged the king to get Wallis to reconsider her situation, but the king replied that he had 'no rights to interfere with the affairs of an individual' and the prime minister realised that he had a very difficult situation on his hands.

For a while the king was allowed to carry on his affair, but the situation changed when he was chastised by Dr Blunt, the Bishop of Bradford, for his carefree lifestyle when storm clouds were gathering over Europe. The newspapers chose to break their code of silence and the affair made headline news.

Edward had made it quite clear that he wanted to marry Wallis and place her on the throne by his side, and foolishly he believed that his people would come round to his way of thinking. Wallis became the target of a hate campaign and had to suffer bricks and stones being hurled through the windows of her London apartment. Meanwhile, Edward was hopelessly in love with Wallis and seemed unable to perform even the simplest of duties. He started turning up late for appointments or cancelled them at the last minute. An emergency meeting was held at Buckingham Palace, aware that there would be no easy way to get Edward to give up Wallis Simpson.

The king was now faced with three options: he either had to give up Wallis; keep Wallis and face the resignation of his entire government; or abdicate and give up the throne. After a discussion with his beloved Wallis, Edward decided that he had no option but to abdicate. Edward signed the papers that ended his rule at 10.00 a.m. on 10 December 1936, surrounded by his three surviving brothers. The next in line for the throne was his brother, who became King George VI.

Edward and Wallis married in a simple ceremony on 3 June 1937 and, with a gift bestowed by his brother the king, Edward was allowed the keep the family name of Windsor so that he became the Duke of Windsor and Wallis the Duchess.

Following the abdication, the Duke and Duchess were exiled from Great Britain and, although many people believed it would only be for a few years, the exile lasted for the remainder of their lives.

Edward died on 28 May 1972 at the age of 77, while Wallis lived for another 14 years still secluded from the rest of the world. She died on 24 April 1986 at the age of 89.

PRINCESS MARGARET AND
FORBIDDEN LOVE

Margaret, born on 21 August 1930, was a beautiful child who was full of personality and born to shine. Had she not been born into a royal line she could have pursued her true passions in life, but as a member of the House of Windsor she was made to tow the line and give up her one true love.

Much of Margaret's childhood was spent at Windsor Castle during the harsh years of World War II. To try and relieve some of the boredom she devised practical jokes and as she reached her teenage years loved to flirt with the soldiers. She was wilful, spirited and charming, a stark contrast to her more dutiful and staid older sister, Elizabeth. She was very affectionate and able to wrap her father round her little finger. At the age of 16 Margaret was invited to go on a tour of the Commonwealth with the rest of her family and seeing her father's health take a turn for the worse, suddenly made her realise the role she was expected to play as a member of the royal family.

Accompanying the family on the tour was a man named Group Captain Peter Townsend, a loyal servant who knew he had an important role to play in protecting the royal family. He was 16 years older than Margaret, married with two sons, and at the time paid no particular attention to the younger of the two sisters. Margaret was thoroughly enjoying the tour and took full advantage of all the world had to offer.

Margaret's father, King George VI, died in his sleep on 6 February 1952, about five years after their tour of the Commonwealth. Margaret, who was 21 at the time, was devastated by his death, something which she never fully recovered from. The Queen Mother appointed Peter Townsend as comptroller of the household, a position which meant he had considerable contact with Margaret. With Margaret still reeling from the loss of her father and Townsend struggling over the failure of his marriage, the couple found increasing solace in each other's company. When Townsend was finally divorced he was given custody of their two sons. In 1953 Townsend accepted his next royal assignment, this time at Sandringham. It was during this time that the relationship with Margaret really developed and they declared their love for one another. However, being older and wiser, Townsend was aware that the relationship was doomed, realising that it would not be accepted by the all-powerful 'establishment'. Until Margaret was 25, she would need the queen's permission to marry and after that she would also require Parliament's as well. Her uncle, Edward VIII, had been forced to abdicate and she knew full well that this would still be fresh in their minds.

Aware of the delicate situation, Margaret and Townsend managed to keep their love affair secret for the next few months. It wasn't until her sister's coronation on 2 June 1953 that a reporter noticed a rather familiar behaviour between the couple. After that they were caught on more than one occasion recklessly frolicking and showing careless intimacy. They became virtually inseparable and yet they were aware all the time that they were living on borrowed time. Aware that Margaret's love affair was scanda-lous, Prime Minister Winston Churchill intervened by sending Margaret on a tour of Rhodesia with her mother. Townsend was sent on an assignment to Belgium the day before Margaret was due to return to England. It was hoped that their affection would cool during his absence, but they didn't account for the old adage 'absence makes the heart grow stronger'. Despite the obstacles put in their way, the pair managed to keep their love alive with letters, long-distance phone calls and liaisons at houses of loyal friends. Churchill made it clear that parliament would not allow them to marry under any circumstances and Margaret knew she was faced with a tough decision. If she gave up her life as a royal she felt Townsend would feel forever guilty for not providing her with the same standard of living. Reluctantly, they came to the decision to end the relationship and Townsend helped Margaret write her 'official' letter of decision.

I would like it to be known that I have decided not to marry Group Captain Townsend. I have been aware that, subject to my renouncing my rights of succession, it might have been possible for me to contract a civil marriage. But mindful of the Church's teachings that Christian marriage is indissoluble, and conscious of my duty to the Commonwealth, I have resolved to put these considerations before others. I have reached the decision entirely alone and in doing so I have been strengthened by the unfailing support and devotion of Group Captain Peter Townsend. I am deeply grateful for the concern of all those who have constantly prayed for my happiness.

For Margaret, she had lost the two men she truly loved in quick succession and somehow her eyes lost a lot of their original sparkle. She made the very painful decision to put duty and family in front of the desires of her heart.

Margaret married photographer Anthony Armstrong-Jones (bestowed with the title Earl of Snowden and Viscount Linley by the queen) on 6 May 1960. Many believed that Margaret never truly recovered from her broken heart, and although the marriage lasted 16 years, it was often the subject of controversy. After their divorce Margaret lost much of her former vitality, and ill health forced her to scale down many of her public engagements. Suffering from repeated bouts of depression and several strokes, Margaret died on 9 February 2002, a very much loved member of the House of Windsor.

A DASHING PRINCE

Prince Andrew was born on 19 February 1960, the third child and second son of Queen Elizabeth II and Prince Philip. Even during his school years at Gordonstoun, Andrew was the subject of several romantic rumours, resulting in the tabloids giving him the nickname 'Randy Andy'. Having been described as the most dashing, daring and handsome of the

Queen's sons, it is not surprising that he had a stream of girlfriends, but none caused the same sensation as his affair with a soft-porn star called Koo Stark.

When Andrew had completed his A-levels in 1979 he joined the Royal Navy and quickly saw active service. His squadron was scheduled to sail to the Falkland Islands on HMS *Invincible*, from where he flew missions in Sea Kings. In 1997 Andrew took a desk job in the Ministry of Defence and finally retired from the Navy in July 2001.

Already being headlined as the ladies' favourite, it was no surprise when he was seen out with a stunning brunette. The girl in question was Koo Stark, the daughter of film producer Wilbur Stark, with a promising career ahead of her in films and as a photographer. Koo is thought to have met Andrew at a party held by writer Nigel Dempster, and the chemistry was there right from the start.

Andrew was smitten and introduced his new girl-friend to the queen and the queen mother at Balmoral and she was an instant hit, particularly with Prince Philip, who always had an eye for a pretty lady. However, she quickly fell out of favour with the royal family when they learned of Koo's involvement in soft-porn films in 1977, called *Emily* and *Cruel Passion*. Her relationship with Prince Andrew was quickly worldwide news – after all it's not every day that one of the queen's sons goes out with an actress who has been seen doing naughty things on film.

The family immediately put pressure on Andrew to end the affair, but the prince was besotted and found it hard to let go. They wrote impassioned letters to each other and talked about their future together, but deep down they both knew their relationship was doomed. Koo's past had caused too much of a stir in the Windsor family, and under direct orders from the queen, Andrew reluctantly ended the affair in 1983. He was banned from having any contact with Koo, and the telephone operators at Buckingham Palace were told not to put any calls from her through to the prince. Although it caused a minor scandal in the House of Windsor at the time, had they realised what major waves one Sarah Ferguson would cause later on, they would probably have gladly accepted Koo into their family circle.

Andrew and Sarah Ferguson had been childhood friends because her father was the manager of Prince Charles's polo team. In 1985 Sarah was invited to a house party at Windsor Castle to celebrate the Royal Ascot horse races, and it is believed that the romance started that same week. By March 1986 they were engaged and on 23 July 1986 they were married in Westminster Abbey. Many believed the couple were still feeling the effects of previous love affairs –

Andrew for Koo Stark and Sarah for a former racing driver Paddy McNally. Despite this the crowds turned out to see the wedding of the year and 500 million television viewers tuned in to see the latest royal love match. Everyone was happy that the dashing prince had settled down at last and the beautiful red-haired princess had captured his heart.

However, after the initial excitement of a new relationship, the couple started to have problems. Andrew loved his life in the services and missed the excitement when he was home, and his periods away from Fergie, as she was affectionately known, became longer and longer. In 1987 he went back to sea on HMS *Edinburgh,* which drove an even deeper wedge between the couple.

To try and get over the loneliness, Fergie took to travelling around the world in a rather carefree manner and initially the press were kind to her. However, she soon became the subject of criticism – her clothes, her weight, her personality all made her a worldwide laughing-stock. She became miserable and despite frequent requests to be allowed to live like other military couples, the Windsors would not allow it for security reasons. Fergie threw herself into charity work and even learned to fly a helicopter to try and win favour with her husband, but the rift grew deeper.

While her own world was falling apart, Fergie was

unaware that her father, Major Ron Ferguson, had secrets of his own. In May 1988 he was exposed by a Sunday newspaper as being a frequent visitor to a massage parlour who offered 'extra services' for those who wanted it. Although the royal family supported the major, Andrew then had his own doubts that he had chosen the wrong person to be his wife.

When their first daughter, Beatrice, was born in 1988, it not only took the pressure off her father's scandalous behaviour, but it also seemed to briefly reunite the royal couple. Their second daughter, Eugenie, was born in 1990, but to Fergie's dismay it did not keep Andrew at home – it appeared that the sea was still his first love. Once again Fergie's behaviour was plastered all over the front pages of the tabloids, knocking her for her frumpy image compared to the beauty and style of her rival Princess Diana.

Downhearted and feeling badly treated by both the press and the royal family, Fergie sought for affection elsewhere. Fergie first met Texan businessman Steve Wyatt in Houston, Texas, in 1989, while she was pregnant with her second child. She immediately fell under his spell and after that the couple made love whenever and wherever they could. Wyatt was heir to an oil fortune and owned his own private jet, and the couple had romantic holidays in Morocco and the south of France. They threw caution to the wind, not afraid to be seen together and even romped in the gardens of 'Southyork', the mansion Fergie shared with Andrew in Sunninghill, Berkshire.

However, the holiday in France came back to haunt Fergie when 120 photographs of the two of them together were mysteriously found in a London apartment and then printed in a daily newspaper. For Andrew it was the final straw and he told the queen that he wanted to get out of the marriage, adding that it had been a mistake right from the start. Although the queen tried her hardest to get the couple to reconcile their differences, her efforts fell on stony ground – little did she know there was much worse to come.

Fergie had turned to writing, and published a series of children's books about *Budgie the Helicopter*. Despite their success, the Duchess found herself heavily in debt as a result of her jet-set lifestyle. In 1992 Fergie had a new man in her life, John Bryan, who called himself her 'financial adviser'. Although he was advising Fergie about her finances, it soon became evident that he was offering other more personal services and once again the panic button went off in Buckingham Palace. In August 1992 Fergie and Bryan went away together with the children to a villa in the south of France. Unbeknown to them, a cunning member of the French paparazzi had hidden in the bushes at the edge of the villa and managed to capture them in compromising positions. He took photographs of Fergie going topless by the pool and also, more incriminating, one of Bryan sucking the duchess's big toe. All this took place not only in front of the two young girls, Beatrice and Eugenie, but also in the presence of two bodyguards. Rather a funny way of managing Fergie's finances!

Andrew and the royal family reeled in discomfort from the press releases, and Fergie's already low status was now at rock bottom. It was the final straw and Fergie was seen leaving Balmoral in her car, banished from the House of Windsor.

A few months later, Major Ferguson added to the misery with another exposé, this time from his previous involvement with a 26-year-old stable-girl called Lesley Player. She had written a book about her affair with the major and also given explicit details about Fergie's romps with Steve Wyatt.

To add even more fuel to an already raging fire, John Bryan gave book publishers a taste of excerpts from diaries he claimed to have kept during his four-year affair with Fergie. Royal insiders were convinced that it was a ploy to exert pressure on Fergie to get cash out of her, and the queen's advisers were put under pressure to hand over money so that Fergie could buy her ex-lover's silence.

The couple's divorce finally became official in April

1996, and Andrew and Fergie were given joint custody of their children. However, despite the major rift and everything that has happened over the years, the couple have amazingly managed to stay friends and in 2004 Fergie was photographed with the queen for the first time in over a decade. Seemingly, that was one series of scandals that the royal family were able to put behind them.

PRINCESS ANNE

Princess Anne was born in 1950 and is the second child and only daughter of Queen Elizabeth and Prince Philip. She was given the title princess royal by her mother in June 1987 and it could be said that she is the most austere of the queen's children. She is known to have a temper and will not suffer fools gladly, and she has made it plain on more than one occasion that she will not put up with media prying into her private life. Cameramen have often been the brunt of her sharp tongue and she soon gained herself the reputation of being a frosty royal.

After a string of boyfriends, Anne finally settled down and married Captain Mark Phillips at Westminster Abbey on 14 November 1973 with all the usual pomp and ceremony. Phillips was a lieutenant and later captain in the 1st Queen's

Dragoon Guards and was considered to be an ideal match for the princess royal, being described as a 'tweedie' sort with a love for countryside pursuits.

The following year Anne was the target of a failed kidnapping, and to this day remains the closest any individual has come to abducting a member of the British royal family. The incident occurred on 20 March 1974, when Anne and her husband were returning to Buckingham Palace after a local charity event. Their car was forced to stop by a man driving a Ford Escort, who jumped from his car and started firing a gun. Anne's private detective responded with amazing speed and jumped out to shield the princess. However, his gun jammed and he was shot in the head and chest. Their chauffeur was also shot as he tried to disarm the man. Anne managed to dive out of the car on the far side and the gunman was eventually stopped by a passer-by who punched him in the back of the head. The man who attempted the kidnap was Ian Ball, who doctors later judged to be mentally unstable.

With the knowledge that Anne loved the country, the queen bought the couple their own mansion at Gatcombe Park in Gloucestershire, where Anne's two children Peter and Zara were born. Although the public saw Anne leading the idyllic life, in reality domestic life in the country disagreed with her. She became bored, not satisfied as her role as wife and mother. She threw herself into her work as a representative of the royal family and made a name for herself with her charity work. For the first time there was a chink in the armour, allowing the people to see the human side of a person who truly cared about what was happening around the world. However, with this new-found fame came the whispers of marital problems.

The problem first came to light when Anne and Mark were attending the Olympic games as part of the equestrian team. They no longer shared the same bedroom and it became obvious that they barely tolerated one another. It wasn't until the disclosure of a former royal bodyguard that anyone realised just quite how serious their differences had become.

Peter Cross was Anne's former minder and in 1985 he threatened to sell his story that he had had a 'special relationship' with Anne. He intimated that she was in love with him but the royal family managed to weather the storm because he was soon exposed as a man who had had numerous affairs. Despite this the marriage between Anne and Mark did not survive the scandal, and the couple only stayed together allegedly for the sake of the children and the reputation of the royal family.

In 1986 Timothy Lawrence was employed by the queen as an equerry. He a tall and handsome naval officer who not only caught the eye of the princess royal but also stole her heart. Unhappy in her marriage, the new man in her life seemed to bring back some of her old sparkle. The world, however, did not learn about the attraction between Anne and Commander Lawrence until 1989. A number of letters written by the commander to Anne had been stolen out of his suitcase and sent to *The Sun* newspaper. For some reason the paper decided not to print the contents of the letters and returned them to Anne, averting yet another crisis in the royal family.

Shortly afterwards Buckingham Palace released a statement that Anne and Mark were to separate, but with no plans for a divorce. The couple remained friends, but there was still more trouble ahead. In March 1991 Heather Tonkin, a 40-year-old teacher from New Zealand, claimed that Captain Mark Phillips was the father of her six-year-old child and launched a paternity suit against him. She alleged that she had received several thousand pounds in maintenance money, which had been cleverly disguised as equestrian fees but wanted more knowing that Mark was about to receive a tidy sum following his separation from Anne. Although the paternity suit was eventually dropped, it is believed that the matter was settled out of court to save any further scandal.

Princess Ann became the second member of the

royal family, after Margaret, to get divorced. It was all finalised on 13 April 1992. On 12 December 1992 the princess royal married Timothy Lawrence in a small family ceremony at a modest parish church in Crathie, Scotland. Exchanging vows that they would stay together until 'death do us part' may now seem to be just meaningless words, as rumours that Princess Anne and Commander Laurence were leading separate lives surfaced in 2001.

DAUGHTER OF AN SS MEMBER

Princess Michael of Kent is the youngest child of the late Baron Günther von Reibnitz and Countess Szapary. She is a descendant of four European monarchs on both sides of her family. The princess gradually climbed the social ladder but it wasn't until she moved to the United Kingdom that she really received any recognition. Her marriage to an Old Etonian banker lasted only a few years, but it did introduce her to an exclusive London set, which included Prince Michael of Kent.

When the news broke of Marie Christine von Reibtnitz's engagement to Prince Michael of Kent, the queen is said to have commented: 'She sounds far too grand for us', and the Catholic divorcee claimed she didn't receive a very warm welcome. Since her marriage to the prince in 1978, the princess has not been scared to speak her mind, describing the decor at Windsor Castle as 'awful' and also that the queen's corgies 'should be shot!'. Princess Anne reportedly nicknamed her 'Princess Pushy', a term that has been mercilessly used by the press whenever the opportunity arises.

The princess's reputation was taken down a further notch when it was revealed that her father had been a member of Hitler's notorious SS. Apparently he had been one of Hitler's servants, those men who were responsible for the death of many prisoners of war and civilians in the Nazi's evil death camps. Although there is no evidence that her father was actually involved in the genocide or the atrocial medical experiments carried out by the SS, he did join voluntarily and was closely connected with the SS 'Lebensborn' programme. This project was one of the most secret and perhaps terrifying of the Nazi programmes. The goal was to coax girls of 'racially pure' origin to have babies in secret, which would then be given to the SS to raise, in an effort to produce the perfect race. When the news broke it hit royalists hard and there was a public outcry. The idea that someone could enter the House of Windsor with a father who had been a member of the SS was simply unthinkable. Buckingham Palace called an immediate meeting between the queen and Princess Michael.

Advised by her minister, the queen decided there should be no recriminations or disgrace, and told the princess that she could not be blamed for the actions of her father. Princess Michael publicly spoke on television the following day saying:

> *Here I am, 40 years old, and I suddenly discover something that is really quite unpleasant. I shall just simply have to live with it.*

It was indeed a great blow for the princess who had always worshipped her father like a hero. However, she did go on to say that she had a document that proved his membership of the Black Guard was purely honorary, adding that he never actually wore a uniform. Princess Michael did manage to survive the scandal, but she continues to be outspoken and often makes herself very unpopular. A recent event in the United States did nothing for the reputation of the royal family when she turned to some roudy black diners in a New York restaurant and said "You need to go back to the colonies!' Of course the princess vehemently denies she ever made such a racist remark. It appears that Princess Michael of Kent will always be famous for outspokenness, even down to defending Prince Harry recently for wearing a Nazi costume as a fancy dress. Which is ironic, considering the revelations about father.

CHARLES AND DIANA

The House of Windsor has certainly seen its fair share of inglorious days, but the scandal that rocked it to the very core was the divorce of Prince Charles and Princess Diana.

When Charles, the Queen's eldest son, announced in 1981 that he was engaged to a kindergarten teacher of aristocratic birth, it rekindled the public's interest in the British monarchy. The fact that she was 12 years his junior and someone with a spotless past was cause for a national celebration and Lady Diana Spencer immediately became the public's sweetheart. With her coy looks and complete look of innocence, it was felt that she was a wise and suitable choice to act as Prince Charles's royal ambassador and Buckingham Palace were delighted. The wedding would hopefully improve their long-suffering reputation after a spell of recent transgressions and scandals. Diana was the daughter of one of the queen's oldest friends, the Earl of Spencer, and also the younger sister of one of Charles's previous girlfriends, Sarah Spencer. Diana proudly showed off her engagement ring which was white gold with an oval sapphire in the middle and 14 diamonds round the outside. Her face was lit up with excitement and expectation, but little did she know what torment lay ahead of her.

On 29 July 1981 over 600,000 people crowded the route that Diana took from Buckingham Palace to London's St Paul's Cathedral, and a further estimated 750 million people followed the fairytale wedding on their television screens. There was an air of excitement everywhere: for the first time in 300 years an English girl was betrothed to a British heir to the throne. It was indeed the wedding of the century with Diana riding in a glass coach; Britain had never seen such extravaganza. Diana waved and smiled to her fans, but it was more the wave of a film star than someone who was about to become a member of the royal family. In the House of Windsor everything had to be far more discreet and this was a painful lesson she was soon to learn.

Buckingham Palace and its loyal followers were delighted when Diana gave birth to the first of their two sons, William Arthur Philip Louis on 21 June 1982. Her natural aptitude towards motherhood not only delighted her new family, but was greeted with delight by her adoring public who were not used to such a hands-on approach by a member of the royal family. However, by the time their second son, Harry, was born two years later, details of their not-so-happy marriage had become public knowledge. There were even rumours that Harry was not Charles's son and cruel headlines ran the story 'An heir and a spare', intimating that he was the result of some illicit liaison. There is no doubt that they had both been unfaithful to each other. Charles, who had been quite open about his long-term love affair with Camilla Parker-Bowles, who was the wife of one of his dearest friends, was not prepared to stop seeing her even after his betrothal to Diana. He had been in love with Camilla since he had been a young man of 23 and it would appear that nothing would sway his affections. Diana, who it is believed truly loved Charles at the beginning, almost called the wedding off when she discovered an expensive bracelet intended for Camilla to show her where his true affections lay.

Diana cleverly hid from her public the torment she must have been going through. No one except her closest associates were aware of the emotional breakdowns and suicide attempts that went on behind closed doors. Diana was a people person and she resolved that she would not let her unhappy marriage be her undoing. Instead she threw herself into her royal duties: touring the Commonwealth; visiting drug abuse centres; inspecting troops; visiting hospitals where lepers were being treated and became a patron of the National AIDS Trust among hundreds of other official duties. She became the people's princess and she was adored wherever she went.

The news that all was not well was met with shock horror when a tell-all biography of Diana's private life of hell hit the shelves in 1992. The palace had tried their hardest to hide the ever-widening divide between the prince and princess, but now it had become public knowledge and there was worse to come. British intelligence, aware that the news was out, decided to release to a London newspaper a taped telephone conversation between Diana and one of her close male friends, James Gilbey. *The Sun*'s reporters knew they were sitting on dynamite and on 14 August the so-called 'Squidgy' tapes were splashed all over the tabloid. The next day they offered a phone line for the public to listen to them – they received over 60,000 calls. They listened to Gilbey passionately declaring his love for the princess in which he lovingly referred to her as his 'squidgy'.

Still reeling from the scandal of the tape, the realm then had to face a counter-attack that sent more shockwaves through Buckingham Palace. In September 1992 an Australian publication printed a transcript from an alleged sexually explicit telephone conversation between Charles and Camilla, in which Charles said something about wishing he was a tampon so that he could be inside her. This latest revelation left the prince and princess with no other choice but to give the prime minister leave to announce their official separation.

Added to the already considerable misery of their dirty laundry being washed in public, the House of Windsor had to face another disaster before the end of 1992. On the night of 21 November a fierce fire raged through Windsor Castle, threatening one of the world's greatest collections of art. It took 250 firefighters 15 hours and 1.5 million gallons of water to douse the flames, while the queen and the duke of York desperately helped rescue priceless works of art. Over 100 rooms were damaged in the fire, which in itself became the topic of an intense public debate. As the castle was owned by the British government and not the royal family, it meant that the taxpayer would have to meet the £40 million restoration fee. However, to settle the dispute the queen agreed to meet 70 per cent of the costs and opened Buckingham Palace to the public to try and generate extra funds. The queen was visibly distressed by everything that had taken place in 1992 and described it has her *Annus Horribilis*, which no one can deny was a most miserable year for the Windsor family.

For a while Diana withdrew from the public eye and her official duties but it wouldn't be long before she was back making headline news. In June 1994 Prince Charles agreed to a television documentary in which he admitted he had committed adultery. In October the same year three more new tomes arrived on the shelves of high street bookshops, detailing the obvious sham of Charles's and Diana's marriage. One of the damning books was a memoir by life guard officer James Hewitt, who claimed he had had a torrid five-year affair with Princess Diana.

In November 1995 Diana decided to come forward with her side of the story, and in an interview on a BBC news show, *Panorama*, she openly admitted that it was Charles's on-going affair with Camilla that had led to her health problems and the eventual downfall of the marriage, and that it was true about her affair with James Hewitt. She added at the end, and probably to the delight of all her fans, that she did not intend to 'go quietly'.

With the foundations of Buckingham Palace visibly cracking, a British bookmaker set odds at 5:1 that the monarchy would collapse by the turn of the century. In the meantime, it was the messy job of the royal solicitors to try and work out some sort of amical agreement to release Charles and Diana from their marriage vows. In July 1996 everything was finalised and although, technically speaking, Diana would no longer be a member of the royal family, she would be allowed to keep the title of the princess of Wales and some of the royal perks that went with it. It went without saying that she would still have a major say in the raising of her two sons.

Diana definitely left the palace a much stronger and wiser woman, and with a $26 million settlement to boot. Her name and pictures were always splashed all over the newspapers, whether it was to do with her constant charitable endeavours or her personal affairs. She openly admitted that the constant intrusion by the press affected her deeply and that had it not been for her two sons, she would have left her native country a long time ago.

No one could believe it when the news broke on 13 August 1997 that Diana and her latest beau, million-aire Dodi Fayed, had been killed in a car crash in a Paris tunnel. The chauffeur of the Mercedes car was also killed as a result of being pursued at high speed by paparazzi on motorbikes. Although Diana was cut from the wreckage and rushed to hospital, doctors were unable to save her life. The whole of Britain went into shock and hundreds of mourners gathered at the princess's London home of Kensington palace to lay flowers at the gates. Diana's bodyguard, Trevor Rees-Jones survived the crash and tests later showed that the driver, Henri Paul, had taken both drugs and quite a large amount of alcohol just prior to the accident.

In the period when Britain was mourning the loss of their princess, some members of the royal family were criticised for their visible lack of concern, which once again showed the monarchy in a poor light. There has been much controversy and conspiracy theories regarding the death of Princess Diana and today the matter has never been truly resolved. There is no doubt she will never be forgotten for as Tony Blair so rightly said 'People everywhere . . . they liked her, they loved her, they regarded her as one of the people.'

HOUSE OF GRIMALDI

There was a time when Monaco was little more than an unwelcoming rocky peninsula, but today it is a thriving principality thanks to the ancient sovereign House of Grimaldi. Monte Carlo, the main city of Monaco, is today best known for the chink of the chips on the gambling tables and the beautiful women basking on its sun-kissed beaches. Much of Monaco's current popularity is due to the marriage of its ruler, Prince Rainier, to the beautiful Hollywood actress Grace Kelly. A fairytale wedding, a beautiful castle, and three children – and yet the House of Grimaldi had its fair share of scandal.

GRACE KELLY AND THE PRINCE

Grace Kelly was born on 12 November 1929 into the family of a self-made millionaire, so money was never a problem throughout her life. She attended a Catholic school, but against her parent's wishes pursued a career in acting. She graduated from the

American Academy of Dramatic Arts in New York and quickly received not only television parts but offers from Hollywood. Her first movie was *Fourteen Hours* (1951), where she played only a minor role, but her first major picture came the following year with *High Noon*, in which she played the young bride of a sheriff played by Gary Cooper. After that the offers flooded in, and in 1954 she appeared in an incredible five films, taking the leading role in each one. This was to be the year that changed Grace Kelly's life completely. She won Best Actress Award for her part in *The Country Girl* and after attending the Oscars in Hollywood, flew to the south of France to attend the Cannes film festival.

Grace met the wealthiest bachelor in the world, Prince Rainier, at the Cannes film festival in May 1955, when she was asked to be photographed next to him for the magazine *Paris Match*. She was 26 years old and he was just coming up to his 32nd birthday. After the photo shoot, the prince invited Grace back to his gardens and the first sparks of a romance were kindled. By December that year, their engagement was announced with a wedding scheduled for April 1956. However, before the wedding could go ahead the prince made several harsh demands. He wanted a substantial dowry from the Kelly family, and after much haggling they finally agreed to pay $2,000,000.

Grace was also required to take a fertility test; Rainier's previous girlfriend had proved to be infertile and he subsequently broke off the engagement. Grace also had to give up her career in films and finally had to sign an agreement to relinquish any rights to their children should the relationship end in divorce.

Grace's last film was a remake of the 1940s *The Philadelphia Story* and having tied up any loose ends in the United States, she set sail for France to join her fiance. Their engagement had already caused a lot of interest in the media and Monaco was buzzing, waiting to catch sight of their new princess. Grace, her family and 50 of her friends arrived on 4 April 1956 on board the USS *Constitution*. The prince's yacht sailed out of the harbour to pick them up and take them back to the beautiful, pink, 235-roomed palace high on the hills of Monaco overlooking the Mediterranean Sea.

The first part of the wedding ceremony took place on 18 April in the throne room of the palace. It was a civil ceremony, which was required by Monegasque law. The religious ceremony took place the following day in St Nicholas Church. Because Grace had been forced to break her seven-year contract with MGM studios, they were given the rights to film the wedding, which was to be later released as a movie. The wedding was a stunning spectacle with Grace looking every part the princess. Guests at the wedding included Cary Grant, Aga Khan, Gloria Swanson, David Niven, Aristotle Onassis, Ava Gardner and several heads of state and diplomats.

Officially now Her Serene Highness Princess Grace of Monaco, Grace and her new husband sailed off in his luxurious yacht the *Deo Juvante II* with stops in Villegranche, Spain and Corsica. On arriving back from the honeymoon, Grace found out that she was pregnant and although she struggled with her new lifestyle for a while, she threw herself into renovating the palace and creating a brand new nursery. Princess Caroline was born on 23 January 1957 and the prince and his subjects were delighted to have an heir to secure their principality. Prince Albert was born a year later on 14 March and Princess Stephanie seven years later on 1 February 1965. Grace was a devoted mother and an exceedingly popular princess, but like most families the raising of children proved to be quite traumatic on more than one occasion.

PRINCESS CAROLINE

Princess Caroline was the golden child who wanted for nothing. She was beautiful and the press followed her wherever she went. This unfortunately caused a scandal when she was 21 years old, as she was pictured topless at the Monte Carlo Beach Club, which was the place where the rich and famous loved to hang out. The prince and princess were seething and tried to confine their daughter to the palace grounds by cutting off her allowance, but she was a wilful young woman who was not about to be tamed.

Before the incident at the beach club, Caroline had started an affair with an infamous French playboy by the name of Philippe Junot against her parent's wishes. Although they did their best to keep the couple apart, Caroline was defiant and, because she had already reached the age of consent, agreed to marry Junot.

While Princess Caroline prepared to marry Junot, who was 17 years her senior, on 28 June 1978, reporters from all over the world tried to think of ways of trying to break the security surrounding the wedding. The prince was making every endeavour to keep the affair totally private but it was becoming more and more difficult. Because Monaco was such a small principality, everything that happened to the royal family was headline news, and the media didn't want to miss out on such a prestigious story. Right up to the end the prince was hoping that his daughter would change her mind, but Caroline was adamant that the wedding was to go ahead and admitted afterwards that she had gone through with it 'to spite mama'.

The marriage was a disaster and only lasted for 831 days. No sooner had the couple returned from their honeymoon, than Caroline found out that her rake of a husband had made approaches to some of the seedier tabloids to sell some nude photographs he had taken of his wife on honeymoon. The divorce was a long and painful affair, with Caroline applying to the Catholic church for a Papal annulment. This was not granted until 12 years later.

Hardly over the traumas of her marriage break-up, Caroline was forced to overcome an even greater tragedy when her mother was killed in a tragic car crash on 13 December 1982. Grace was driving with her daughter Stephanie, when their car careened off the winding roads of France leading to Monaco. Although Stephanie was able to get out of the car once it had stopped rolling, her mother wasn't so lucky. Apparently, Grace had suffered a minor stroke, which had caused her to lose control of the vehicle, and the following day she was pronounced dead. Caroline suddenly stepped into her mother's shoes and blossomed into the principality's new first lady. She took on a number of high-profile roles and fulfilled each new role with a sense of duty, a side not previously seen in her character.

On 29 December 1983, Caroline found love again and married 23-year-old Italian Stefano Casiraghi, the son of a wealthy businessman. The wedding, compared to her first one to Junot, was a low-key civil ceremony, possibly due to the fact that Caroline was already pregnant with their first son Andrea Albert Pierre, who was born on 8 June 1984. In 1986 Charlotte Marie Pomeline was born and one year later, Pierre Rainier Stefano.

Despite outward appearances, friends of Caroline's say that it was not a happy union. Casiraghi continued to have an affair throughout their marriage with the daughter of a famous European aristocrat. As if that wasn't bad enough, he accrued massive debts and Caroline was forced to put up a considerable amount of her late mother's jewellery to try and stop the banks from foreclosing on her husband's business. Then tragedy struck again when Caroline's husband was killed in a speedboat racing accident.

Caroline retreated from public life with her three children and took to wearing black all the time. She lost a considerable amount of weight and rumours were going round that she was suffering from an eating disorder. Two years later Caroline was back in with Vincent Lindon, a French actor and the son of a rich industrialist. The relationship lasted for five years, but the couple never married.

In 1999 Caroline was hitting the headlines once again with a very controversial romance with Prince

Ernst August of Hanover. He was a direct descendant of King George III and already married with two children. Gossip spread fast that they were having a secret relationship, which was confirmed when the prince divorced his wife of 16 years and became Caroline's constant companion.

The couple married on Caroline's 42nd birthday in a quiet civil ceremony, which gave her the title of Princess of Hanover. The couple have since had a child, Alexandra, and Caroline now concentrates mainly on charity work and has won herself a lot of respect in her home of Monaco.

PRINCESS STEPHANIE

Stephanie, the youngest of the Rainier children, was a headache to her parents and rocked her family with scandals. She was beautiful and sensuous and bickered constantly with her older sister. Perhaps one of the more resourceful of the Rainier children, Stephanie managed to bounce back after each new escapade. Even from an early age she showed signs of some of the traits that have secured her reputation today.

Stephanie finished high school in 1982, but was not interested in going on to higher education. She had a flair for design and became an intern in the Dior house of fashion. However, the fatal accident in

September 1982 that killed her mother temporarily put a stop to her career. There were rumours that Stephanie was actually driving the car, but that has never been proved and she is the only person who has a clear idea of what actually happened that day. However, she has continued to remain silent on the subject, leaving the cause of the accident a complete mystery. Affected badly by the trauma of her mother's death, Stephanie has had a very turbulent private life. She tried her hand at fashion designing, modelling, being a recording artist and even owning her own business. Her boyfriends have included a racing car driver, Hollywood actors, businessmen and many others, and yet it was her relationship with her own bodyguard, Daniel Ducruet, that caused the worst scandal. Prince Rainier became concerned when photographs were released of Stephanie lying around a pool naked, with none other than her bodyguard. Ducruet, 33, was a former Monaco policeman who was obviously doing far more than just protecting Princess Stephanie.

In 1991 Stephanie fell pregnant and Ducruet immediately dumped his girlfriend, Martine Malbouvier, who had a four-month-old son by the bodyguard. Prince Rainier was heartbroken and said to a friend, 'How could Stephanie do this to me? I have forgiven her for much of her wild behaviour, but this is too much.' He disowned his grandchildren, Louis, who was born on 26 November 1992 and a little girl, Pauline Grace born on 4 May 1994.

Stephanie eventually convinced her father to allow her to marry Ducruet, but before the ceremony on 1 July 1995 in Monaco, he was made to sign a prenuptial agreement that stripped him of custody rights to any of his children. A very wise move as just a couple of month's after the couple's first anniversary, Ducruet was caught on camera cavorting around a pool with Muriel Houteman, the reigning 'Miss Topless Belgium'. The short-lived marriage was over. Ducruet was immediately banished from the Court of Monaco and forbidden from seeing his children. Ducruet was later awarded £20,000 in damages after he made allegations that it had all been a trap designed to disgrace him.

After her quickie divorce was granted, Stephanie embarked on a string of brief affairs which included the footballer Fabien Barthez and screen heartthrob, Jean-Claude Van Damme. Then the newspapers got hold of another story – that Stephanie was romantically linked with yet another of her bodyguards, a former Paris policeman Jean Raymond Gottlieb. Just a few months into the affair, Stephanie was pregnant again and gave birth to her third child, Camille Marie Kelly, who was born on 15 July 1998.

Although it is believed that Gottlieb is the father, Stephanie refused to have the father's name put on the birth certificate and so this has never been confirmed.

Prince Rainier had simply had enough of his daughter's unbefitting behaviour and ordered her to leave Monaco. She went to Auron, the ski resort, where she had an affair with a barman, Pierre Pinelli, and was even photographed waiting on tables at his restaurant. However, the affair was short-lived.

Stephanie's predilection towards low-life friends put her life in danger. For years she had associated with a crowd that both bought and used large amounts of coccaine. When she was approached by the police, she made a deal with them that she would be immune from prosecution in return for supplying them with information. One of her associates was linked to the cartels of Colombia and subsequently the Sicilian Mafia, which made Stephanie a target after she turned in a ruthless drug runner by the name of Giovanni Felice and 12 other known dealers. Prince Rainier, forgetting his past differences with his daughter, immediately stepped in and gave her a safe refuge. She was placed in a luxury penthouse in Monaco with armed bodyguards 24 hours a day. Although she did receive several threatening phone calls, one of which said that her young son was a target, the threats were thankfully never carried out. In August 2000 a cocaine dealer Eskander Laribi was shot dead outside a Nice post office. His girlfriend arrived at the scene driving a car that belonged to the princess, but because of her diplomatic immunity Stephanie was prevented from standing as a witness in the subsequent trial.

After Stephanie's life of living on the edge, she embarked on one that was totally bizarre. In 2000 she had a romance with a leading Swiss circus owner and elephant trainer called Franco Knie. The affair became public in 2001 when Knie announced that he was leaving his wife for the princess. Stephanie spent several months touring with the circus, living in Knie's caravan together with her children. However, the affair ended abruptly in 2002 when it was reported that Stephanie was having an affair with her father's butler, Richard Lucas, who was also married with two children. In 2003 it was rumoured that she was having a fling with the palace's head gardener and also her sister's ex-husband Philippe Junot.

Stephanie married a Portuguese trapeze artist on 12 September 2003, ten years her junior and a member of the Circus Knie. This marriage ended in divorce on 24 November 2004, and *Hello!* magazine published photos of her with a new man, married croupier Franck Brasseur. Since then she has been linked with several other men, including her current boyfriend, French actor and musician Merwan Rim.

Prince Rainier died on 6 April 2005 of heart, lung and kidney failure. Since his death Stephanie has settled down considerably and has become involved in the fight against AIDS.

Prince Albert, as the sole male in the line, is left as heir and successor. Albert, a dedicated sportsman, formed the Monaco national bobsled team in 1986 and competed in five Olympic games. Albert never married and is still considered today to be one of the world's most eligible bachelors.

However, Albert's slate is not entirely clean as just one month after taking over as sovereign of Monaco, he announced that he was the father of a two-year-old boy born to an air stewardess by the name of Nicole Coste. Apparently he had met Nicole on an Air France flight in 1997. The following year, Albert also admitted he had a daughter, who was the result of a romantic tryst with an American waitress by the name of Tamara Rotolo. Unfortunately, neither child is in line for the throne, as the principality's constitution states that only *direct* and *legitimate* descendants are considered to be rightful and legal heirs.

PART NINE

SPORTS
PERSONALITIES

O. J. SIMPSON

The murder trial of a former American football star, Orenthal James Simpson (better known to his fans simply as 'O. J.') dragged on for nine months in true Hollywood style in 1995. It was played out in court like an extremely tacky novel, with 11 formidable lawyers representing the easily recognizable sportsman standing in the dock. Unbelievably 91 per cent of the American population watched the trial on television, while a further 142 million tuned their radios to hear the eventual outcome of possibly the world's greatest true life soap opera.

Simpson was standing trial for the double murder of his ex-wife Nicole Brown and her friend, Ronald Goldman, but the proceedings turned into a political fight as to whether a black man could find justice in a legal system predominantly controlled by whites. Sadly the focus on the two hapless victims was totally overwhelmed by the team of polished lawyers who seemed willing to try any tack to turn their client into a political pawn.

THE EVENTS UNFOLD

The evening of 12 June 1994 was shrouded in fog and the howling Akita dog pacing up and down the street in a distressed manner, added to the eeriness. Steven Schwab, who lived in South Bundy Drive in Los Angeles, was walking his own dog at around 11.00 that night, when he came across the Akita. It was acting strangely and its fur and paws were covered in blood. At first the man presumed the dog had been injured, but on closer inspection could find no wounds. His neighbour Suka Boztepe agreed to look after the dog until morning, but was not happy when the Akita continued to pace up and down, whining continually. Eventually he decided to take the dog out for a walk in the hope that he could settle it down for the night. The dog was powerful and dragged Boztepe to the gates of number 875, where it just stood staring into the darkness.

Boztepe tried to focus his eyes and cautiously walked a little way down the path. He stopped abruptly when the dog let out a pitiful cry, and could just about make out the outline of a body lying at the foot of some stone steps. Boztepe retraced his steps and immediately contacted the LAPD.

Two police officers arrived at the three-level condominium at a little after midnight. The first thing the officer noticed in his torchlight was a large pool of blood, and then he saw the first body. It was a woman, lying face down, pressed up against the steps that led to the front door of the condominium. She was covered in blood, which appeared to have gushed out of wounds to her upper body and throat. Just a little to her right, hidden partially by a bush, lay the body of a man, who was also steeped in blood.

The woman turned out to be Nicole Brown Simpson, the ex-wife of the retired football player O. J. Simpson. She was the owner of the condominium and on searching the property, the LAPD found Brown's two children fast asleep in their bedrooms. At this time the identity of the dead man was uncertain. When the forensic team arrived they discovered a number of objects close to the bodies. There was a dark blue knitted cap, a set of keys, a beeper, a white envelope speckled in blood and also a bloodstained leather glove. Leading away from the bodies was a set of bloody footprints that continued to the back of the property.

O. J., being Nicole's former husband, was immediately placed on the list of suspects, although there was no evidence at the time that linked him directly with the scene of the crime. Meanwhile, O. J. himself, was on board an American Airlines flight to Chicago, unbeknown to the police.

When the police arrived at O. J.'s gated estate at Rockingham Avenue just 3 kilometres (2 miles) from where the bodies had been found, they noticed a 1994 white Ford Bronco parked bizarrely outside the property. As one of the officers took a closer look, he noticed in the beam of his torch what appeared to be a blood spot on the door near the driver's handle.

The lights in the house were blazing and the police felt sure someone was in the house. However, despite several efforts to arouse someone, they received no response to either their phone calls or knocking on the door. Without a search warrant they were unable to break into the property, so they decided to walk round the side of the property to a row of three bungalows. They managed to raise the occupants of two of the bungalows, Arnelle Simpson, O. J.'s daughter and a friend, Kato Kaelin.

When Arnelle learned that her stepmother had been murdered she called a close friend of her father's, Al Cowling, who was able to tell her the police the whereabouts of her father. The police placed a call to the O'Hare Plaza Hotel in Chicago, informing O. J. that his wife had been murdered. Although evidently distressed at the news, the policeman thought it was strange that O. J. never asked any details about the murders, apart from enquiring about the safety of his children. He told the police he would catch the next available flight back to Los Angeles.

Because of O. J.'s status, the police were aware that the news of the double murder would make the headline news, so they thought it apt to break the news to Nicole's parents before they heard about it on the morning news. They arrived at Dana Point in Orange County just before 6.30 a.m. and sadly passed on the news to Nicole's father, Louis Brown, that his daughter was dead. As the policeman attempted to comfort Brown, a woman's voice started crying out in another room – 'O. J. did it! O. J. killed her! I knew that son of a bitch was going to kill her!' The outbreak came from Nicole's own sister, Denise.

Back at Rockingham Avenue, the police had found another leather glove covered in blood, which seemed to be an exact match to the one found beside the body of Nicole. On further investigation they found what appeared to be spots of blood on the ground near two cars parked on the driveway. The trail led them out of the gates and stopped at the back of the white Ford Bronco parked outside the estate. When the police peered through the window of the car they noticed other blood spots on the driver's door and some on the passenger side of the vehicle. On returning to the garden, the police found the trail of blood took them right up to the front door. With all the evidence to hand the investigating officers returned to their station to prepare a search warrant to enter the home of O. J. and seize and relevant clues.

As soon as O. J. returned to Los Angeles he was taken in for questioning. When asked about a deep cut to his right hand, O. J. initially claimed he did not know how it had happened. When asked again later in the interview about the cut, O. J. said he might have received the injury when he reached inside his Ford Bronco on the night of the murders. Then he changed his mind and said it had most probably happened when he had broken a glass in his Chicago hotel room on hearing the news about the death of Nicole. Although the initial interview was not very forthcoming, the police eventually accumulated enough evidence against O. J. and they issued a warrant for his arrest.

THE CHASE

O. J. contacted his attorney, Robert Shapiro, and asked him to make a deal with the police, which allowed him until 10.00 the following morning to turn himself in. However, when the allotted time came and went and there was no sign of O. J., the police informed Shapiro that they would be going to his house to pick him up. When they arrived O. J. was nowhere to be found, but he had left behind a letter addressed to 'To Whom it May Concern'.

> *. . . Don't feel sorry for me. I've had a great life, great friends. Please think of the real O. J. and not this lost person. Thanks for making my life special. I hope I helped yours. Peace and love, O. J.*

At around 6.20 that evening, a man phoned the police and said he had seen O. J. driving around in a white Ford Bronco, apparently belonging to a close friend of the star, A. C. Cowlings. The police put together a posse of cars and went in hot pursuit, followed by a news helicopter and several curious members of the public. It couldn't in any way be described as a fast chase through the streets of Los Angeles – to the contrary it was more of a crawl, and ended with O. J. being arrested in his own driveway. Inside the car the police discovered a false beard and moustache, a loaded gun, a passport and $8,750 in cash.

THE TRIAL

The prosecution believed that their case was so strong against O. J. that they had no doubt that the jury would find him guilty of murder. However, a series of major blunders cost the prosecutors their case. After the initial hearing, when O. J. categorically denied any connection with the murders, the trial opened on Tuesday, 24 January 1995.

Despite the dismal weather on the first day of the trial, everyone was intrigued and wanted to be there to watch what turned out to be a total farce. Over the next 99 days, the prosecution presented 72 witnesses, many of them friends and relatives of his ex-wife. The majority suggested that O. J. had both the motive and the opportunity to carry out the murders, and pointed out to the court that he already had a history of domestic violence. Despite the prosecution supplying endless pieces of evidence which could have placed O. J. at the scene of the crime, the defence used every tactic to prove that the evidence provided was 'contaminated, compromised and ultimately corrupted'.

The prosecution felt the case was slipping away from them and decided to use a piece of circumstantial evidence, the bloodstained gloves found at O. J.'s property and by the side of Nicole's body. The judge instructed O. J. to put the gloves on, but the star seemed to struggle to get them to fit. 'They don't fit. See? They don't fit,' O. J. claimed. The damage had been done and the seed of doubt had been planted in the jury's minds.

O. J.'s defence team worked like a well-oiled piece of machinery and earned themselves the nickname the 'Dream Team'. Day by day they undermined the evidence submitted by the prosecution, raising more and more doubts until eventually they virtually forced an acquittal. It would be a forensic expert by the name of Henry Lee, that finally won O. J. his acquittal by firmly planting doubts leaving a final impact on the jury.

By the time the teams put together their closing arguments, the case had already gone down in Californian history as the longest trial in front of a jury. The American public watched and waited with baited breath to hear the outcome of the trial that had become their favourite soap opera. At 10.00 a.m. on 3 October 1993, the jury announced their verdict:

> *We the jury in the above entitled action find the defendant, Orenthal James Simpson, not guilty of the crime of murder.*

From O. J. could be heard an audible sigh, but from the friends and family of his ex-wife, there were cries of 'Oh my God! Oh my God!'

O. J. was ordered to pay compensatory damages of $8.5 million and punitive damages of $25 million.

WHERE ARE THEY NOW?

Despite being a broken man, today O. J. lives well on a substantial pension plan set up by the former football star when he was still making millions. This type of pension is exempt from civil court judgements, which means he can live quite comfortably off $25,000 a month.

Nicole's parents, Louis and Juditha Brown, became embroiled in a protracted court battle with their former son-in-law, in an attempt to win custody of the couple's two young children, Justin aged 10 and Sydney aged 13. Their daughter, Denise Brown, focuses her attention on the plight of battered wives and travels around the country speaking of domestic violence.

As for the Akita dog, who alerted people to the plight of its master, she now lives with Nicole's parents in Orange County. She is a great playmate for the Simpson children when they go to visit.

In November 2006, O. J. published a book entitled *If I Did It* and the publisher, Judith Reagan, told the Associated Press, 'This is an historic case and I consider this to be his confession!'

DAVID BECKHAM

David Beckham is one of Britain's most iconic athletes whose name and face are instantly recognisable around the world. He is married to Victoria Beckham, otherwise known as Posh Spice, and, as a family they symbolise fame, beauty, success and fortune – something which most people can only dream of. Always in the limelight, the epitome of the perfect family, it is not surprising that the tabloids jumped on the news of David Beckham's infidelity.

THE YOUNG SPORTSMAN

He was born David Robert Joseph Beckham on 2 May 1975, in the East End of London at Leystonstone. His father, Ted, was a kitchen fitter and his mother, Sandra, a hairdresser. Both his parents were avid supporters of Manchester United, and realising their son was a natural athlete they enrolled David in Bobby Charlton's football school in Manchester. He quickly showed his natural aptitude for the sport. He was given a place in a training session at FC Barcelona and by the age of 16 was playing for Manchester United as a trainee. Between 1992 and 2003, David made almost 400 appearances for Manchester United and scored 85 goals.

His success on the football field, his good looks and his marriage to Spice Girls star, Victoria Adams, meant that the name Beckham was never out of the news. Both David and Victoria were snapped up by the fashion industry and they quickly became a worldwide phenomenon. However, with all the positive press came the bad, and the Beckham's perfect image was tarnished for a while with not just one accusation of infidelity, but two.

A BLOT ON THE COPYBOOK

The Beckhams were going from strength to strength and when David signed a four-year contract with Real Madrid in July 2003, worth an estimated $40 million, it seemed the couple were set for life. To outsiders, the Beckhams wanted for nothing – plenty of money, three beautiful children, a wonderful home – but cracks started to appear in their idyllic facade. David was accused of sending text messages to a Malaysian-born model named Sarah Marbeck. The

29-year-old lived in Australia and claimed that she had had a two-year affair with the soccer star after meeting him in Singapore in July 2001. She claimed that after just four hours of meeting, the couple took part in a romantic embrace.

During the supposed affair, Victoria fell pregnant with the couple's second son, Romeo, and was said to have been devastated when she found some rather lurid text messages between David and Sarah. When Sarah was approached by the *News of the World*, she claimed that the world's most famous footballer had told her that he was in love with her.

> *I know I meant something to him because, on and off, we continued our relationship month after month after month. . . . When we made love David told me, 'I know what we are doing is wrong but I can't help it'. The first time he took me to bed he kissed me everywhere. I looked down and there was David Beckham kissing my breasts, David Beckham!*

MORE CRACKS

More cracks appeared in April 2004 when David – now at the top of his game as England captain – was caught sending saucy text messages to his personal assistant, Rebecca Loos, the daughter of a Dutch diplomat. Loos claimed that not only had they had a sexual relationship for some time, but she also said that she felt she was falling in love with him. As his PA Loos was constantly with David and had recently helped him move from Manchester United to Real Madrid, an upheaval which hit the family hard.

Loos claimed that the constant separation from Victoria, who had refused to move to Madrid, had caused David to seek solace in the arms of another woman. She claimed that he needed someone to help him through a difficult time in his life and that he was trapped in a sexless marriage.

When David heard what Loos had said, he said that her claims were 'ludicrous', while Victoria reportedly called her a 'lying cow'.

Both women were paid handsomely for their stories, Ms Loos an alleged $800,000 for her confession, making Beckham supporters more inclined to believe that David was the innocent victim of two money-grabbing women.

The accusations put the marriage under a lot of strain, and with Victoria abroad for much of the time, David was left to face the malicious rumours alone. To try and cement their relationship, David and Victoria decided to take a holiday and flew to Courchevel in France, followed by the paparazzi.

They showed the world they were still very much in love, while others tried to say they were just doing it to quash the rumours.

MOVE TO LA

In July 2007 David Beckham played his last game for Real Madrid, ending his contract with the club. He announced to the press that he had signed a five-year contract to play for the Los Angeles Galaxy to start on 1 July 2007 through to June 2012. Victoria was said to be elated with the prospect of living in LA and immediately started house-hunting for the perfect home. However, the foundations of the Beckham marriage were to be rocked once again when a model threatened to spill the beans about her affair with the soccer star in 1998.

The star of *Love Island*, Emma Ryan, claimed that she had had a six-week fling with David, although she said they had never actually slept together. She reportedly claimed that David wished to see her naked and exchanged several naughty text messages with the model.

It is alleged the relationship started in Manchester in August 1998, when David was a rising Manchester United star. Emma told the *Daily Star*, 'He wanted to see me naked and couldn't wait to play a game of strip Scrabble. Beckham's people tried to make out it was just a brief fling. But the truth is, it was much, much more. Now I'm determined the whole world will know the truth. It was a love affair. We both had very deep feelings for each other.'

This latest revelation came at a time when it was believed the Beckhams were trying for their fourth child. Only time will tell whether the Beckham's move to Los Angeles will cement their relationship. With the reunion of the Spice Girls in 2007 meaning that Victoria is away from home even more, who knows whether David will need to find a little TLC elsewhere.

MIKE TYSON

At first glance the career of Michael Gerard Tyson, better known as 'Mike', reveals the man as one of boxing's all-time greats. He was a former two-time US world heavyweight boxing champion, being the youngest man to ever win the heavyweight title. However, these impressive statistics cannot hide the real man behind those famous boxing gloves.

Tyson was born in to a working-class family in the notorious Brownsville section of Brooklyn. His father, Jimmy Kirkpatrick, deserted the family when Tyson was only two years old, leaving his mother, Lorna Smith Tyson, to raise her family the best way she could. Tyson was repeatedly ridiculed for his high-pitch voice and lisp as a young boy, which resulted in him using his fists in retaliation. His love of fighting saw him expelled from junior high and he spent the next few years in and out of detention centres for petty crime and violence. By the time Tyson was 13, he had been arrested 38 times.

Tyson's natural ability in the boxing ring was first spotted by an ex-boxer by the name of Bobby Stewart. Stewart was also a counsellor at the juvenile detention centre where Tyson was under remand and, seeing the young boy's potential and physical advantages, believed that boxing might be the way to calm the wild spirit raging within. He trained the young Tyson for several months and then introduced him to the legendary Cus D'Amato.

D'Amato immediately saw the boy's potential and removed him from the reform school to start some serious training. D'Amato was a well-known boxing trainer whose protégés included Floyd Patterson and José Torres. Tyson looked up to D'Amato, who not only became his legal guardian but also his father substitute as well. As an amateur, Tyson became a formidable opponent and his rise to stardom was rapid. His professional debut was on 6 March 1985 in Albany, New York, when he defeated Hector Mercedes by knocking him out in the first round. Tyson went from strength to strength, winning 19 of his first 22 fights by knocking out his opponents, many of them in the first round. His winning streak attracted media attention, which resulted in him being hailed the next great heavyweight champion of the world.

However, the death of D'Amato in November 1985 at the pinnacle of Tyson's career is thought to have set the young boxer on the road to ruin. Without this influence in his life, Tyson struggled to stay out of trouble although further fame and fortune were to come first.

When still only 20 years old, Tyson was given his first title fight against Trevor Berbick for the World Boxing Council (WBC) heavyweight championship. He took Berbick in the second round, making Tyson the youngest heavyweight to ever win the coveted title. From then on expectations were high, and Tyson embarked on an ambition to fight every single top heavyweight in the world.

PROBLEMS OUTSIDE THE RING

Although there is no doubt that Tyson was a major success inside the boxing ring, his life away from the ropes was becoming turbulent. In 1987 Tyson was charged with assault, but managed to settle out of court. It was alleged that he hit a parking attendant when the man tried to intervene because Tyson attempted to kiss a woman employee. This was to be the first of many scandals to rock the life and career of the world famous boxer. The same year, Tyson beat James 'Bonecrusher' Smith and became the World

Boxing Association (WBA) heavyweight champion.

On 8 February 1988 Tyson married the actress Robin Givens, but it wasn't long before her family started to accuse Tyson of domestic violence. Robin and her family demanded access to Tyson's fortune so that they could put a down-payment on a $3 million house in New Jersey. The relationship was stormy to say the least and, within a year, the marriage was over. Added to this Tyson sued his manager, Bill Cayton, for breaking their contract and ended up by settling out of court.

In late 1988 Tyson fired his longtime trainer Kevin Rooney, but without his expertise Tyson's skills slowly start to deteriorate, and instead of using the skill that brought him to stardom he went straight in for a knockout. This did nothing for Tyson's reputation, which was further knocked when he broke his right hand in a street brawl with former opponent Mitch Green. In 1997 Green won a lawsuit over the incident and was awarded $45,000.

Tyson seemed to have lost his direction and was found unconscious after driving his car into a tree in the driveway of his former guardian and mentor, D'Amato. The newspapers had a field day, claiming that the boxer had lost his mind and that he had tried to commit suicide. Tyson's wife didn't help by going on television and claiming that her husband was a manic-depressive and that their marriage had been sheer hell, while Tyson sat meekly beside her without saying a word. That seemed to flip Tyson over the edge and the police had to be called out to the home he had shared with Robin, after he started to throw furniture out of the window and forcing his wife and her mother out of the property. After that incident his wife sued for divorce and Tyson became embroiled in a year of bitter legal wrangles. The divorce was finally granted in 1989 and Tyson had to face yet another assault charge and a speeding offence before Tyson's professional life really took a turn for the worse.

In 1990 Tyson had to face a huge upset when he lost his world heavyweight title to James 'Buster' Douglas, and from there his life goes from bad to worse. Firstly, he was sued by a former aide to his ex-wife, Phyllis Polaner, for sexual assault and harassment. Later the same year he had to face a civil jury in New York, who found him guilty of committing battery against Sandra Miller, after he allegedly grabbed her, propositioned her and insulted her at a nightclub. She received minimal damages on the grounds that Tyson's behaviour was not considered to be 'outrageous'. Just three days later Tyson was sued by Lori Davies when it was alleged he tried to grab her buttocks while she was dancing at the same nightclub as Miller. Tyson was eventually fined $100.

In 1991, Tyson was in the news again when he admitted being the father of an eight-month-old girl born to Kimberly Scarborough. But all these minor scandals were nothing compared to the bombshell that was about to hit.

A SPELL IN PRISON

In February 1992 Mike Tyson was facing a jury in Indianapolis after being charged with the rape of an 18-year-old beauty pageant contestant, Desiree Washington. Tyson walked into the courtroom, much the way a boxer would walk into the ring, and sat at the defence table for the majority of the 14-day trial. As the jury foreman read out the verdict, Tyson sat with his hands in his lap, his muscles visibly tensed and no expression on his face. Although his fight promoter, Don King, had not been present throughout the trial, he arrived to hear the verdict being read.

Miss Desiree, who had also been absent during most of the trial, sat in the front row of the gallery with her mother, and watched and listened in complete silence. She claimed to have met Tyson while she was taking part in the beauty pageant and that he had lured her back to his hotel room and forced her to have sex with him. The prosecutors had attempted to portray the accuser as a naive and star-struck woman who had been fooled by a man who used his celebrity status to influence her. Tyson's team had desperately tried to convince the court that the young woman had known exactly what she was getting into when she agreed to go to his hotel room in the early hours of the morning on July 19. They added that Miss Desiree had had plenty of time to leave before Tyson started making sexual advances towards her. They claimed that when she realised she was being treated as a one-night stand, Miss Desiree wanted to get her revenge and decided to prosecute to cover up her humiliating experience.

Unfortunately Tyson's defence lost its case and he was found guilty of rape and and other charges and given a six-year jail sentence. Tyson served three years of his sentence and allegedly studied philosophy and Islam during his time behind bars. He felt angry at the injustice he had received in the court and worried that his reputation as a ladies' man had gone down the pan. When he was released in 1995, it appeared that Tyson had benefitted from his spell in prison as he seemed a much calmer person.

Tyson returned to fighting later that year with two comeback bouts against Peter McNeely and Buster Mathis Jr, both of which he won with ease. Tyson's management received criticism for giving him opponents that were so easy to defeat, and felt they were both unworthy components for Tyson's return to the ring. Tyson regained his WBC title easily by defeating Frank Bruno in March 1996, knocking him out in the third round. He also won back the WBA belt by beating the champion Bruce Seldon in just one round in September 1996. It appeared the good guy was back and his fans loved him, but everything was about to change.

TYSON FIGHTS HOLYFIELD

During Tyson's spell in prison, Evander Holyfield lost his titles and had gone into semi-retirement. Tyson's camp decided to lure Holyfield back into the ring on 9 November 1996. Holyfield, who was given virtually no chance of winning by the bookies, amazingly beat Tyson when the referee stopped the fight in the 11th round. The public demanded a rematch, believing that Tyson should have won the fight, but no one could have predicted the outcome of the much awaited fight.

The rematch was scheduled to take place on 28 June 1997 at the MGM Grand Arena in Las Vegas. The press were calling it 'The Sound and the Fury' and as the clash of the titans was about to start the excitement in the crowd reached fever pitch.

Tyson walked through the crowds wearing his

usual black trunks and shoes without any socks. The fight started quite cautiously, but Tyson received a cut above his right eye as a result of a clash of heads and this seemed to change the complexity of the fight.

When the two men emerged from their corners at the beginning of the third round, Tyson was without his gumshield and was clearly frustrated and irritated. No one has noticed his missing gumshield, with the exception of Holyfield. Holyfield pointed towards Tyson's mouth and then looked towards his trainer, and Tyson had to return to his corner. As soon as the gumshield was in place Tyson charged out of his corner, immediately catching Holyfield with a ferocious combination of punches. The crowd started to go mad chanting both their names.

Suddenly, with just 40 seconds left in the round, the fight took an ugly turn. Tyson managed to get Holyfield in a clinch, spat out his gumshield and then for no explicable reason bit a large chunk out of his opponent's right ear.

The entire stadium gasped, unable to believe what they have just seen, as Tyson spat the piece of his opponent's ear onto the floor. A bewildered Holyfield stood in the middle of the ring clutching the side of his head with blood pouring down his shoulder. The referee abruptly stopped the fight and Holyfield was taken to his corner for much needed medical attention. The referee turned to Tyson and said, 'One more like that and you're gone,' and amazing the fight resumed. The crowd were going mad in a wild fury of emotion. Almost immediately the two fighters were in another close clinch and to everyone's amazement Tyson found Holyfield's left ear and bit that as well, ripping away an even larger piece.

Following the second incident all hell broke lose, with Tyson now in an uncontrollable rage taking a swing at a policeman who had stormed into the ring. As Tyson was led away from the ring, the whole place became a war zone with missiles and abuse being aimed at the boxer from all sides.

Holyfield had to undergo plastic surgery to repair his ear, while Tyson was immediately suspended and his purse withheld. This was just another phase in the crazy and uncontrolled life of the once extremely popular and successful boxer. The world of boxing now saw Mike Tyson as a volatile and dangerous character, and it took him another 18 months before he could convince the authorities to allow him to fight in the ring again.

MORE TROUBLE

In August 1998 Tyson was back in trouble when two motorists claimed that he had assaulted them following a traffic accident in Maryland. By February 1999 Tyson was back in jail, but this time it did nothing to stem his anger and instead he was placed in solitary confinement for 25 days after he threw a television across a room. Tyson was eventually released in May 1999 after serving less than a third of his initial one-year sentence.

Tyson's comeback fight was yet another soap opera, as his bout with Orlin Norris had to be declared a 'no-contest' after Tyson knocked his opponent out after the bell. Tyson's reputation, if not already in tatters, left him unable to find a fight in his home country and he sought contests abroad.

Tyson had three fights in the UK, after much controversy as to whether he should be allowed entry into the country. After several more fights, Tyson stunned the boxing world by admitting that he was ready to quit on 11 June 2005. He told the press that he 'no longer had the fighting guts or the heart anymore'.

TYSON FACES COCAINE CHARGE

In December 2006 Mike Tyson brushed with the law once again when he was arrested and charged with driving under the influence of drugs and possession of cocaine. Tyson, now 41, was arrested in Scottsdale,

Arizona, after he was seen to be driving erratically after leaving a nightclub. During a roadside search they found three bags of cocaine and he later admitted to having used marijuana that day as well as an anti-depressant. Tyson was sentenced to 24 hours in jail and ordered to do 360 hours of community service.

Tyson will always be remembered for his many sporting achievements, but his outrageous and often controversial behaviour in his private life has always kept him very much in the public eye.

GEORGE BEST

George Best is best remembered as being one of the greatest football players in the history of the game. Sadly though, he died prematurely in November 2005, aged just 59, without ever realising his full potential. Although it was no great shock to hear of his demise following a string of alcohol-related illnesses, it made the loss of the British footballing legend no less sad.

A RARE TALENT

George Best was born on 22 May 1946 in Belfast, Northern Ireland. His father, Dickie, was a shipyard worker and his mother, Annie, was the athlete of the family. She was an international hockey player and many believed that George inherited his skills of amazing balance and ball control from his mother. George was the eldest of four children and loved nothing more than to kick a football round the streets where he lived with the other kids in the neighbourhood.

George's incredible skill with the ball was first noticed when he played for the Cregagh Football Club in Belfast. With grass to play on instead of the rough pavements of home, George was able to manipulate the ball the way he wanted. His seniors watched in amazement as he manouevred the ball around the defenders – stopping, spinning, accelerating and then shooting with either foot – a skill rarely seen. Talent scout Bob Bishop and assistant coach for Manchester United, Jimmy Murphy, could hardly believe their eyes and they invited the 15-year-old lad to train with their team.

Despite being excited about the prospect of training, and possibly playing for his dream team, George only survived one night in Manchester, before fleeing home after feeling terribly homesick and rather overwhelmed. His father was extremely angry and told his son that opportunities like that only came along once in a lifetime, especially to a young boy from a council estate. He immediately phoned Matt Busby, the coach for Manchester United, and told him that his son would be returning very shortly.

Busby was very understanding of the situation and decided that George needed a father figure. He was put up in a boarding house run by a woman named Mary Fullaway, who made sure he had a home away from home. George settled and started to show the coaches just how well he could play. By the age of 17 he was offered a contract and just four months later was promoted to play for the big club.

His first major game for the club was a success and he won the hearts of the crowd. The new Man U player seemed to have them eating out of his hand, as he always seemed to be one step ahead of his opponents. His skill and fame went from strength to strength and in 1968 George was voted Footballer of the Year.

By now George's fame had spread worldwide and there wasn't a shop in England that didn't sell something that his picture on it. He received as many as 10,000 letters a week from his fans and for once, the crowds that came to watch him play included hundreds of screaming teenage girls. His popularity was likened to that of a pop star and many people described him as the 'fifth Beatle', not only wooing his fans with his incredible skill but also with his charm and good looks.

With all the fame, however, came pressure and frustration, especially among his fellow teammates. Many of them resented the preferential treatment that George received and others frustrated when he always seemed to try and score rather than pass the ball to a more appropriate player. With his face splashed all over the front of the tabloids, women literally threw themselves at his feet and George was finding it harder and harder to balance his football with his glamorous status.

ROAD TO RUIN

When Busby announced he was going to retire in 1969, George obviously missed his mentor and started behaving erratically. Not only would he miss some training sessions altogether but he also started misbehaving and disregarding the better knowledge of his elders. His regular drinking binges had already started to affect his level of play and the team's new coach, Wilf McGuinness, decided he had no alternative than to suspend the young player for a month.

Although George continued to be a high scorer for his team, his extravant lifestyle started to take its toll and as good as the 1960s were for the young star, the 1970s proved to be bad – very bad.

Instead of getting his thrill on the football pitch, George sought his excitement elsewhere, spending his money on drink, women and fast cars. George's initial run of luck at the gambling tables earned him $50,000, but he would spend the next several years trying to replicate that win. He never succeeded and got deeper and deeper into debt. All the time he was losing money, George was also trying to run a nightclub and a boutique, but as quickly as he made a profit he quickly wasted it away until the situation became very serious.

By 1972 the then coach of Man U, Tommy Docherty, was tired of George's behaviour on and off the pitch and threw him off the first team. Although he attempted a comeback, by 1974 the 27-year-old Best was sacked by his club for excessive drinking and failure to turn up at training sessions and matches. At a time when George should have been the pinnacle of his career, he had played his last game at Old Trafford and left under a shroud of scandal.

Although only a young man, George's body was starting to suffer from alcohol abuse and he struggled to make a comeback in 1974 when he signed to play for Dunstable. The club were delighted when their normal crowd of 200 was boosted to over 5000, but now overweight and desperately unfit George could only display a few of his former talents.

When no further offers came his way, George decided to try his hand overseas and signed a contract with the Los Angeles Aztecs. The club's owner, John Chaffetz, aware of what he was taking on, wasn't even certain whether George would turn up, but he stepped off the plane wearing a T-shirt that said, 'Who the Hell's George?'

This time George was determined to get back in

shape and finally earned himself a position with the scoring leaders. His teammates were thrilled to get to play with such a footballing legend and for a while he thrilled the American crowds.

George met his first wife, Angie, a former *Playboy* Bunny and model, at a dinner party in Los Angeles in 1975 when he was about to sign up for the Aztecs. It was love at first sight for both of them. Although Angie was worried about her boyfriend's constant womanising and drinking, George eventually persuaded her to marry him on 27 January 1978. George, true to form, was drunk at the wedding and spent his wedding night gambling and drinking. They had a son, Calum, who was born in 1981, but George's continual adultery and drinking drove the couple apart.

By 1984 George was drinking himself literally to death and was arrested for drunk driving and assaulting a police officer and spent that Christmas behind bars. In 1991, George appeared on the BBC chat show hosted by Terry Wogan, but he was clearly drunk, incoherent and used abusive language – his world was falling apart around him. He later apologised and openly admitted that his alcoholism was out of control. Despite the fact that George's reputation had gone to pot, many of the old football fraternity refused to turn their backs on him. He still managed to make a decent living from appearance fees and doing some writing for magaines and newspapers. In 1995 George married Alex Pursey, a former air hostess and model, who was aware of his erratic behaviour but who believed she could help him mend his ways. However, all the functions he still attended meant he had plenty of opportunities to drink and by 2002, George's liver had deteriorated to such a point that he required a liver transplant. It was hoped that George's near brush with death would help him fight his battle against alcoholism, but the respite was short-lived. By 2003 he was seen out drinking again and he received a lot of criticism for his lack of respect. Many felt that he shouldn't have received the transplant if he wasn't prepared to help himself.

In 2003 Alex Best took part as a contestant on the reality television show *I'm a Celebrity, Get Me Out of Here!* on which she openly made allegations about their marriage. It appears even she had had enough of his behaviour and was no longer prepared to support him.

On 3 January 2004, George was convicted yet again with a drunk driving offence and was banned from driving for 20 months.

George seemed hell bent on destroying himself and on 2 October 2005, was admitted to intensive care at the private Cromwell Hospital in London. By November his condition had deteriorated and on the morning of the 20th, the *News of the World* published a picture of George Best lying in his hospital bed, alongside a message 'Don't die like me.'

George lost his fight for life on 25 November 2005, ironically a day after the government passed a law allowing bars to stay open 24 hours a day. George was buried in Belfast and tens of thousands of fans attended the service. More than half a million people lined the streets as the hearse drove by, proving that no matter how bad his behaviour was, George Best will always be remembered for the good times and the remarkable skill he showed on the football field. Many believe that we only got a glimpse of the level of his genius.

DIEGO MARADONA

Like his British counterpart, George Best, Diego Maradona is possibly one of the greatest footballers to put on a pair of boots. However, on the flip side of the coin he is also considered to be one of the sport's most controversial figures.

Born on 30 October 1960, among the slums of Buenos Aires, Diego Armando Maradona reached the dizzy heights of professional football at the age of 15. He was originally spotted by a talent scout at the age of 11, when he was playing for a junior football club, Estrella Roja. One of his greatest skills was his ability to dribble the ball at top speed and being able to deliver lethally accurate passes to his teammates.

By the age of 16, Maradona joined the senior national squad for Argentina. Despite his remarkable talent, the coach César Menotti, decided that Maradona was too young to play in the 1978 World Cup, and the bitterly disappointed teenager had to watch his team take the gold medal from a television screen at home.

Determined to make an impact on his team, Maradona gave the game everything he could offer and was eventually picked to join the squad for Spain in 1982. In the first round of the World Cup, Argentina lost to Belgium, but successfully beat Hungary and Salvador to progress to the second round. In the second stage of the tournament, Maradona was closely marked by the Italian Claudio Gentile, but let his frustration overflow when he felt he had been manhandled unfairly. This resulted in him being sent off, which meant he was unable to unleash his full potential and his team failed to take the title.

However, his skills had not gone totally unnoticed, and he was signed to play for Barcelona for a then record transfer fee of £5 million. However, a bout of hepatitis and a badly timed tackle by an opponent, seriously jeopardised his career. Maradona's will-power and physical strength allowed him to make a quick recovery and within 14 weeks he was back on the pitch. It is rumoured that it was during his time at Barcelona that he was introduced to the drug coccaine, to which he later became addicted. Following frequent disputes with Barcelona directors, Maradona demanded a transfer in 1984, and went to play for the Italian club, Napoli, for £6.9 million.

Maradona made his return to the World Cup in 1986 in spectacular fashion, leading his team to victory. As captain, he led his team into the quarter final against England. It was his skill and dominance of the match that truly cemented the man as a legend, but it also caused much controversy. Maradona scored the first goal, but replays later showed that he had scored with the aid of his hand. Unnoticed by the referees and despite cries from the crowd, the goal was allowed. Just five minutes later, Maradona single-handedly took the ball through the entire English defence and scored his second goal. After the match, when confronted by the video tape, Maradona simply replied, 'Even if there was a hand, it must have been the hand of God'.

Maradona took his skill with him to Napoli, helping them reached unprecedented success and winning the UEFA Cup in 1988/1989. However, his personal life was not such a major success. No one knows when his coccaine addiction really started to become a problem. It is thought that he might have started experimenting while in Barcelona, but it was probably the organised crime outfits of Naples in the 1980s that caused it to become a major problem. Added to the drugs, Maradona was also at the centre of a scandal over an illegitimate son that he had fathered in Italy. Maradona was married to the woman he described as 'the love of my life', Claudia Villafane, with whom he had two daughters, but the scandal – together with many alleged infidelities – meant that the couple divorced in 2004.

In 1990 the world was watching Maradona as he captains Argentina once more in the World Cup. However, an ankle injury severely hampered his performance and he was a far less dominant figure than four years earlier. The most memorable of the matches was the semi-final against Italy, which was played at Maradona's home club in Naples. Maradona felt humiliated when the fans started to boo him during the match and after their failure to win the tournament, his career hits an all-time low.

In March 1991 he tested positive for drugs and was banned from playing football for 15 months. After his ban he returns to Napoli and later transfers to Sevilla for one year. By 1994 Maradona's career as a professional footballer was over when he was suspended again for failing a drugs test.

Maradona decided to take a new career path and tried his hand at coaching, but failed miserably. Downhearted and fighting a drug addiction, Maradona returned to his old football club, Boca Juniors and played with them until his last match on 25 October 1997. Just five days later, on his 37th birthday, Maradona announced to the world that he would be retiring from football.

Maradona spent a large part of the 2000s battling

with his addiction to cocaine, periodically entering rehab to try and conquer the problem. The highlight came in 2001 when Maradona played his farewell match against a selected team of some of the greatest footballers in the game. It was a highly emotional day witnessed by over 60,000 fans. Maradona walked out onto the pitch with his daughters, Dalma and Giannina, and one of his nephews. The crowd were excited and screamed loudly to their idol, 'Diegooooo, Diegooooo,' in recognition of one of the best football players of all time. The event finished with fireworks, songs and a lot of tears from Maradona.

In 2004, Maradona suffered a severe heart attack, exacerbated by a tendency towards obesity. He survived the attack, but his old demons came back to haunt him and he started drinking to try and drive them out. He was in and out of hopsital for the new few years, even undergoing a gastric bypass operation in 2005, after which he appeared to be notably thinner. In 2007 Maradona announced on Argentine television that he had kicked his addictions and that he was now completely clean.

Like George Best, Maradona was an exceptionally tortured genius. His controversial lifestyle both on and off the pitch left him both loved and hated, but the name Maradona will always be easily recognisable even in the remotest of places. However, despite his undoubtable skill, the Argentine soccer player has stirred global controversy of unparalled magnitude. This controversy stopped him getting the FIFA title of Best Football Player of the Century because the association found his personal image unacceptable. The award eventually went to Pelé.

THE BLACK SOX
SCANDAL

The Black Sox scandal describes a number of events that took place around and during the 1919 World Baseball Series, which resulted in the most famous scandal in the sport's history. Eight players from the Chicago White Sox (who later became nicknamed the Black Sox) were accused of throwing (or intentionally losing) the series against their opponents the Cincinnati Reds. Exact details of the extent to which each man was involved have always been a little cloudy, but the charges were serious enough to have the players permanently banned from professional baseball for life. The eight men involved were – 'Shoeless' Joe Jackson, pitchers Eddie Cicotte and Claude 'Lefty' Williams, infielders Buck Weaver, Arnold 'Chick' Gandil, Fred McMullin and Charles 'Swede' Risberg, and outfielder Oscar 'Happy' Felsch. Ironically, because of the raised interest in baseball just after the war, the bigwigs decided to make the series a 'best-of-nine' play-off instead of the usual 'best-of-seven' and discussed ways of making it an unforgettable series. Little did they realise what bad timing this was, as baseball was about to make a spectacle of itself without their help.

FORMATION OF THE WHITE SOX

The White Sox team was formed in 1900 under the ownership of Charles Comiskey and were originally called the White Stockings. In their first year they won the league championship and by 1906 the White Sox won the World Series by defeating the Chicago Cubs by four games to two.

During the next four years the team had no major achievements, but in 1910 Comiskey decided to build a new ballpark for his team and put every effort into building a really strong squad. To boost his team in 1915 he bought three star players – outfielder Joe Jackson, second baseman Eddie Collins and centre fielder Happy Felsch.

Two years later the White Sox were playing at their best and won the World Series, and by 1919 had the best record in the American League. Comiskey had succeeded in his dream – building one of the most powerful teams in the history of baseball.

Despite their outstanding success there was a lot of dissent among the players. Regardless of their plush grounds and facilities, the team were payed poorly and it is believed that it was Comiskey's stinginess that was largely to blame for the scandal that was about to erupt. Many said that if they had received decent wages the players would never have agreed to throw the series. Comiskey was also known to constantly break his promises, teasing his players with offers of big bonuses if they won – but these were idle promises that he never intended to keep. When the team did win, all they received was the odd bottle of cheap champagne and a slap on the back. To add insult to injury, Comiskey even had the gall to charge the players a fee for laundering their dirty uniforms. In protest the players decided to leave their uniforms unwashed and for several weeks turned out onto the pitch in dirty gear, but Comiskey physically removed the clothes from their lockers and then fined his players. Unfortunately, without a union to back them up and a clause in their contract that stopped them from transferring to another club, there was little they could do about their conditions.

As if things weren't bad enough, the White Sox players squabbled amongst themselves and none of them seemed to be able to form a bond. The team was divided into two separate cliques – one led by second baseman Eddie Collins and the other by first baseman Chick Gandil. The Collins' 'team' were the educated, sophisticated bunch who seemed able to negotiate a fairly decent salary. By contrast, Gandil's bunch were a far less polished group who were payed a much smaller remuneration – and the resentment grew.

The United States was disrupted by World War I in 1918, and interest in baseball hit an all-time low. The World Series of 1919 was a light at the end of the tunnel and, at a time when the country was starting to return to normal, interest in the sport was being revived. Fans eagerly followed the games and plans were made to make it the best series ever.

The 'fixing' of games was not a new concept, as gamblers were often visibly present at the ballparks. It was widely believed that players often supplemented their meagre wages by agreeing to throw single games, but it had never gone as far as affecting a World Series. By 1919, the number of gamblers at the grounds had dramatically increased and Comiskey decided to post signs throughout his park stating:

NO BETTING ALLOWED IN THIS PARK

Needless to say the signs were ignored and, with player resentment running at an all-time high, several of the team received offers that were just too good to refuse.

THE FIX

By most accounts it appears that Chick Gandil was the ringleader in the 'fix'. A small-time gambler by the name of Joseph Sullivan had allegedly been making money on inside tips from Gandil for some years. A few weeks before the 1919 World Series, Gandil approached Sullivan about the possibility of arranging a fix for the entire series. He told Sullivan that for a fee of $100,000, Gandil and his teammates would ensure that the White Sox lost. Gandil, who was reaching the age of retirement at 33, decided that he would have one last shot at making some big bucks. Sullivan agreed to his terms, realising that he could make a lot of money out of the fix himself, and set about raising the money.

Gandil had the difficult task of getting his teammates to cooperate. Because the stakes were high, Gandil needed to make sure that he could convince enough players to go along with the fix to make it work. Two of Chicago's pitchers, Ciccotte and Williams, had won 52 games between them that season, so Gandil was desperate to get them to agree.

Comiskey was the key figure that convinced the players to go along with Gandil's fix. He had promised to pay Cicotte a bonus of $10,000 if he won a total of 30 games. However, to make sure he wouldn't reach this figure, Comiskey decided to rest Cicotte for the remainder of the pennant games. This meant that Cicotte only played 29 games and was not therefore eligible for the promised bonus. Cicotte agreed to go along with the fix so long as he received the sum of $10,000 up front. Williams and Risberg were willing participants and a third man, McMullin, demanded a piece of the action when he overheard Risberg talking with Gandil.

The two players whose involvement in the fix is most disputed are Weaver and Jackson. Although many people believe that Jackson was an innocent bystander who got caught up in the fix, as far as the grand jury was concerned he was an equal conspirator. It is alleged that Gandil offered to pay him $20,000 for his part in helping to throw the series. However, Jackson became frustrated when he hadn't received any money by the end of the third game and flew at Gandil saying that the players were being stitched up by the gamblers. Lefty Williams eventually paid him $5000 in cash at the end of the fourth game. Weaver, who attended several of the meetings of the conspirators, apparently refused to take any part.

Because Sullivan did not have the resources to come up with the money, he had to recruit several other infamous gamblers into the plot – a former featherweight boxing champion Abe Attell, ex-White

Sox pitcher 'Sleepy Bill' burns and New York Giant first baseman Hall Chase. However, the main benefactor was the infamous businessman Arnold Rothstein, who was also a famous kingpin of organised crime in New York. He was also well known as a big time gambler who would put big money on anything that he could fix.

THE WORLD SERIES

The Chicago White Sox were hot favourites to win the 1919 World Series and the odds against them favoured five to one. The day before the series opened, the rumours of a fix were rife. As the money started to change hands, the odds quickly shifted towards the White Sox opponents, the Cincinnati Reds and the same night Cicotte found the sum of $10,000 in cash in his hotel room.

As arranged the White Sox lost their first game, but the players did not receive the $20,000 in cash that Gandil had promised them. Used to broken promises, the players took a lot of persuading before they would agree to lose the second game, but Gandil promised that the money would be forthcoming by the end of the day. The White Sox lost 4–2.

Those players not involved in the fix were starting to get suspicious. After all they were used to winning and couldn't understand why some of their team were playing so badly. Catcher Ray Schalk and manager Kid Gleason approached Gandil and Williams and chastised them for their appalling performances. After the match Gandil went to see Abe Attell to collect the $40,000 that he owed him and his teammates. Attell only handed over $10,000 and the players started to have second thoughts about continuing to lose their games.

The White Sox won their third game with ease ,which caused many of the big time gamblers to lose a lot of money. This time it was Attell who felt he had been betrayed and refused to hand over any more money. Sullivan, on the other hand, managed to raise $20,000 before the start of the fourth game which convinced some of the players that it was still worth throwing the next game. Cicotte made several serious errors and the White Sox lost games four and five.

By this time, however, the gamblers had missed another payment and the players decided once and for all that it wasn't worth losing the series if there was to be no money at the end of it. At least they were guaranteed $5000 each if they won, so the White Sox went on to win both games six and seven. The players were all playing to save the series, and it seemed as though at last it was within their grasp.

This is were Rothstein stepped in. He knew that he

was about to lose an awful lot of money and he decided to do something about it. With his investment at risk, Rothstein sent one of his henchmen to see Williams, who was set to pitch in the eighth game. He told Williams that Rothstein wanted the series to be over by the end of the day and threatened Williams and his wife with death if the fix didn't go ahead. Williams was petrified, the threats had worked, the White Sox lost 10–5 – Cincinnati were handed the World Series on a plate.

A sports writers for the *Chicago Herald and Examiner*, Hugh Fullerton, had been following the series carefully and had kept his ear to the ground regarding rumours of a fix. He decided to drop hints in his newspaper column and urged other club owners to do something about the gamblers' illegal involvement in baseball. The majority of people believed it was impossible to fix such an important fixture. Club owners, on the other hand, who knew better, refused to acknowledge that there was a problem, believing that their fans would stay away if they got a sniff of any underhand dealings. It is possible that the whole sordid affair would have blown over if the problem had not continued to grow in the forthcoming years. During the next baseball season, other teams started to take advantage of the illicit 'windfalls' and rumours spread that major teams such as the New York Giants, New York Yankees, Boston Braves and Cleveland Indians had been throwing games in return for cash.

FACING THE GRAND JURY

The White Sox were enjoying a profitable season in 1920 when they were called before the Grand Jury at Cook County, Illinois. Comiskey, who was trying to cover his tracks, suggested that Jackson and Cicotte should be the first people to testify and that they should admit to everything.

By now the scandal had gone public, with the front pages of every tabloid covering the story. They made sure they covered every single detail of the trial, giving their readers something worth reading. At the conclusion of the hearing, indictments were handed down against eight of the White Sox players, together with gamblers Hal Chase, Abe Attell, Joe Sullivan, Bill Burns and quite a few of Rothstein's henchmen. It is reported that Rothstein made as much as $270,000 on the 1919 Series but, probably because of his under-world connections, he was not indicted. He did, however, get his come-uppance when he was later murdered by a rival gambler who accused him of fixing a poker game.

The White Sox players who had been indicted

were immediately suspended for the rest of the season and had to face trial which began in June 1921.

The trial never really answered any questions as it was a farce right from the start. The confessions of Jackson, Cicotte and Williams went mysteriously missing and the facts regarding the fix were carefully manipulated, distorted and sometimes subject to outright lies. After one month the jury, due to lack of concrete evidence, found a verdict of not guilty.

The missing reports peculiarly turned up four years later in the hands of Comiskey's lawyer, George Hudnall, who offered no explanation as to how he had got hold of them.

After 1920, club owners were scared that baseball might not survive the massive scandal that had erupted and decided to clean up their acts. Federal Judge Kenesaw Mountain Landis was appointed as an independent commissioner, and was given dictatorial power over baseball to try and restore the public's faith in the game. Although the White Sox players had been acquitted, Landis decided to give them all a life-time ban and never allowed them to play a professional game again.

ROSIE RUIZ

On 21 April 1980, 23-year-old Rosie Ruiz was the first woman to complete the Boston marathon. Amazingly, she had set a record time for a female runner – two hours, 31 minutes and 56 seconds. What was even more amazing was that she appeared remarkably sweat-free, was not out of breath and showed no signs of having just run the gruelling 42.2 kilometre (26.2-mile) course. It is quite incredible to think that in these days of electronic monitoring and checkpoints that anyone would have the affront to attempt such an obvious hoax, but in the early 1980s such sophisticated monitoring was not available.

As Ruiz climbed the victory podium and accepted her wreath completely relaxed and unperturbed by what she had just done, race officials began to question her victory. The main problem was that no one had actually seen her start the race and she appeared nowhere on the video footage or indeed any of the numerous photographs taken at various stages of the race. The first time people remembered seeing her face was in the last half mile of the course. There was no evidence whatsoever to prove that she had completed the course and finally a few members of the crowd came forward to confirm that they had seen her jumping over a fence to join the race during its final section. Obviously far fresher than any of the other runners, Ruiz sprinted easily to victory over the finishing line.

When she was questioned by reporters why she didn't seem to be suffering the normal effects of fatigue, she simply replied, 'I got up with a lot of energy this morning!'

Meanwhile the real winner, Jacqueline Gareau of Canada, who had completed the race in a creditable two hours, 34 minutes and 28 seconds, was essentially being ignored by the media as they rushed to speak with Ruiz. This had the effect of robbing Gareau of the limelight and her moment of glory, although she was later honoured in a special ceremony a couple of weeks later.

As the race officials prepared to announce the disqualification of Ruiz from the race – having learned that she had dropped out early and hopped on the subway, only to rejoin the runners in the last mile – they also found out that she had cheated during the earlier New York marathon. It was during that race that she had qualified to run in Boston. She had apparently used the same tactics of riding on the subway. Freelance photographer, Susan Morrow, later reported that she remembered meeting Ruiz on the subway during the New York race and accompanied her to the last section of the course. They walked together to the finishing area, where Ruiz identified herself as an injured runner. She was taken to the first aid station where volunteers marked her down as having completed the marathon.

Of course this is not the first time that a marathon runner has claimed victory dishonestly. In September 1991 spectators noticed that the winner of the Brussels marathon, Abbes Tehami, had somehow managed to shave off his moustache while taking part in the race. It eventually came to light that Tehami had only completed the last part of the marathon – his coach had started it for him.

OTHER THEORIES

As with many scandals, people like to offer their opinion on what really happened. The case of Ruiz winning the marathon is no exception to the rule. Many officials believe that what really happened is that she didn't actually intend to win the race, but wanted to finish in a respectable time. It is believed that after she was mistakenly marked as having completed the New York marathon, Ruiz was too embarrassed to tell her trainer what had really happened. On the day of the 1980 Boston marathon, wanting her trainer to believe she was better than she actually was, Ruiz walked from her hotel to Kenmore Square, which is about 1.6 kilometres (1 mile) from the finishing line. However, it is thought that she joined the race too early, not aware that she was actually in front of all the other women runners. The fact that she was unable to give details about any prominent landmarks along the course seemed to prove that it was not planned at all and that she had never intended to steal first position. Many experts believe that if she had really intended to pull the perfect ruse, she would have studied these points so that she would be ready to answer such questions.

Ruiz quickly faded from the public eye after her title was stripped from her, even though she continued to claim that she had not cheated and insisted that she had run the full distance in both races. She was also sacked from her job at the New York-based Metal Traders Inc. because the yellow shirt she wore during the race was a gift from her boss and was emblazoned with the company's logo.